U.S. POLICY
IN POSTCOLONIAL AFRICA

PETER LANG
New York • Washington, D.C./Baltimore • Bern
Frankfurt am Main • Berlin • Brussels • Vienna • Oxford

F. Ugboaja Ohaegbulam

U.S. POLICY IN POSTCOLONIAL AFRICA

Four Case Studies in Conflict Resolution

PETER LANG
New York • Washington, D.C./Baltimore • Bern
Frankfurt am Main • Berlin • Brussels • Vienna • Oxford

Library of Congress Cataloging-in-Publication Data

Ohaegbulam, Festus Ugboaja.
U.S. policy in postcolonial Africa: four case studies
in conflict resolution / F. Ugboaja Ohaegbulam.
p. cm.
Includes bibliographical references (p.) and index.
1. United States—Foreign relations—Africa—Case studies.
2. Africa—Foreign relations—United States—Case studies.
3. Conflict management—Africa—Case studies.
4. Africa—Politics and government—
1960- —Case studies. I. Title.
DT38.7.039   327.7306'09'045—dc22   2003025258
ISBN 0-8204-7091-0

Bibliographic information published by **Die Deutsche Bibliothek**.
Die Deutsche Bibliothek lists this publication in the "Deutsche
Nationalbibliografie"; detailed bibliographic data is available
on the Internet at http://dnb.ddb.de/.

Cover design by Joni Holst

The paper in this book meets the guidelines for permanence and durability
of the Committee on Production Guidelines for Book Longevity
of the Council of Library Resources.

Printed in the United States of America

This book is dedicated to my wife, Emma,
whose support in all my endeavors
has been and continues to be invaluable.

Acknowledgments

I express my sincere gratitude to several people who graciously gave their time and energy to help me research and prepare this book. My colleague, Earl Conteh-Morgan, assisted me in several ways in locating critical sources and in commenting on aspects of the manuscript. Kris Bezdecny of the Department of Geography, the University of South Florida (USF), helped me in the production of the maps included in the volume. I recognize and thank Professor Joseph Harrington, editor, *The New England Journal of History* for granting me the permission to include in Chapter 9 the contents of my earlier article "The Clinton Administration's African Crisis Response Initiative: An Examination of a Post-Cold War United States Africa Policy" published in the journal's volume 58, number 3 (Spring 2002). I am indebted to Mr. Scott Fisher of ACOTA, U.S. Department of State, for the bulk of the information included in the section on Sequel to ACRI, Chapter 9.

Delores Bryant, office manager, Department of Government and International Affairs (USF), was invaluable to me in many critical ways in conducting the research and producing the book. To her I am eternally grateful for her encouragement, support, patience, and understanding beyond the call of duty.

I recognize with deep gratitude Marianne Bell, supervisor, Information Processing Center, College of Arts and Sciences (USF), not just for her painstaking role in preparing the camera-ready copy of the manuscript, but also for her advice and assistance throughout the process of writing the book. Finally, I am grateful to the Department of Government and International Affairs for providing the opportunity and facilities that were crucial in writing and producing the book.

F.U.O.
Tampa, Florida

Table of Contents

Document, Maps, and Tables

Document

Maps

Tables

Abbreviations

ACOTA—African Contingency Operations Training and Assistance
ACRI—African Crisis Response Initiative
AFRC—Armed Forces Revolutionary Council
ANC—African National Congress
BONUCA—United Nations Peace-Building Office in the Central African Republic
CAR—Central African Republic
CODESA—Convention for a Democratic South Africa
CIA—Central Intelligence Agency
DRC—Democratic Republic of the Congo
ECOMOG—Economic Community of West African States Monitoring Group
ECOWAS—Economic Community of West African States
EPLF—Eritrean People's Liberation Front
EPRDF—Ethiopian People's Revolutionary Democratic Front
FAA—Angolan Armed Forces
FAR—Rwandan Armed Forces
FLEC—Front for the Liberation of the Enclave of Cabinda
FNLA—National Front for the Liberation of Angola
FNLC—Congo National Liberation Front
FRELIMO—Mozambique Liberation Front
GURN—Government of Unity and National Reconciliation
ICTR—International Criminal Tribunal for Rwanda
IFOR—Implementation Force
IGAD—Intergovernmental Authority on Development
IMET—International Military Education and Training
MINURSO—United Nations Mission for the Referendum in Western Sahara

MONUA—United Nations Observer Mission in Angola
MONUC—United Nations Mission in the Democratic Republic of the Congo
MPLA—Popular Movement for the Liberation of Angola
MUNICI—United Nations Mission in Côte d'Ivoire
NATO—North Atlantic Treaty Organization
NEPAD—New Partnership for Africa's Development
NPRC—National Provisional Ruling Council
NSC—National Security Council
NSSM-39—National Security Study Memorandum-39.
OAU—Organization of African Unity
OFR—Operation Focus Relief
ONUC—United Nations Operations in the Congo (Democratic Republic)
PDD-25—Presidential Decision Directive-25
PLAN—Namibian People's Liberation Army
RDF—Rapid Deployment Force
RENAMO—Mozambique National Resistance Movement
RPF—Rwandan Patriotic Front
RUF—Revolutionary United Front
SADC—Southern Africa Development Community
SADR—Saharan Arab Democratic Republic
SPLA—Sudanese People's Liberation Army
SPLM—Sudanese People's Liberation Movement
SWAPO—Southwest African People's Organization
UNAMIR—United Nations Assistance Mission in Rwanda
UNAMSIL—United Nations Assistance Mission in Sierra Leone

UNAVEM—United Nations Angola Verification Mission

UNHCR—United Nations High Commissioner for Refugees

UNICEF—United Nations International Children's Fund

UNITA—National Union for the Total Independence of Angola

UNMEE—United Nations Mission in Ethiopia and Eritrea

UNMIL—United Nations Mission in Liberia

UNOB—United Nations Office in Burundi

UNOGBIS—United Nations Peace-Building Support Office in Guinea-Bissau

UNOL—United Nations Peace-Building Office in Liberia

UNPOS—United Nations Political Office for Somalia

UNSC—United Nations Security Council

UNTAG—United Nations Transition Assistance Group

USAID—United States Agency for International Development

ZANU—Zimbabwe African National Union

ZAPU—Zimbabwe African People's Union

CHAPTER 1
U. S. Role in World Affairs

A nation's role in world affairs depends on a variety of domestic and external factors. These frequently include how the nation perceives its national security interests, whether in regional or global terms. Since the United States emerged as a world power in 1898 and particularly after the end of World War II, its leaders have consistently perceived its national security interest in global terms. That perception was part of the energy that successfully fueled U.S. dedication for about fifty years to the containment of communism and Soviet ideological expansion. It is the same force that is operating in the war against terrorism and the proliferation of weapons of mass destruction.

Forces that Influence/Constrain U.S. Foreign Policy

Developments in the world outside the United States play a critical role in influencing or constraining the role that country plays in the world. For example, after the end of World War II, American leaders believed that their nation was threatened by fundamental changes in the international environment. The major powers of Western Europe—Britain, France, and Germany especially—lay exhausted and economically debilitated by the war. Communist and Soviet ideologies, antithetical to Euro-American values and the socio-political system, had become entrenched in Eastern Europe and were threatening to expand to other regions of the world. Non-self-governing territories in various regions of the world—in Africa, Asia, and the Caribbean—were militantly demanding independence from Western European colonial powers that had been U.S. allies in the war against the Axis Powers and remained its major trading partners. To address these developments, U.S. leaders adopted and implemented the Marshall Plan for the recovery of Europe and a policy, including the formation of the North Atlantic Treaty Organization (NATO), of containing communism and Soviet ideological expansion. At the same time the Marshall Plan or European Recovery Program was not entirely altruistic but had strong elements of American self-interest. It was designed not only to achieve the recovery of Europe and to minimize the appeal of communism to a devastated Europe. It was also intended to redound and, in fact, did redound, to the economic benefit of the United States since Europe was America's best trading partner. The plan thus served as an indirect subsidy to the American economy as European nations used the loan to buy American goods.

The collapse of Euro-communism in 1989 and the subsequent disintegration of the Soviet Union in 1991 brought about a fundamental structural change in the external setting of American foreign policy. Therefore, among other policies, post-World War II American policy towards Eastern Europe and the entire former Soviet bloc was altered from a policy of animosity and containment of communism to one of cooperation and a willingness to be helpful in their economic and social transformation. Cold War regulations which had been designed to restrict the communist bloc's access to American market, exports, aid, and commercial credits were eliminated. New consulates and embassies were set up in the former Soviet bloc countries—the Commonwealth of Independent States—while some of their counterparts in Africa were closed. Resources available to the Department of State, the premier foreign policy bureaucracy, were reduced by about thirty percent. Also, American foreign aid programs, which had been designed largely to contain communism, were slashed. U.S. support for authoritarian regimes in Africa that oppressed their citizens in the guise of their role as America's partners in containing Soviet expansionism was curtailed where it was not totally withdrawn.

When in 1990 Saddam Hussein of Iraq attempted to upset the political *status quo* in the oil-rich Persian Gulf by invading, conquering, and occupying Kuwait, the George H.W. Bush administration mobilized the international community in a successful war against Iraq in 1991. By doing so the administration defeated a menace to vital U.S. interest in the oil-rich region. In this century, terrorist attacks on the New York World Trade Center and the Pentagon on 11 September 2001 briefly tempered George W. Bush's unilateralism as he sought allies in the war against terrorism. The terrorist attacks produced more ramifications. Over night, they transformed George W. Bush and shifted U.S. foreign policy from post-Cold War norms of internationalism and respect for international law and institutions towards a new doctrine of preemption, scuttling the traditional strategies of deterrence and containment

This, accordingly, was how in 2002 the Bush administration declared its intention to force a regime change in Iraq and to help transform that country into a democracy. The leader of Iraq, Saddam Hussein, it said, was oppressing his people and was not complying with UN demands that Iraq disarm and destroy its weapons of mass destruction. The administration believed that Iraq constituted an immediate threat and danger to the international community as well as to U.S. interests in the Persian Gulf. Later, the administration added that it would undertake a unilateral preemptive strike against Iraq to thwart the threat and enforce UN Security Council resolutions requiring Iraq to destroy its weapons of mass destruction. The international community, including America's European allies Germany and France, in addition to Russia and the People's Republic of China, refused to endorse the pronouncements and intentions because of their inherent danger and the precedent they would establish. Many members of the UN opposed any U.S. unilateral action against Iraq. Any actions against Iraq, opponents argued, should be multilateral under UN auspices. The administration persisted in its intentions in spite of internal division, especially between the Department of State, which opposed the idea, and the Department of Defense, which advocated it.[1] To emphasize its resolve to carry out its intentions and to assure the world that the nation was united on the issue, the administration drafted a resolution which it requested Congress to pass to authorize it to pursue its goals in Iraq. After a lengthy debate and modification of the draft resolution, Congress resolved to give the president an enabling authority. However, as international opposition and internal division within the administration persisted, the administration was persuaded to work through the United Nations. Eventually UN Security Council Resolution 1441 was passed, calling upon Iraq to comply with UN demands and to allow UN inspectors into its territory in order to resolve the issues raised by the Bush administration diplomatically.

Impatient with the inspection process and what it resolutely insisted was Iraq's noncompliance with UN Security Council resolutions requiring it to disarm, the Bush administration decided to disarm it by force with or without the UN. It sought a second resolution from the UN Security Council to disarm Iraq by force. When it was unable to muster the required nine votes in the Security Council and was faced with a veto threat from France and Russia, it abandoned the resolution and invaded Iraq on 13 March 2003. By doing so it provoked the wrath and disgust of the vast majority of the international community.

American statecraft grows out of domestic imperatives. This inextricable linkage is obvious from the impact of American values, interest groups, and the vagaries of domestic politics on American foreign policy. Thus domestic forces also influence or constrain America's role in the world. Examples of such domestic forces include the U.S. Constitution, political institutions and bureaucracies, individual personalities in office and their characteristics, values and principles, and available human and material resources. The United States is a unique society with multiple centers of power or interest groups. Groups such as farmers' associations, the business community, organized labor, U.S.-based multinational corporations, ethnic and other pressure groups, academic and professional associations, exert pressure on U.S. foreign policy managers as they seek to promote or enhance their specific interests. Jewish-American, Cuban-American, and Irish-American pressure groups, for example, exert significant influence on U.S. policy towards the Middle East, Cuba, and Northern Ireland, respectively.

Except for TransAfrica which is relatively new, Africa lacks a powerful constituency able to exert pressure on U.S. national security bureaucracies, the Congress, and the presidency on behalf of its nations. The "Free South Africa Movement" of the 1980s that culminated in the implementation of the U.S. Comprehensive Anti-Apartheid Sanctions Act of 1986 was the exception. In recent years, however, a strong majority of Americans have come to believe that Africa is important to the United States, and most feel that the United States does not pay enough attention to that continent. Whether this recent perception will be translated into political action or pressure in the interest of African states remains an open question.

The U.S. Constitution is a critical force that influences American foreign policy. The principles of *rule of law—constitutionalism, power sharing,* and *official accountability*—enshrined in it have an enormous impact. Government officials have only the authority and power that the Constitution gives to them. They are at the same time accountable to the American people through a variety of ways, including periodic elections and sensitivity to public opinion, in the performance of their constitutional duties. Also the Constitution's division of institutional responsibility for the making and implementation of American foreign policy between the legislative and executive branches affects the U.S. role in world affairs. This is illustrated by frequent tension between the two branches in treaty and war-making and by the legislative branch's use of its powers of legislation, budget, and investigation to influence the direction of foreign policy and the U.S. role in world affairs.

The administrative structures, institutions, and leadership of the national government also affect the U.S. role in world affairs. This, among other reasons, is a function of the career and socialization experiences, corporate connections, worldview, values and norms, interests and visions political leaders and bureaucrats bring with them to national office. These are not always in harmony one with the other. They often collide. Fundamental differences between Cyrus Vance and Zbigniew Brzezinski, the Carter administration's secretary of state and adviser on national security affairs, respectively, caused a major political problem for the administration's foreign policy. Similarly, ideological and personality conflicts and internecine warfare within the foreign policy teams of the Ronald Reagan and George W. Bush administrations resulted in foreign policies that were contentious and fragmented.

Traditionally, the Departments of State and Defense tend to clash on foreign policy issues because of the differing personalities and perspectives of their leaders.[2] There was division within the George W. Bush administration on a variety of foreign policy issues between the two foreign policy bureaucracies. As indicated above, the Department of State was very cautious about a quick unilateral U.S. military action to disarm Iraq of its weapons of mass destruction, but the Department of Defense and Vice President Dick Cheney and his national security staff advocated such action. There was also division between the two on U.S. policy on North Korea, the Israeli-Palestine peace process, and over the reconstruction of postwar Iraq. In the conflict in Kosovo during the Clinton administration, the Department of State called for military action while the Pentagon opposed such intervention. Similarly, in 1994, Pentagon officials vehemently opposed UN humanitarian intervention in Rwanda to prevent or limit the scope of the genocide in that Central African country. Earlier in the 1960s the Europeanists and the Africanists in the Department of State disagreed over the Kennedy administration's approach to the decolonization of Portuguese colonies in Africa. Also in 1962, when the National Security Council (NSC) proposed U.S. support for self-determination in Angola and offered economic assistance to Portugal in exchange for the measure, the Pentagon characterized such a proposal as precipitous and overly aggressive. The policy, it said, "would produce repercussions in Portugal and possibly Spain that could undermine the American strategic capability to respond to the Berlin, the Middle East and African crises."[3]

Differing approaches to strategic intelligence, especially by the Central Intelligence Agency (CIA) and the Defense Department, and the tendency of presidents and their senior advisers to politicize intelligence and to prefer that the CIA report whatever will suit their policy tend to produce a clash as to the management and direction of foreign policy.[4] In 2002, when he was dissatisfied with what the CIA was telling President Bush on Iraq, Defense Secretary Donald Rumsfeld set up his own intelligence unit to analyze reports from the CIA and other agencies. It is also typical of presidents to reject CIA analysis for information from other agencies, such as the Federal Bureau of Investigation (FBI), that supports their policy.[5]

Division in cases such as the ones identified here is not necessarily bad as it gives the president clear choices and places the responsibility for the ultimate foreign policy decision in his or her hands. However, differences may lead to or provide evidence of disarray when they are not properly handled.

Again, the structure of the American political system as a federation of fifty states imposes on the national government an obligation to take into account the interests of its component units, which may clash with each other or with those of the national government, as it formulates and implements its foreign policy. This necessity creates problems of consultation and coordination for the national government which may impact and protract the process of decision-making. The vagaries of domestic politics, political partisanship, and the quest for political office, especially the presidency, constitute additional influences and constraints. Presidents typically base their decisions—whether on domestic or foreign policy—on political calculations rather than a vigorous process of resolving competing interests and principles. Thus, the vagaries of domestic politics tend to negate the adage that politics stops at the water's edge. As a consequence of all these variable forces, U.S. foreign policy has frequently been distorted by bureaucratic disagreements, infighting and partisan sniping, and quest for reelection, hijacked by foreign lobbyists and domestic special interests, and held hostage by irresponsible and xenophobic members of Congress.

A grasp of how these forces impact America's foreign policy behavior is essential to any comprehensive understanding of U.S. role in conflict resolution in postcolonial Africa, the focus of this study. Equally important is a knowledge of the goals and objectives American leaders seek in their conduct and management of their nation's foreign policy and role in world affairs.

Goals and Objectives of U.S. Foreign Policy

America's foreign policy or role in world affairs seeks to achieve a range of virtually endless goals and objectives which U.S. policymakers define as being in their national interest. However, foreign policy is resource driven. Therefore, since resources—human and material—to promote competing goals and objectives are usually limited, priorities have to be established and definite choices made from the range of goals and objectives.

The primary goal is the promotion of American national security. However, there is no single national security interest but rather a cluster of national security interests including the preservation of American independence, territorial integrity, fundamental institutions, values and traditional way of life; the promotion of the physical and economic security and well-being of

American citizens; the preservation of America's international authority and diplomatic independence. These and other interests may be perceived by U.S. leaders as vital or subsidiary. Any developments that might affect the physical security of America and the lives of its citizens and for which American leaders are willing to risk American lives fall within the definition of vital national security interests. Such interests are mostly nonnegotiable.

Subsidiary national interests are those leaders are willing to negotiate. They may include:

    i.   Ensuring prestige and credibility
    ii.   The promotion of a relatively stable international system
    iii. The promotion of good working relations with friends and allies
    iv. Expansion of democratic government and free market economy
    v.   Finding answers to humanitarian and ecological problems
    vi. Finding methods of dealing with the proliferation of weapons of mass destruction

These and other interests perceived by leaders as subsidiary can be elevated to a vital national security interest.

Essential to the promotion of both vital and subsidiary national interests are peace and prosperity, stability and security, democracy, and a credible defense system. Hence, American leaders factor these into their calculation of the national security interest.

It is important to understand that there is no a priori definition of national interest. U.S. national interest is whatever U.S. policymakers define as such and are willing to make sacrifices to achieve. As a concept, national security is a tool policymakers of a nation apply in their efforts to influence the world environment to their own nation's advantage. Hence, "American foreign policy is not a mechanical calculus of the nation's interests. Instead, determination of those interests is the product of a complex political process anchored in tradition and colored by contemporary developments at home and abroad."[6]

Traditionally, U.S. policy makers have not perceived America's interests in Africa as fundamental or vital. As a result they have tended to relegate Africa to the bottom of their foreign policy priorities. This tendency was most evident prior to World War II when the United States had only "three legations, three consulates-general, eight consulates, and one consular agency on the continent,"[7] and when most official decisions on African issues were made in the Department of State's Division of European Affairs even though those issues had been theoretically assigned to the Division of Near Eastern Affairs. However, Africa began to assume greater strategic significance to America after the United States was drawn into World War II. North Africa provided the Allied troops a place to regroup after Nazi occupation of France. Central and southern Africa had vital minerals, such as uranium, that were essential to Allied war efforts. West Africa straddled important Atlantic sea lanes. There had been fear during the early stages of the war that Germany might invade the Western Hemisphere from West Africa.

After the war, it became generally recognized that the United States did have economic, geostrategic, and political interests in the continent. Africa is a major producer of many primary products—oil, gold, diamond, cobalt, uranium, for example—essential to America's continued industrial growth and production. It offers America, in spite of its many traumas, a market for its products and investment. Its location makes it geostrategically important to the United States as a power that perceives its interests in global terms. In this context, U.S. perception of the threat of communism and Soviet ideological expansion after World War II enhanced the significance of Africa to the United States. Hence, the continent became part of the theater of the Cold War. In the same regard, the Horn of Africa especially has been viewed by U.S. policy makers as essential to the war on terrorism and the effective operation of America's Rapid Deployment Force (RDF), which was organized in 1980 after the Soviet invasion and occupation of Afghanistan to be a strike force capable of moving swiftly into the Persian Gulf to protect U.S. interests in the oil-rich region. Three of RDF's bases are located in Mombasa, Kenya; Berbera, Somalia, and Diego Garcia in the Indian Ocean. Also until its closure in 1974, among other reasons, as a consequence of the development of satellites, Kagnew in Ethiopia was one of America's strategic intelligence-gathering stations. After the tragic events of 11 September 2001, the U.S. government upgraded its geo-strategic and military interests in Djibouti in the Horn of Africa as part of the global war against terrorism.

Africa's voting strength in the UN General Assembly accorded it some significance to the United States during the Cold War and today as it wields its influence as the sole superpower. Africa is also significantly important to the United States because of the political and (especially) economic interests of its NATO allies and chief commercial partners in Africa. Nineteenth-century Western imperialism incorporated African societies into the global economic and political order as appendages of Western Europe. Therefore, American policy makers considered Africa as primarily a European sphere of interest.

Thus, the United States always followed the lead of European powers in African issues and developments.

This tendency persists. In fact, the end of the Cold War diminished whatever strategic importance Africa had in the perception of leading U.S. strategic thinkers. In a debate between Jeffrey Gedman and Ronald Asmus, it was said that "what fires the imagination of [America's] strategic thinkers [in the post-Cold War era] are projects like the coming unification of Korea, the challenge of China, stability on the [Indian] subcontinent, and…the future of the Middle East and the [Persian] Gulf. In relative terms, Europe matters less."[8] Africa, from its conspicuous absence from the list, it can be deduced, mattered not at all. Indeed, during his presidential campaign in 2000, George W. Bush said: "While Africa may be important, it doesn't fit into the [United States'] strategic interests, as far as I can see them." Thus, political attention and available personnel and material resources (foreign aid) are shifted away from Africa whenever there are competing interests. For example, after the end of the Cold War in 1989, U.S. administrations downgraded Africa in favor of the former communist countries of Eastern Europe and the former Soviet republics—the Commonwealth of Independent States. In the early years of the new millennium, U.S. political interest and aid assets were diverted to the Middle East, Afghanistan, and Iraq, and its support for African development, humanitarian, refugee and public health needs as well as peace processes and agreements was considerably reduced. In view of this, U.S. interest in the continent has been essentially a function of America's war against terrorism which, since the terrorist attacks on the New York World Trade Center and the Pentagon, became a major preoccupation of the Bush administration. (See Chapter 9.)

Occasionally, American leaders engage in trade-offs and balancing acts between American values and what they regard as their economic and national security interests. For example, during the Cold War they tolerated growing human rights abuses and political mismanagement in such African countries as Ethiopia, Liberia, Somalia, Sudan, and Zaire (Democratic Republic of the Congo) for strategic or ideological reasons. Inadvertently, they encouraged those abuses through their sympathetic political support of the offending governments with foreign aid and by receiving their leaders at the White House and extending to them other visible forms of cooperation. The African recipients of such cooperation used the approbation associated with them—particularly economic and military assistance—as a means of legitimizing themselves with their people and their neighbors and intimidating potential domestic opposition.

The practice of trade-offs and balancing acts continued after the end of the Cold War. In two instances George W. Bush demonstrated a split personality as to the promotion of democracy abroad. After 11 September 2001 Bush, who during the 2000 campaigns for the presidency had proclaimed himself a realist, sought closer ties with autocratic regimes throughout the Middle East and Asia as allies in his war against al Qaeda, but Bush the "compassionate conservative" proclaimed that democracy is the only true solution to terror. Again, in April 2002, Bush demonstrated his eagerness to accept the (eventually aborted) military overthrow of Hugo Chavez, the elected president of oil-rich Venezuela. He spoke of a "forward strategy of freedom" in the Middle East, urged the rulers of Egypt and Saudi Arabia to press for democracy, but he continued to arm and fund undemocratic governments in both countries because he perceived them as his putative allies on the war on terrorism. For him, "anti-terrorist tactics mandated strategic alliances with tyrants—on the model of U.S. support for Saddam Hussein in the 1980s, when Iran was [America's] greater enemy."[9]

It is obvious, therefore, from these that while some basic Euro-American values—freedom, democracy, economic liberalism and respect for human rights—are being corrupted in practice, the rhetoric of promoting them continues to be espoused. Moral language is thus used to cloak a traditional or concocted national security agenda. Hence, in several instances, a disconnect existed between American values and American foreign policy behavior.

This practice is in accordance with the views of a school of thought known as *realism* regarding the concept of national security and the conduct of foreign policy on the one hand and the promotion of foreign policy goals on the other. Realists stress raw self-interest or the use of power—military power, economic power, and credible deterrence—to protect and promote national security interest. In their view, national security interest is whatever enhances or preserves a state's security, economic and military power, and influence. Therefore, considerations in the conduct of foreign policy are largely derived from what is good for the state and its place in international politics. In such conduct and management of national security, realists place *less faith* in the international community and multilateralism and *more faith* in state power and unilateral action. Further, realists such as Clarke Cochran insist that foreign policy goals should be framed "in terms of whether the national interests in question are achievable and in terms of an analysis of the costs of achieving them in relation to the benefits to be derived."[10]

Another philosophy—moralism or idealism—stresses that moral values, principles, international law, and pragmatism should be the major guides to

American foreign policy decisions and behavior. Therefore, idealists tend to de-emphasize power and war in pursuit of national interest and seek to make the world as it ought to be. They believe that multilateral organizations, such as the League of Nations or the United Nations, should be the major venues through which the United States promotes its ideals, and that international law should be the nation's main policy tool; that force, preferably, should be used as a last resort and only when it is untainted by any hint of national interest. Their premises are best encapsulated in Woodrow Wilson's crusade during and after World War I to make the world safe for democracy. Especially in his Fourteen Points, Wilson called for a new world order of collective security, of "open covenants of peace openly arrived at" after which there would be no more secret diplomacy but freedom of the seas, removal of barriers to trade, self-determination of peoples, general disarmament, and collective security. Historically, American foreign policy has encompassed political realism, moral idealism, and pragmatism. Public support tends to erode very rapidly when any of the three bases appeared to be absent.

The realities of the post-Cold War international system have promoted U.S. national security interests and its role in the world. With its overwhelming military superiority, impressive resource base, and technological skill, the United States is better able to pursue its interests than most other members of the international community. Even so, America is constrained now, as it was in the past, in use of its unique power and position by domestic as well as external forces. For example, despite the overwhelming nature of its military power, the United States is not, does not desire, and does not have the resources to be, the omnipotent policeman of the world. Although the George W. Bush administration defied the UN Security Council and launched a war against Iraq, it did so only after the Council deprived it of the legitimacy of that measure by rejecting its call for a second resolution to authorize war against Iraq. As generally expected, U.S. armed forces easily defeated Iraq and occupied its territory. However, those forces did so at a high price, including strained relations with America's NATO allies, the yet-unknown outcome of the occupation of Iraq, and the very dangerous precedent that the United States alone can act as prosecutor, judge, jury, and executioner. Although a majority of the American public supported the administration's unilateral action in Iraq, it is unlikely that it will support a costly and protracted occupation of the country.

The preceding discussion provides some understanding of the fundamental operative forces of U.S. foreign policy. Its purpose is to facilitate an appreciation of U.S. role in conflict resolution in postcolonial Africa and to underline the fact that U.S. foreign policy is neither a social welfare nor a purely humanitarian venture. This means that issues of conflict resolution in Africa or elsewhere will arouse U.S. concern mainly when American security interests are at stake. This is the essence of President William Jefferson Clinton's Presidential Decision Directive-25 (PDD-25), which stipulated the conditions under which U.S. armed forces would participate in multilateral peacekeeping or peace-enforcement missions under UN auspices. A similar guidepost for U.S. foreign policy was emphasized by John Quincy Adams when he served as U.S. Secretary of State. In a Fourth of July 1821 speech, Adams said:

> Whenever the standard of freedom and independence has been or shall be unfurled, there will be America's heart....But she does not go abroad in search of monsters to destroy. She is the well wisher to the freedom and independence of all. She is the champion and vindicator only of her own.[11]

The guideposts underline the critical element of enlightened self-interest. Again, this element is illustrated by President Clinton's statement before a National Summit on Africa in Washington, DC, in February 2002. On that occasion Clinton said:

> Because we want to build a world in which our security is not threatened by the spread of armed conflict, in which bitter ethnic and religious differences are resolved by the force of argument, not the force of arms, we must be involved in Africa.[12]

When an American president departs from these traditional guideposts, he does so either because of bad advice or as a result of his own personal ambition or ideology. Since the disintegration of the Soviet Union, the United States has remained the sole superpower, the preeminent world leader. Yet, as demonstrated by Clinton's PDD-25 and George W. Bush's unilateral rejection of the Kyoto Protocol on global warming and the international criminal court and his abrogation of the ABM Treaty in pursuit of a national missile defense system, American national security interest, not the interest of the international community in general, remains the major goal of American foreign policy.

This book examines the dimensions of the U.S. role in conflict resolution in postcolonial Africa by focusing on four specific cases—conflicts in the Horn of Africa (1962–1994), Western Sahara (1975–2003), Angola (1975–1993), and genocide in Rwanda (1994). Chapter 2 provides a succinct survey of armed conflicts in postcolonial Africa in order to identify the circumstances that precipitated U.S. action. Chapter 3 briefly surveys the origins of U.S. role in general in these conflicts, and Chapter 4 documents U.S. intervention. Chapters

5, 6, 7, and 8 examine that role in specific African conflicts. Chapter 9 looks at the Clinton administration's African Crisis Response Initiative (ACRI). Chapter 10 summarizes the dimensions of the U.S. role as well as its lessons and legacies.

Notes

1. Steven R. Weisman, "Powell at New Turning Point in His Evolution on Iraq," *The New York Times* (13 March 2003), wysiwyg://4Dhttp://www.nytimes.com/200...14/international/middleeast/14POWE.html.

2. Robin Wright, "White House Divided Over [Iraq] Reconstruction," *Los Angeles Times* (2 April 2003), wysiwyg://56/http://www.latimes.com/new...358865.story?coll=l%2Dhome %2Dheadlines.

3. George Wright, *The Destruction of a Nation: United States' Policy Toward Angola Since 1945* (London: Pluto, 1997), p. 38.

4. See James Risen, "Iraq Arms Report Now the Subject of a C.I.A. Review," *The New York Times* (4 June 2003), http://www.nytimes.com/2003/06/04/international/world special/04WEAP.html?th; James Risen and David Johnston, "Split at CIA and F.B.I on Iraqi Ties to Al Qaeda," *The New York Times* (1 February 2003), wysiwyg://36/http:// www.ny times.com/ 200...02/international/middleeast/02INTE.html.

5. See Pat M. Holt, "U.S. Intelligence: Seeing What It Wants to See in Iraq," *Christian Science Monitor* (7 November 2002), wysiwyg://60/http://www.csmonitor.com/2002/ 1107/p11s01-coop.html.

6. Eugene R. Wittkopf et al., *American Foreign Policy: Pattern and Process*, 6th Edition (Belmont, CA: Wadsworth, 2003), p. 12.

7. David A. Dickson, *United States Policy Towards Sub-Saharan Africa: Change, Continuity and Constraint* (Lanham, MD: University Press of America, 1985), p. 3.

8. "Debate: The Future of U.S.-German Relations," An Examination of the Troubled Strategic Relationship Between Washington and Berlin by Jeffrey Gedman, director of the Aspen Institute Berlin, and former Clinton [State Department] official Ronald D. Asmus, http://www.nytimes.com/cfr/international/slot2_070203.html.

9. Benjamin R. Barber, "Commentary, American Dream, Super-Sized," http://www.latimes. com/news/opinion/com...039.story?coll=comment-opinions.

10. Clarke E. Cochran et al., *American Public Policy: An Introduction*, 7th Edition (Belmont, CA: Wadsworth, 2003), p. 402.

11. Pat M. Holt, "Bush: A Liberator or Conqueror?" *Christian Science Monitor* (5 December 2002), wysiwyg://63/http://www.csmonitor.com/2002/1205/p09s01-coop.html; F. Ugboaja Ohaegbulam, *A Concise Introduction to American Foreign Policy* (New York: Peter Lang, 1999), p. 154.

12. President William J. Clinton, Africa and America: Partners in the New Millennium: Statement before National Summit on Africa (Washington, DC, 16–20 February 2000).

CHAPTER 2
Armed Conflicts in Postcolonial Africa

Destructive conflicts have turned Africa, the most diverse of all the continents in the world, into a continent unable to turn its trend of diversity into opportunities for development.

Conflicts…[may be] used as vehicles for social change in order to promote justice, peace, sustainable development, democracy and human rights. Competition for power and resources is entirely natural, it is the essence of the political process. The problem, therefore, is not the eradication of *conflict* but the limitation on those forms of conflict that utilize violence. The challenge is about how to manage this competition without plunging a society into a spiral of violence and how to build patterns of development, institutions, and political cultures that can mediate such competition peacefully and routinely. If this competition results in gross imbalance in the allocation of resources and some ethnic, clan, religious, regionalist and nationalist groups begin to fear for their future and physical safety, a series of dangerous and difficult to resolve strategic dilemmas arise that contain within them the potential for tremendous [and destructive] violence. [Africa's case][1]

Africa has been the scene of many armed conflicts since the 1950s when the European colonial empires began to collapse,[2] earning the continent, already the world's poorest region, the notoriety of being the world's most war-ravaged region and thus most heavily burdened with conflict-generated problems—such as fatalities, flows of refugees and displaced persons, and adverse developmental, environmental, and psychological impacts—which are not easily measurable on an accountant's spreadsheet. During the last decade of the twentieth century alone, thirty African countries experienced violent and destructive conflicts.[3] Many of those countries grappled with continuing civil war or the threat of renewed fighting. At least twenty of the continent's fifty-four countries were beset by armed conflict during the last year of the twentieth century and the first of the new millennium.

War continued in former Zaire (Democratic Republic of the Congo, DRC) after the dictator Mobutu Sese Seko was overthrown in 1997. Laurent Kabila, leader of the armed revolt against Mobutu, was himself assassinated in January 2001. Not long after the ouster of Mobutu, the Kabila-led liberation movement split into warring factions, which attracted intervention by six neighboring countries. Angola, Zimbabwe, and Namibia intervened on the side of Kabila's government; Rwanda, Uganda, and Burundi on the side of the rebel factions. A cease-fire agreement negotiated in Lusaka, Zambia, in 1999 between Kabila and the rebels who controlled about one-half of the country had not been enforced by the time of Kabila's death. All six interventionists had vested interests in the war and were motivated by greed, a grab for land and resources. A panel appointed by the UN Security Council charged Uganda, Rwanda, and Burundi especially with "systematic and systemic," "mass-scale looting" of the DRC, extracting diamonds, gold, timber, elephant tusks, and other resources from the war-torn nation.[4] The Rwanda government, in particular, was also driven by security concerns, viewing the war in the DRC as an extension of the struggle between the Tutsi-led government and the Hutu rebels. Thus, ignoring peace accords it signed in Lusaka, Zambia, it fought Hutu rebels, known as Inter-hamwe, in North and South Kivu Provinces of the DRC, supporting its activities with revenues from mines and other resources it controlled in the region.

Angola, which supported Kabila in the DRC, was itself embroiled in a civil war with the National Union for the Total Independence of Angola (UNITA) over political succession after the collapse of Portugal's African empire in 1975 until Jonas Savimbi, the leader of the rebel movement, was killed in 2002. In 1999 the war spread sporadically into Namibia, whose government had authorized the Popular Movement for the Liberation of Angola (MPLA) government of Angola to operate on its territory against UNITA rebels. Besides the civil war with UNITA, the Angolan government fought and continues to fight separatists in Cabinda (population 250,000), who began their quest for separatism in 1961 during Portuguese colonial rule. Separated from the rest of Angola by a sliver of the DRC, Cabinda is rich in oil reserves and is Angola's major source of revenue. It produces about 70 percent of Angola's oil and almost all of its foreign exchange earnings. The enclave also provided Angola with a strategic base to guard against rear base operations by UNITA rebels against the government.

In Algeria, Muslim fundamentalists waged a campaign of terror after the cancellation of elections they believe they had won in 1992. Punitive actions by the government escalated the number of massacres in the country to more than 100,000 since the beginning of the troubles.

In Central Africa, Burundi has had no peace. It remains in the grip of a bitter civil war between the Tutsi and Hutu rebels. The Hutu make up 85 percent of the population, but the Tutsi, 15 percent of the population, control the government and the army as well as much of the economic life of the country.

Map 2.1 Africa in 2003

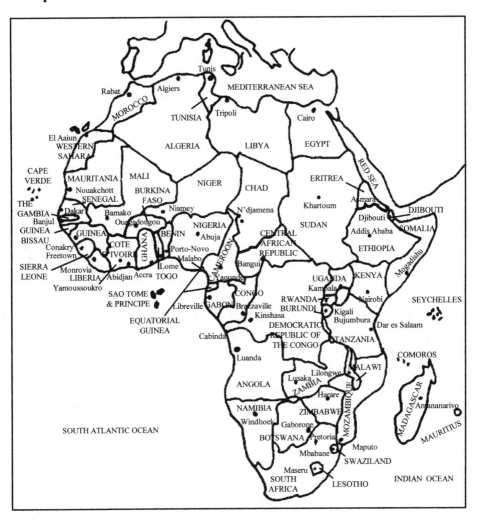

The volatile imbalance resulted in killings for forty years on both sides. More than 200,000 people in the country have died since the most recent bout began in 1993. The rebel groups rejected a peace agreement signed in Arusha, Tanzania. Violence, therefore, continues in the country. Still recovering from the 1994 massacre of an estimated 800,000 Tutsi and moderate Hutu, Rwanda remains politically tense. As of October 2003, about 100,000 of its nationals remain in prison awaiting trial for their part in the 1994 massacres. Rwanda intervened on the side of the rebels in the civil war in DRC at the same time that it battled against Hutu rebels in the east of the former Zaire. Uganda, too, fought on three fronts—against rebels in two areas in the north and west of its territory and in the civil war in the DRC in support of rebels against the late Kabila's government until its withdrawal in March 2001.

The Horn of Africa, labeled the arc of instability by political observers in the 1970s, remained a zone of armed conflict until the dawn of the twenty-first century. War, anarchy, and political instability were the characteristic features of the region as the new century began. Eritrean nationalists waged a war of national liberation against Ethiopia for more than three decades. In May 1998, five years after Eritrea won its independence from Ethiopia, war erupted again between the two countries and raged until a settlement was reached in 2001.

Somalia, after waging irredentist wars against Ethiopia for more than fifteen years, descended into anarchy in the 1990s as a result of wars among its clans. Because of one region's secession and war among the militias of rival clans, there was no authoritative body to maintain effective control and to fulfill the normal functions of a state until August 2000, when a transitional government was set up. As of 2004 most of the protagonists have not recognized the provisional government set up in 2000. War and famine have claimed more than one million lives in Sudan where a civil war has raged since 1983 between the Arab Muslim-dominated government in the north and resource-rich southern Sudan.

In Chad, rebel forces have continued to fight government troops in northern Tibeste since October 1998. Despite a cease-fire agreement in 1991, Morocco and Polisario nationalists are deadlocked on the modalities of a UN-prescribed referendum to resolve the dispute on sovereignty over the former Spanish Sahara.

A civil war (which devastated Sierra Leone for eleven years, beginning in 1991, and invited the Economic Community of West Africa's Monitoring Group [ECOMOG] and UN intervention) spread conflict and suffering into Guinea by September 2000. Interethnic and religious tension became a permanent experience of Nigerians. The introduction of the Islamic law code—*Sharia*—in northern Nigeria in 1999 provoked violence in the north and the southeast of the country which left more than 2,000 people dead. Continued violence between some southwest and northern elements took an additional toll in 2000. The thirty-month civil war (1967–1970) in the West African nation had already caused much devastation and the death of more than one million people. Elsewhere in West Africa, Senegal especially, political and economic stability remained elusive as the new century began. For over eighteen years separatists in the southwest region of Senegal's Casamance have remained in open rebellion against the government. In Côte d'Ivoire, several years of divisive ethnic politics preceded a military coup in December 1999 in which General Robert Guei overthrew the regime of Henri Konan Bedie. The coup marked the onset of a period of instability, violence, and economic uncertainty. The election of Laurent Gbagbo as president in 2001 did not restore stability. His victory rapidly turned into political and ethnic fighting between his supporters and those of the opposition leader, Alassane Ouattara. In November 2002 northern Muslims and southern Christians began to fight each other for control of the government. France, the former colonial authority, intervened militarily and diplomatically to establish a fragile peace. Subsequently, it was to work with a West African force to give advice and monitor the uneasy peace in January 2003.

These hot spots tended to set off chain reactions. The brutal war in Sierra Leone, for example, started as an offshoot of a civil war in Liberia and spread several years later to neighboring Guinea. As noted above, the war of political succession in Angola spread to Namibia in 1999. The 1994 Rwanda conflict spread to DRC, and six neighboring countries intervened in the civil war in the DRC shortly after the ouster of Mobutu in 1997.

These armed conflicts in Africa consumed enormous internal and external funds. Thus, scarce resources were devoted to waging war and to emergency relief and reconstruction instead of towards the sustainable development programs required for the solid foundation for long-term peace and prosperity which African societies sorely need. In addition, the wars and conflicts adversely affected the populations. The recruitment of child soldiers caused incalculable traumas; while the planting of land mines not only maimed the limbs of civilians—men, women, and children—but also undermined food production and the entire agricultural sector of the economy. The UN and the major powers of the world, not just the African states themselves, were fully aware of these facts. By March 2001, the UN had four peacekeeping missions in Africa: UN Mission for the Referendum in Western Sahara (MINURSO), UN Assistance Mission in Sierra Leone (UNAMSIL), UN Mission in Ethiopia and Eritrea (UNMEE), and UN Mission in the Democratic Republic of the Congo (MONUC). A fifth mission in Côte d'Ivoire—MUNICI—began in 2003 to help enforce a fragile cease-fire in the West African nation's eight-month civil war. Six more missions were established before the end of the year. The additions included: UN Office in Burundi (UNOB), UN Peace-Building Office in the Central African Republic (BONUCA), UN Mission in Liberia (UNMIL), UN Peace-Building Office in Liberia (UNOL), UN Peace-Building Support Office in Guinea-Bissau (UNOGBIS), and UN Political Office for Somalia (UNPOS).[5] Yet, because of lack of international political will and the relative disengagement of the United States from security issues on the continent, the major powers did little, beyond these, compared to their responses to other violent conflicts in Kosovo and East Timor, to contain the warfare that ravaged Africa unchecked.

Initially, the armed conflicts in Africa were wars of national liberation from imperial control by European powers. Algerian nationalists successfully fought such a war against France and French settlers in Algeria, especially for about eight years (1954–1962). A similar protracted war of national liberation was waged for thirteen years (1961–1974) in Angola, Mozambique, Guinea-Bissau, and Cape Verde Islands against Portugal. That war culminated in the collapse of Portuguese colonial empire in Africa in 1974. But its political and economic ramifications persist in the former colonies of Portugal, especially Angola, where they have been most magnified.

In southern Africa—Zimbabwe, Namibia, and the Republic of South Africa—African nationalists waged guerrilla wars and organized violent resistance movements against white minority domination in order to establish majority rule and multiracial government. Those violent conflicts took their toll in both human lives and various aspects of social life until their resolution in Zimbabwe (1980), Namibia (1990), and the collapse of apartheid in South Africa (1990). In Zimbabwe, control of arable land by whites, a major cause of the original conflict between whites and blacks during the colonial period, remains a source of the contemporary conflict.

Before the end of apartheid in South Africa in 1990, the violence had spread to neighboring countries in the region. After its independence from Portugal in 1975, Mozambique permitted the Zimbabwe African National Union (ZANU) and the African National Congress (ANC) South Africa to use its territory as a base of operation against white minority governments in Zimbabwe and the

Republic of South Africa, respectively. Zambia, like Mozambique, provided Zimbabwe African People's Union (ZAPU) and the ANC bases in its territory for operations against the same white minority regimes. Angola, similarly, allowed the Namibian People's Liberation Army (PLAN), the military wing of Southwest African Peoples Organization (SWAPO), to carry out guerrilla operations against South Africa. The UN revoked South Africa's political mandate over Namibia in 1966 and, at the same time, declared its continued presence in the territory as an illegal occupation.

These measures provoked further violence in southern Africa. The white minority governments of Zimbabwe and South Africa mounted violent raids at will against Zambia, Angola, and Mozambique. Both intervened in a civil strife in Mozambique by creating, training, and arming a rebel group—Mozambique National Resistance Movement (RENAMO)—against the government and people of Mozambique. For about ten years the apartheid regime in South Africa used RENAMO and its policy of "destructive engagement" to wreak havoc on the population, economy, and infrastructure of Mozambique.

The vast majority of the violent conflicts in Africa occurred after independence was conceded by the European imperial powers. Most of them, including more than eighty violent changes of government, were internal. (See Table 2.1.) This is a global trend: Most violent conflicts in the contemporary world are intrastate rather than interstate. Interstate wars in the continent have been few, infrequent, and brief: Ethiopia/Somalia; Kenya/Somalia; Uganda/Tanzania; Algeria/Morocco; Egypt/Libya; Libya/Chad; Ethiopia/Eritrea—out of concern for self-preservation and in accordance with the injunction by the Organization of African Unity against African nations intervening in the domestic affairs of sister states and fighting each other directly. So far, ethnic irredentism, dispute over territory and natural resources, rivalry for power and economic advantage, and alleged subversive activities were most common causes of the interstate wars that have been waged. (See Table 2.2.)

During the last two decades of the twentieth century, the nature and scope of internal wars in Africa, as in other regions of the world, changed dramatically. The combatants were not just regular armies of established states or rebels and mercenaries but also warlords, paramilitary bands, and armed militias and private security groups who engaged in criminal activities and routine massacre of civilians without any concern whatsoever for reprisals. An alarming trend began in the 1990s. Weak governments, unable to rely on their armed forces or the erstwhile Cold War-style armed intervention by the superpowers, hired private military companies to deal with challenges from rebel groups. These

Table 2.1: Intra-African Conflicts (1959–2000)

Conflict	Date	Issue	Outcome
Algeria	1992–2001	Civil War, Government vs. Islamic Militants	Quiescent; More than 100,000 Deaths
Angola	1975–2002	Political succession Cabinda Separatism	MPLA Government Ongoing War
Burundi	1959–61; 1963–67; 1973; 1996–2002	Ethnic Strife (Tutsi vs. Hutu)	Quiescent
Central African Republic	1996–98	Revolt Against Political and Economic Mismanagement	Quiescent
Chad	1977–81	Civil Strife	Settled; Strife in Tibeste
Comoros	1997–2000	Secession	Ongoing
Congo-Brazzaville	1997–98	Military Rebellion against Government	Settled
Congo, Democratic Republic	1960–65; 1977–78, 1996–2002	Secession; Government vs. Rebels Supported by Rwanda and Uganda	Secession Ended Mobutu; Over-thrown; Ongoing
Ethiopia	1962–91	Secession (Eritrea); Internal Rebellion	Independence of Eritrea; Overthrow of Mengistu
Guinea-Bissau	1998–99	Army Mutiny; Civil Strife	Settled; ECOMOG Intervention
Lesotho	1998	Election Violence against Government	Settled; Intervention by RSA and Botswana
Liberia	1989–97	Civil War	Settled (by ECOMOG)
Mozambique	1976–87	Civil Strife	Settled
Nigeria	1966–70; 1995–99	Civil War (Secession); Civil Strife	Secession Ended; Quiescent
Rwanda	1959; 1972–73; 1994	Ethnic Strife; Hutu vs. Tutsi	Quiescent
Sierra Leone	1998–2001	Civil War; Government vs. Rebel Movement	Lome Accord

Somalia	1991–94	Secession; Intra-Clan Strife	Quiescent
Sudan	1964–72; 1985–2002	Civil War (South vs. North-Dominated Muslim Government)	Settled (1972); Renewed; Ongoing
Tanganyika	1964	Army Mutiny	Settled
Uganda	1981–86	Civil Strife/Military Revolt	Overthrow of Obote; Ongoing

Table 2.2: Interstate African Conflicts (1962–2000)

Conflict	Date	Issue
Algeria-Morocco	1963–65	Territory
Benin-Niger	1963	Territory
Ethiopia-Somalia	1964–78	Ethnic Irredentism
Kenya-Somalia	1964–72	Ethnic Irredentism
Ghana-Burkina Faso	1972	Territory
Ghana-Neighbors	1965	Subversion
Ghana-Guinea	1966	Subversion
Rwanda-Burundi	1966–73	Subversion
Equatorial Guinea-Gabon	1972	Territory
Guinea-Côte d'Ivoire	1966–67	Subversion/Seizure of Diplomats
Guinea-Senegal	1971	Subversion
Tanzania-Uganda	1978/1979	Subversion/Territory
Sudan-Ethiopia	1977–80	Territory
Benin-Gabon	1977	Territory
Burkina Faso-Mali	1977	Territory
Eritrea-Ethiopia	1998–2000	Territory

private military companies, such as Executive Outcomes (from South Africa), engaged in a variety of operations in the zones of conflict. They organized weapons transfers, trained palace and security guards, formed business partnerships with corrupt politicians, guarded mineral mining sites, and received payment for their services in mining concessions and oil contracts.[6] For all the belligerents, including the government, the rebels, and the private military companies—Executive Outcomes, Sandline International (based in London), and Military Professional Services, Incorporated (based in Alexandria, VA)—land mines, grenades, and small arms and light weapons such as AK-47 assault rifles and machine guns became the major weapons of choice. With these weapons they maimed civilians, halted agricultural production and a significant amount of social interaction, and wiped out much of the infrastructure of the nation in conflict and the morale of its society. These weapons reached the belligerents in various ways. Combatants in the internal violent conflicts only needed the ability to pay or, alternatively, an external sponsor who was able to pay.[7] The rebels in Angola, DRC, and Sierra Leone, for example, did not even need money as the leaders were able to obtain arms through trading timber, diamonds, and other natural resources smuggled out of the country.

In violation of several international agreements, including the African Charter on the Rights and Welfare of the Child, that prohibit the participation of minors in armed conflict, both governmental and nongovernmental belligerent groups in Angola, Burundi, the Democratic Republic of the Congo, Liberia, Mozambique, Sierra Leone, and Uganda abducted, recruited, trained and armed children in order to increase their ranks and to terrorize the civilian population.[8] According to Amnesty International and other human rights groups, the estimated number of soldiers and rebels under eighteen years in Africa was 13,900 in 1996 and 66,250 from 1998 to the first quarter of 2000.[9] This has become a global trend. *Human Rights Watch World Report 2001* estimated that 300,000 boys and girls were fighting in armed conflicts in approximately thirty countries during the last decade of the twentieth century. According to the Report, 75,000 of those children were participating in conflicts in Asia and the Pacific, placing the region second only to Africa in the use of children as soldiers.[10]

While, increasingly, the belligerents cautiously avoided direct confrontation with each other, they made the civilian population their targets. Thus, civilians suffered more casualties than the combatants themselves both physically and psychologically. In addition the warlords (for example, Charles Taylor of

Liberia, Foday Sankoh of Sierra Leone, and Jonas Savimbi of Angola) cloaked themselves as nationalists but were, in fact, terrorists. They used modern communications equipment—cell phones, websites and electronic media—to mobilize ethnic loyalty for widespread violence. They looted their nation's resources such as diamonds and timber through smuggling and clandestine relations with legitimate companies. By such means they readily obtained arms and weapons in exchange for diamonds or other commodities. They had no abiding interest in conflict resolution but rather intended to continue violent conflict in order to maintain their loot and wealth.[11] In this objective they were joined by their bedfellows, profiteers outside Africa who gained from the wars devastating the continent. The alien profiteers not only supplied rebel groups such as the Jonas Savimbi's UNITA and Foday Sankoh's Revolutionary United Front (RUF) with arms, they also provided international networks for arms and diamonds trafficking in violation of UN sanctions.[12] For these reasons international sanctions and mediation achieved negligible results. What generally were the major causes of the wars?

Major Causes of Conflicts

Although international politics and external economic forces fanned and exacerbated the conflicts, their root cause was the dynamics within postcolonial African societies themselves.[13] A major element of those dynamics is the political and economic decay of a significant number of these states. Political decay, as in West Africa and the Great Lakes region, created a power vacuum in those governments that had only nominal control over their territories and little power over means of coercion. Economic decay aggravated the situation for, in the absence of a viable legal-administrative structure, violence was the only way of securing access to national resources. Furthermore, economic decay provided the warring factions with an endless supply of fighters, including unemployed adolescents and child soldiers who saw few other career prospects in the poverty-stricken and war-torn nations.

While there were similar causes—such as the inordinate political ambition of such individuals as Jonas Savimbi, Charles Taylor, and Robert Mugabe; a struggle for the control of national resource endowments in such countries as Angola, the Democratic Republic of the Congo, Liberia, and Sierra Leone; a lack of economic opportunity and political participation; ethnic and religious animosities; a history of political abuse; and corrupt leadership—no general theory of the causation of conflicts applies across the entire continent. The dynamics within nations differed, among other reasons, according to their history, different levels of political, social, and economic conditions, and development. Each troubled African nation has had its own unique experience since independence. The dynamics within each nation had several components. The UN secretary-general, Kofi Annan, provided an insight into some elements of the dynamics when he identified the reasons for the high incidence of violent crisis in Africa. According to him, it

> is a question of management. It is a question of leadership. It is a question of greed. It is a question of ethnic conflicts, which are sometimes based on one group's perception that [it is] not being treated fairly, it is being discriminated against by the state, or by the group that wields power, sort of "winner-takes-all" approach to the political process.[14]

The UN secretary-general added:

> The nature of political power in many African states, together with the real and perceived consequences of capturing and maintaining power, is a key source of conflict across the continent. It is frequently the case that political victory assumes a "winner-takes-all" form with respect to wealth and resources, patronage, and the prestige and prerogatives of office...political control becomes excessively important, and the stakes become dangerously high. This situation is exacerbated when, as it is often the case in Africa, the State is the major provider of employment and political parties are largely either regional or ethnically based. In such circumstances, the multiethnic character of most African states makes conflict even more likely, leading to an often violent politicization of ethnicity.[15]

The situation in Nigeria, Africa's most populous country, illustrates these elemental dynamics. The country's greedy leaders have consistently mismanaged the nation's economy and political process. Official corruption is pervasive and endemic. The leaders persistently use ethnicity, including the politics of ethnic security, to ensure their political survival. The election of President Moshood Abiola on 12 June 1993 was annulled by the military mainly because of his region and ethnic origin. The political administration of Lagos, the former capital of the country for over seventy years, is now exclusively the preserve of the native national group despite the contributions of other Nigerian nationalities to its growth and development. The adoption of the Islamic legal code, *Sharia*, by some states in the north widened a religious cleavage between Christians and Muslims. A perennial source of conflict, the cleavage caused the violent death of hundreds of Nigerian citizens in February and May 2000 during bloody clashes between Christians and Muslims over the adoption of *Sharia*. In November 2002, more than 200 Nigerians were killed when Muslim extremists took exception to a newspaper editorial ridiculing their opposition to the hosting of a Miss World Pageant at Abuja.

Furthermore, for over two years, militant Ijaw youths of the Niger Delta, protesting, among other things, the environmental blight and impoverishment of the region, clashed sporadically with the armed forces of the country as they attacked oil companies and installations. In the southwest, Odua People's Congress, a militant group demanding autonomy for the Yoruba ethnic group, was linked to various ethnic clashes in the commercial capital, Lagos, where hundreds of people were killed. After six constitutions had been written and adopted since 1959, persistent demands were made in several quarters in 1999 and 2000 for a sovereign national conference to determine the modalities of the existence of Nigeria as a sovereign state and of the relations among its nationality groups. After political control of the country at the executive/ presidential level shifted to the South in 1999, civilian and military leaders in the North who had controlled Nigeria for nearly forty years, wasted no time in complaining bitterly against "marginalization" of the North. Apparently, they assumed that they no longer controlled the most prestigious and lucrative positions in the federation.

Bad Governance

One major problem within African states is bad governance. Most of Africa's wars have been the result of bad governance, and this is likely to be the case until Africa masters its problems with personal rule, weak leadership, inadequate checks and balances between the major branches of the government—the executive, legislative, and the judiciary—a lack of accountability and transparency, and the absence of an influential civil society. To date postcolonial Africa is suffering from a crisis of leadership. Venal leaders without any modicum of vision, who allow massive declines in their peoples' standard of living while enriching themselves and their cronies, are the curse of the African continent. Unfortunately, African states and governments and the international community have not been willing to speak out against autocracy or political repression in the continent. Idi Amin of Uganda was tolerated. Only a few voices have been raised outside those of the government of the U.K., the European Union, and the U.S. government against Robert Mugabe's exploitation of the land problem in Zimbabwe to prolong his political career. The European Union and the United States imposed visa bans on Zimbabwe's leaders, froze their overseas assets, and halted official assistance to Mugabe's government. Mugabe, however, remained recalcitrant and defiant. He abhors political competition and hurls political opponents into prison when he does not charge them with treason. This typical behavior of African rulers is often compounded by the corrupt activities of a discredited public service and a judiciary stripped of its independence and so perceived as a mere puppet of the ruling elite.

As a consequence of these institutional inadequacies, weak and authoritarian African rulers generate considerable resentment by their authoritarianism and inability to manage factional struggles; by serving the interests of some ethnic groups while neglecting or trampling upon those of other groups; by excluding certain groups from power or inadequately representing some groups in government, the law courts, the military, the police, and other state and political institutions, and the civil service and state employment. The ruthless corruption and reckless misrule of these rulers tend to strip them of their moral authority, and the government they run of its force and legitimacy. These practices tend to aggravate the characteristic poverty and gross income inequality within the state. The resentment that flows from them creates social and political tensions which escalate to violent conflicts. In the words of Adebayo Adedeji, "Civil wars and civil strifes are but violent reactions to the pervasive lack of democracy, the denial of human rights, the complete disregard of the sovereignty of the people, the lack of empowerment and, generally bad governance."[16]

Legacies of Imperial Map-Making and Rule

The legacies of imperial map-making, together with the framework of colonial laws and institutions which emergent African states inherited at independence, form part of the dynamics in postcolonial Africa. The imperial map-makers balkanized African national groups to suit their own interests. At the same time, they amalgamated on paper, for their own administrative and economic convenience, nationalities with differing political cultures and religious traditions. The framework of colonial laws and institutions which African states inherited had been designed to exploit local and regional divisions, not to overcome them. Thus, the pervasive colonial legacy of ethnic and regional particularism continued to promote conventional and guerrilla wars as ethnic groups, clans, or regional parties vied for the control of the state, the major provider of employment and resources for social and economic development. These elements of colonial legacy were notably among the core causes of the civil wars in the Democratic Republic of the Congo (1960–1964), Nigeria (1967–1970), Chad (1977–1981), Sudan (1955–1972; 1983–present), and the tragedies and traumas of Rwanda (1994).

The resumed civil war in Sudan was far more complex. It began in 1983 as a conflict between the predominantly Christian South, which was seeking greater autonomy and religious freedom, and the largely Muslim government of the North. Other issues in the civil war were historical struggles, competition for resources, ethnicity, and politics. The Muslim-Arab-dominated government in the North imposed Muslin law on non-Muslims of the South and controlled and exploited oil deposits in the South. Stubbornly resistant to peacemaking, the war raged for more than twenty years. More than two million Sudanese died as a result of the fighting and war-related famine. Some 4.4 million southern Sudanese were forced to flee their homes. This number represented the largest displaced population in the world and cost the international community one-quarter of a billion dollars a year for humanitarian relief.[17] (See Chapter 4 on U.S. diplomatic intervention in the conflict) In addition, between 5,000 and 15,000 southern Sudanese women and children were reported to have been abducted and sold in the course of the conflict as slaves by Arab militiamen loyal to the northern-controlled government.

Armed disputes over inherited boundaries and natural resources occurred between Algeria and Morocco, Libya and Chad, Nigeria and Cameroon. As early as 1963/64, the Organization of African Unity decided that African states should accept as sacrosanct the boundaries they had inherited at independence; that attempts to revise those boundaries by armed force would open a Pandora's box and would know no end. The probability of such an outcome was very high, given the fact that many African states faced the challenge of forging a genuine national identity from among the disparate and often competing communities within the polities they had inherited. Governments were instead encouraged to pursue economic cooperation and joint exploitation of those natural resources which straddled their borders.

Related to the legacy of boundaries inherited from the colonial powers was the issue of ethnic irredentism. This too was a cause of violent conflict in the Horn of Africa. Compounded by the wider geographic importance of the region, this attempt to reunite Somali people who had been split into five territories by European imperial powers led to protracted conflicts between Ethiopia and Somalia, and Somalia and Kenya.

Underdeveloped Economy

The underdeveloped economy and the commercial relations instituted by colonialism form part of the dynamic roots of the conflicts. European colonial rule incorporated African countries into the world capitalist system, thus, fostering their economic dependency, underdevelopment, and lack of industrial-ization. It transferred from Africa to Europe wealth that should have been used to develop and industrialize the continent, thus creating jobs. The economic infrastructure it provided was never adequate, and large parts of some colonial territories, especially those without mineral resources or good soil for cash crops, were left without roads or railways. Thus, colonialism caused uneven economic and social development in virtually every colony. Industrialization or manufacturing was completely neglected. African countries, therefore, became producers of raw materials and consumers of finished goods imported from Europe or elsewhere overseas to the exclusive advantage of the manufacturers and exporters. Importing manufactured goods eliminated local industries and skills that had once produced those goods, delaying technological development and creating high unemployment rates and poverty. Colonial economic policy also adversely affected agricultural production and self-sufficiency in Africa. It promoted cash cropping and failed to diversify the agricultural economy, fostering thereby mono-crop economies. These negative economic effects of colonial rule are part of the dynamics which have produced unfortunate political and social consequences, including foreign indebtedness and wars throughout postcolonial Africa.

As the UN secretary-general's report on the causes of conflict in Africa stated, colonial economy and the commercial relations instituted under colonial rule created long-term distortions in the political economy of African states.

> Colonial transportation networks and related physical infrastructure were designed to satisfy the needs of trade with the metropolitan country, not to support the balanced growth of an indigenous economy. In addition to frequently imposing unfavorable terms of trade, economic activities that were strongly skewed towards extractive industries and primary commodities for export stimulated little demand for steady and widespread improvements in the skills and educational levels of the workforce. The consequences of this pattern of production and exchange spilled over into the postcolonial state. As political competition was not rooted in viable national economic systems, in many instances the prevailing structure of incentives favored capturing the institutional remnants of the colonial economy for factional advantage.[18]

Thus, wherever poverty is pervasive, as in postcolonial Africa where the state is the major source of wealth and power, wars have been and are being waged purely for economic motives: to control the state and national resources. Protagonists and international arms merchants indulge in wars in order to profit from chaos and lack of accountability. The *Report of the UN Secretary-General* states that "in Liberia, the control and exploitation of diamonds, timber and other raw materials was one of the principal objectives of the warring factions. Control over those resources financed the various factions and gave them the means to sustain the conflict."[19] The Report also found this to be true of Angola "where protracted difficulties in the peace process owed much to the importance of control over the exploitation of the country's lucrative diamond fields. In Sierra Leone, the chance to plunder natural resources and loot Central Bank reserves was a key motivation of those who seized power from the elected Government in May 1997."[20]

Added to various aspects of colonial legacy, competition for scarce land and water resources in central Africa exacerbated intrastate conflict in Rwanda and Burundi and led to war between the DRC (formerly Zaire) and its supporters—Angola, Zimbabwe, Namibia—on the one hand and Rwanda and Uganda on the other. In 1997 Rwanda, plagued by land scarcity, and Uganda joined Laurent Kabila and his rebel forces to overthrow the authoritarian ruler of Zaire, Mobutu Seso Seko. A year later in 1998, the two central African countries joined rebel groups against their former ally, Kabila. Rwanda's goal, ostensibly, was to pursue ethnic Hutu militias that had carried out genocidal attacks in Rwanda in 1994 and continued to use Congo's territory as a base of operations. Rwanda had accused Kabila of not doing enough to deal with the threat posed by the Hutu militias and was prepared to occupy the portion of Congo from which the militias launched their attacks in order to ensure its own security—and, some observers opined, to alleviate its land-scarcity problem. Early in 2000 Rwanda and Uganda began to fight over the control of Congo's mineral-rich region of Kisangani which they had occupied.

In Nigeria, where there had been a thirty-month-long tragic civil war, violent strife recurred when local communities in the Delta region complained that they were not receiving a fair share of the benefits from the region's oil resources and were suffering excessively from the degradation of their natural environment. In a number of other states, conflicts have arisen as a result of diametrically opposed visions of society and the state. For example, the growing and militant demands of religious fundamentalists in regard to how the state and society should be organized and administered such as were voiced in Algeria, Egypt, and Nigeria, were sources of violence. In the Sudan, an ethno-religious conflict which has spawned the deaths of about two million people and uprooted five million others has raged intermittently since 1955.

Imperial Ambition

Imperial ambition, or an alleged desire to reestablish polities severed or dismantled by European colonial map-makers, has been another cause of war in postcolonial Africa. The late King Hassan II of Morocco had such an ambition in Western Sahara, a former Spanish colony. Western Sahara, Hassan held till his death in 1999, was part of the ancient Moroccan empire. His desire to annex the territory on such grounds was challenged by Mauritania, which asserted a similar claim. The ongoing conflict in Western Sahara is the product of the clashing ambitions of Morocco, Mauritania, and Sahrawi nationalists and their supporter, Algeria.

The late Emperor Haile Selassie of Ethiopia wanted to annex Eritrea, the part of Ethiopia seized by Italy in the nineteenth century during the European scramble for Africa. With the help of the government of the United States, Haile Selassie was able to achieve his goal after the United Nations decided in 1952 that Eritrea should become a federated unit within Ethiopia. Haile Selassie violated the terms of the federation, and by doing so, he provoked a war of national liberation that ended in 1993 after more than thirty years. In that year Eritrea became independent. However, five years later in 1998 Eritrea and Ethiopia attacked each other viciously for about two years over a boundary dispute.

Eritrea initiated the war when it invaded a disputed border in May 1998. What President Isaias Afewerki had thought would be a brief campaign kindled a two-year war.[21] In prosecuting the war, the two Horn of Africa countries spent more than $1 billion on arms purchases from Russia, the former Soviet bloc countries, China, and North Korea. For two of the world's poorest nations, whose populations faced severe food shortages caused by drought and worsened by war, this was a needless diversion of scarce resources needed for economic and social development. Thus, the war stalled economic growth in both countries and took its toll in lives; the estimate is 90,000 killed and more than 1 million nationals and residents displaced.[22]

Authoritarian Rule as in Liberia and Sierra Leone

Finally, authoritarian rule throughout Africa has been a persistent and pervasive cause of armed violence. Part of the legacy of European imperial control, authoritarian rule in many a postcolonial African state has been replaced by an even more inept and incompetent military dictatorship. Coups d'état as means of political change plagued postcolonial Africa and contributed to the increased incidence of civil strife, including bloody countercoups, especially in such West African states as Nigeria, Ghana, Sierra Leone, Togo, and Burkina Faso. In the recent past, authoritarian rulers such as Mengistu Haile Mariam of Ethiopia, Sani Abacha of Nigeria, Jaafar Nemeiri of Sudan, and Siad Barre of Somalia, for example, claimed to be motivated by a resolve to promote national reconstruction through speedy modernization and economic development. However, in reality, they all gave priority to consolidating their own power, enriching themselves, and leaving their countries an entirely negative legacy. In this manner, administrative mismanagement by authoritarian rulers, civilian and military alike, by overcentralization of political and economic power and the suppression of political pluralism frequently led to corruption, nepotism, insurgency, and armed conflict.

Two specific West African cases—Liberia and Sierra Leone—exemplify this postcolonial phenomenon. The Liberian civil war (1989–1997), although deeply embedded in the history of the country, was motivated by greed for control of the state and national resources. The struggle found expression through ethnic animosity, which pitted ethnic groups against each other, principally the descendants of American immigrants versus the indigenous people: the Gio/Mano against the Krahn/Mandingo. The armed conflict began on 24 December 1989 when Charles Taylor's National Patriotic Front of Liberia, in a clear bid for power, mounted an attack on the government of Samuel K. Doe.

A former senior Liberian bureaucrat whom President Doe accused of stealing government funds, Taylor had fled to the United States. There he was arrested at Doe's request but successfully plotted his escape to Burkina Faso. Like Blaise Compaore, president of Burkina Faso, who helped him to procure arms from Moammar Khaddafi and Ukraine, Taylor received military training at Libya's World Revolutionary Headquarters in the 1980s. He financed his military purchases and rebellion against Doe with proceeds from illicit sales of Liberian timber to European timber companies.[23] After looting Liberian timber and rubber, he invaded neighboring Sierra Leone in order to gain access to diamond mines with which to finance his campaign. Furthermore, he formed alliances with local insurgents and villagers and gave them arms so that they could help him fight the government of Sierra Leone when it attempted to prevent his invasion.

In his own determination and flat-out lust for power, the autocratic Liberian President Doe responded with every means available. An earlier effort in 1985 by his military colleague, General Thomas Quiwonkpa, to remove him from power had been foiled and the leader executed for his daring. All the other elements in the war—Prince Johnson, Amos Sawyer, and Alhaji Koromah— were greedy for power and control of national resources.

From a historical perspective, the Liberian conflict may be seen as a struggle for power between the indigenous rural dwellers and those of the descendants of American-born Liberians, who, some observers believe, had ruthlessly controlled Liberia from 1847 to 1980. As represented by Charles Taylor, the descendants of the American-born Liberians sought to regain the power Doe had seized from their leader, William Tolbert, in a bloody military coup in April 1980. In 1990 Taylor and his ill-trained and undisciplined insurgents assassi- nated Doe and overthrew his government. Fighting continued for seven more years. It took the military intervention of the Economic Community of West African States Monitoring Group (ECOMOG) and enormous sacrifice in human and material resources by the intervening members of the Economic Commu- nity of West African States, Nigeria especially, to bring the violent conflict to an end. Presidential and legislative elections were held on 19 July 1997. Charles Taylor and his National Patriotic Party won overwhelmingly. Some observers considered his victory a bribe to induce him to accept peace and end the war. However, the flight of most businesses during the seven years of civil strife disrupted formal economic activity. Continued uncertainty about security, heightened by armed clashes since September 1998 between government forces and supporters of factional leader Roosevelt Johnson, slowed the process of rebuilding the social and economic structure of the war-torn country. The Special Court for Sierra Leone—a joint tribunal of the United Nations and the government in Freetown established in June 2001—charged Taylor on 4 June 2003 with bearing the greatest responsibility for war crimes, crimes against humanity and serious violations of international humanitarian law over a ten- year period in West Africa.

A combination of forces—the call by President George W. Bush, together with growing international pressure, on him to step down as Liberia's president, a 4 June 2003 indictment for war crimes by the United Nations' Special Court in Sierra Leone, the tribunal's subsequent 6 June warrant for his arrest, and the prospects of a military defeat by rebels—compelled Taylor to resign on 11 August 2003. After handing over power to Vice President Moses Blah, Taylor departed Liberia for asylum in Nigeria, with the parting words "God willing, I will be back." At an all-party talks later in the month, Gyude Bryant, a businessman seen as politically neutral, was chosen to lead a transitional government until elections in 2005.

Sierra Leone, the western neighbor of Liberia, also was war-torn for more than ten years.[24] The devastating civil war began in March 1991 when Charles Taylor, a faction leader in Liberia's civil war, sponsored a rebel group—the Revolutionary United Front (RUF)—to attack and destabilize the country, then a rear base for ECOMOG, which was preventing him from capturing Monrovia.[25] However, the events which led to the conflict predated the 1991 Taylor-inspired attack. They were rooted in reckless authoritarian misrule, personal greed, ruthless corruption, ineffective police power or collapse of state authority, and social and political discontent, all of which characterized the administrations of Albert Margai (1964–67), Siaka Stevens (1968–85), and Joseph Momoh (1985–92).[26] The repressive measures Stevens adopted against critics and opponents of his regime—disaffected youth, radical students, and university lecturers—forced the dissidents into exile. Some of the dissidents traveled to Libya for military training and later organized the RUF, brutal rebels who systematically slaughtered tens of thousands of Sierra Leoneans and maimed many more during the ensuing civil war.

Three decades of bad government had so blighted peoples' opportunities and hopes that the rebels decided to look at the situation through the barrel of a gun. Foday Sankoh, a former corporal and army photographer who had been imprisoned for his part in a failed military coup and who had also visited Libya for guerrilla training, joined their ranks and became a recruiter of revolutionaries for RUF.[27] His purpose, he proclaimed, was to remove a corrupt elite that had been colluding with foreigners to loot the country's diamond riches and impoverish its people. Soon Sankoh took over the leadership of the military wing of the RUF. He subverted the antigovernment protests and ideas generated by students and disaffected youth for political reform and proceeded to eliminate the intellectuals, such as Abu Kanu and Rashid Mansaray, in the rebel movement. The intellectuals had opposed Sankoh's policy of forced recruitment and drugging of children and his brutal attacks on civilians.

Unable to repel the rebels and protect the people, Joseph Momoh's inept and demoralized government was overthrown by young soldiers led by Captain Valentine Strasser (age 26) in April 1992. Well received by Sierra Leoneans, Strasser's National Provisional Ruling Council (NPRC), started its regime with a promise to restore honest government and to undertake radical social reform. People's expectations were dashed: Strasser quickly acquired the bad habits of his predecessors. Instead of the reform government he had promised, his military junta preyed on its own people. The soldiers broke military discipline and took up terrorism and banditry in rural areas, disguising themselves as RUF rebels or actually cooperating with them. The soldiers finally seized control of key diamond mining areas and had to be driven out by Executive Outcomes, a South African mercenary firm hired by the NPRC. However, for its own selfish reasons, the NPRC failed to prosecute the war effectively against RUF rebels and muzzle the marauding government troops.

By 1994, once they had fully grasped the situation, Sierra Leoneans furiously turned against the NPRC and demanded elections and a return to civilian government. The demand culminated first in confrontations between the NPRC and Sierra Leonean civil society, including women's groups, and subsequently, the overthrow of Strasser by Brigadier Julius Maada Bio, the NPRC vice-chairman, at the end of 1995. To forestall the elections and the return to civilian rule demanded by the public, Bio secretly attempted to reach an understanding with Foday Sankoh to form an NPRC-RUF government. The scheme was thwarted by foreign diplomats, and the elections were conducted as scheduled in early 1996 despite efforts by the NPRC soldiers to intimidate the voters and disrupt the process.

Ahmed Tejan Kabbah, a former UN diplomat, emerged from the elections as the president not for his leadership qualities but because his colleagues believed that they could manipulate him. Given the opposition of the rogue soldiers to civilian government and the RUF insurgency, this did not augur well for the country. Kabbah's actions upon assuming office did not inspire any confidence in a nation in crisis. He succumbed to the old ways of patronage and showed no evidence of a plan to tackle the clear and present danger that the marauding RUF rebels and rogue soldiers posed to Sierra Leone. Furthermore, he failed to address the problems of thousands of displaced persons and refugees as well as destroyed schools and clinics and to engage the public and address its concerns.

Thus, by the end of his first year in office, Kabbah's actions (and inaction) cost him the confidence of virtually every segment of society. The already fractious army was alienated. Kabbah had made Hinga Norman, a Mende retired military officer and leader of the Kamajors, his deputy defense minister. For his security and survival, he had begun to rely more on the Kamajors, traditional Mende warriors, who had defended their region against the army and the plundering RUF rebels.

Arguing that Kabbah had diverted army resources to the Kamajors, rebellious soldiers overthrew his government on 27 May 1997. They released Major Johnny Paul Koromah, who had been imprisoned after a failed coup, to become their leader. Major Koromah and his benefactors terrorized and looted the capital city, Freetown, and invited RUF rebels to form a coalition government, which eventually became the Armed Forces Revolutionary Council/RUF Coalition (AFRC/RUF). Kabbah sought refuge in Guinea-Conakry.

The soldiers' open alliance with the RUF rebels and the plundering of the capital city provoked public hostility against the AFRC and denied the Coalition international recognition as well. Accordingly, in February 1998 Sierra Leoneans cooperated with ECOMOG forces to liberate Freetown from nine months of anarchic terror and wholesale slaughter by the AFRC/RUF. Kabbah's government was restored to power on 10 March 1998, but fighting between the government and AFRC/RUF rebels continued. More than 6,000 Sierra Leoneans, including police officers, judges, human rights activists, journalists, civil servants, government officials, and ordinary citizens, were killed, and the limbs of about 1,500 others amputated. About 700,000 citizens became internally displaced, while about 450,000 others fled the country.[28] Sankoh was tried and convicted of treason in October 1998 and sentenced to death. His fellow rebels stepped up their attacks and mounted an assault in December on Freetown, which they nearly seized in January 1999.

The recapture of the capital city by ECOMOG forces early in 1999 paved the way for an agreement signed in Lome on 7 July 1999, when all the parties agreed to end hostilities and form a national government. The agreement, overseen by the UN, Britain, and, particularly, the United States,[29] made Sankoh a member of the government and protected him and his forces from prosecution for war crimes.[30] It also gave them control over Sierra Leone's diamond mines, their main source of income.

There was a loud outcry within and outside Sierra Leone against the Lome peace accord by individuals and groups who believed that the agreement had empowered people—the RUF rebels—who were hardened war criminals.[31] This proved to be the case when the war resumed in May 2000. Earlier, the rebels had violated a 1996 peace treaty with President Kabbah.[32] This time, in their determination to maintain control over the diamond mining areas, they took hostage about 500 UN peacekeepers who, on a mission to enforce the 1999 truce, were approaching the region. They killed several more people as they moved towards Freetown in defiance of the 1999 Lome peace accord.

The resumption of the war underlined the primary goal of the rebels in the ten-year war—control of Sierra Leone's diamond wealth. "We have always maintained that the conflict in Sierra Leone is not about ideology, ethnic or regional difference," Sierra Leone's ambassador, Ibrahim Kamara, told the UN Security Council after the body voted on 5 July 2000 to impose a worldwide ban on the purchase of rough diamonds from Sierra Leone. The ambassador added: "It has nothing to do with the so-called problem of marginalized youths or, as some political commentators have characterized it, an uprising by the rural poor against the urban elite. The root of the conflict is and remains diamonds, diamonds and diamonds."[33] The rebels' war-making was financed by illicit trade in Sierra Leone diamonds, which was facilitated not only by Charles Taylor of Liberia but also by legitimate international diamond companies.[34]

The war caused the death of more than 500,000 Sierra Leoneans and the displacement of more than a million others, while hundreds of thousands fled to neighboring countries, mainly Guinea and Liberia. The tragic irony of it all is that Sierra Leone is the poorest country in the world. Yet its spectacular mineral wealth, especially its diamonds, provided the reason and the resources for much of the war. Unfortunately, this wealth benefited very few citizens of the country over decades of inequality, corruption, and war, and the vast majority of the population became even more impoverished and dehumanized.

Intervention by British troops helped to subdue the rebels, who had intensified the war in 2000. The war was officially declared over in January 2002 after more than 45,000 RUF fighters handed their weapons to UN peacekeepers. Kabbah won the postwar election the following May. The Special Court for Sierra Leone indicted eleven leading notorious warmongers including Charles Taylor of Liberia, for crimes committed during the war. Three of the indicted Sierra Leoneans, RUF leader, Foday Sankoh, who was among the first to appear before the Special Court, his deputy, and Johnny Paul Koroma, died in 2003.

The Case of Rwanda

The perennial conflict in Rwanda in Central Africa is rooted in the country's political history, starting under a Tutsi monarchy. Specifically, it was the result of excluding specific ethnic communities from effective political participation. In precolonial times, Tutsi monarchs maintained political hegemony over the Hutu majority. German and Belgian colonial overlords, through their policy of "indirect rule" and other administrative practices, political constraints, and discrimination, strengthened the Tutsi hegemony. In the waning years of Belgian imperial rule, political exclusion of the Hutu led to insurrection by that group in 1959 against the Tutsi monarchy. The revolt ended Tutsi political domination and eventually brought the Hutu majority to political power after independence in 1962.

The Hutu revolution had important consequences: exclusion of the Tutsi minority from any meaningful participation in the political affairs of the country and the flight of tens of thousands of Tutsi nationals into neighboring countries. The political change marked the beginning of a cycle of turbulent struggles for power in Rwanda, ultimately resulting in a revanchist invasion by the Tutsi in 1990.

Demographic pressures contributed to the conflict. Rwanda is a very poor and overpopulated country. About 90 percent of its population depends on agriculture for its livelihood. Claiming that there was insufficient land for the population, the Hutu regime of Juvenal Habyarimana refused to allow the repatriation of Tutsi who had fled the country during previous violent clashes and were suffering political and economic disabilities in their lands of exile, especially in Uganda. The situation was made worse by economic decline and hardships experienced by Rwanda and other African countries during the 1980s and early 1990s that became part of the dynamic that produced the Rwanda genocide of 1994 in which about 800,000 Tutsi and Hutu sympathizers were massacred by Hutu extremists during a period of 100 days. (See Chapter 8 for more details.)

External Causes

With the exception of the 1986 U.S. Comprehensive Anti-Apartheid Sanctions Act against South Africa, not one of the major powers ever undertook a coercive or noncoercive humanitarian intervention in any of Africa's Cold War-era conflicts caused by political/economic mismanagement or involving the violation of internationally accepted norms on human rights. During the Cold War, superpower rivalry fueled the conflicts, and efforts to bolster or undermine the governments of African states were a familiar feature of the competition. Authoritarian and oppressive regimes were either supported or opposed in keeping with the interests of the superpowers who were pursuing global hegemony. In the DRC a conflict that began when Moise Tshombe, aided and abetted by powerful Belgian and Western European mining interests, pro-claimed the secession of Katanga after the abrupt ending of Belgium's colonial rule in July 1960 became a Cold War contest between the United States and its allies and the Soviet bloc. In Angola, an internal rivalry for political succession after the collapse of the Portuguese colonial empire in 1974 was aggravated into a prolonged war by the animosity between the United States and the Soviet Union. In the Horn of Africa, on the one hand, American support for Siad Barre of Somalia enabled the dictator to suppress Somali citizens and sowed the seed of the country's tragic collapse. On the other hand, Soviet support for Mengistu Haile Mariam of Ethiopia prolonged a costly civil war that took a heavy toll on human lives and economic and social development. Upon the end of the Cold War, Africans were left to fend for themselves.

With the end of U.S.-Soviet ideological rivalry, emerging corporate interests with a stake in the outcome of the conflicts and commercial sources, including diamonds-for-arms smugglers, increasingly supplied military equipment, light weapons, and information to belligerents. They and their customers who benefit from chaos, and lack of accountability have more interest in prolonging conflicts than stopping them.[35] In a similar fashion, on religious and cultural grounds, the oil-rich Islamic states of the Persian Gulf fueled the wars in the Horn of Africa, especially the civil war in Sudan and Eritrea's prolonged struggle for independence from Ethiopia. Similarly, for the first thirteen years of the war, Saudi Arabia provided the bulk of the finances for Morocco's war against the Polisario in Western Sahara. Consequently, fought with weapons funded by these states and imported through the merchants (formerly from the superpowers and their allies), these wars diverted scarce national resources away from basic needs and social development and led to upward spirals of armaments and military spending. This also meant that the governments had little or no funds left for fighting HIV/AIDS and the other epidemics that are taking heavy tolls on their population.

Collective Impact of the Wars

It is axiomatic that conflicts cause considerable human, social, economic, and environmental destruction and create structural imbalances. The more violent and protracted the conflict, the greater and more pervasive the negative results, especially in terms of economic growth, social costs, social cohesion, mortality rates, and psychological damage. The postcolonial wars in Africa, accordingly, have caused the deaths of more than 10 million people, disabled and maimed hundreds of thousands, even millions, of persons, and produced waves of refugees totaling 8.1 million according to the UN High Commissioner for Refugees (UNHCR) in 1998. About 15 million more have been internally displaced in the affected areas.[36] Most of these victims were noncombatants, including women and children. Additionally, the wars have weakened the affected societies, undermined the process of their national consolidation and economic development. They created a climate of insecurity and political instability, which lowered already marginal intra-African trade, promoted the flight of local capital and skilled manpower, discouraged tourism, and frightened away foreign investment. Furthermore, the wars produced severe consequences that spilled over beyond the region and the affected country, thus making civil war not just the problem of the countries directly affected.

The high levels of military spending required to prosecute the wars diverted funds away from investment in economic infrastructure, education, health care, and social welfare; thus exacerbating the problems of poverty, disease, and social alienation, which are in their own right drivers of internal conflict. The natural resources of the countries at war could have been used to reduce the national level of poverty, but instead they were used to import arms and wage the war. The increase in government military spending is only part of the diversion of resources into violence. The resources rebel groups control also divert resources from productive activities. This diversion causes a double loss: the loss to the area that had previously benefited from the resources and cost of the damage from the war that these resources helped pay for.

During the war, key economic infrastructure is frequently, if not always, damaged, as rebel forces target the physical infrastructure—communication and support lines, airports, ports, roads, and bridges. In Angola, Liberia, and Mozambique, for example, major infrastructures were damaged or looted. The prewar transport system, especially in Angola and Mozambique, was badly damaged, and revenue normally derived from it was lost. In addition, rebel and government soldiers loot and destroy housing, schools, and health facilities. In Angola and Mozambique agricultural production was also disrupted by land mines and thievery by rebel soldiers, who robbed the farms or stole cattle to feed themselves. A conspicuous social cost of all this destruction is a persisting legacy of poverty and misery.

The use of minors—both boys and girls—as soldiers, spies, porters, and sex objects had its own effect on the social and psychological development of a generation of children in societies like Angola, Mozambique, and Sudan with protracted violent conflicts. To the child soldiers, war, which they had experienced all their life, became a normal way of life and thus imbued in them a culture of violence and ensured that gangs and militia would flourish well after the war officially ended. The psychological impact of the war on children traumatized by it and on future generations of Africans is really incalculable.

In many a warring state, the process of political democratic reform which began after the end of both Eurocommunism and the Cold War in 1989 was aborted. Similarly, groups once armed by the ideological rivals became criminalized when they could no longer receive support from their former benefactors.

The intrastate wars produced consequences beyond the borders of the affected state. Refugee flows taxed the resources of neighboring states and the international community in general. As in the cases of Liberia and Rwanda, refugees spilled into sister states within the region, causing additional fatalities, regional political and economic instability, and other repercussions. Furthermore, they reduced the incomes of neighboring states while, at the same time, increasing the incidence of disease in such there as a result of the influx of refugees exposed to infectious diseases. The war in Somalia generated a territory outside the control of any recognized government. Somalia became an epicenter of crime—international terrorism and drug traffic.

With the incidence of HIV/AIDS infection and malaria rising, amidst widespread civil strife and under a heavy debt burden, the African region as a whole took a downward turn. In the first year of the new millennium, people in Africa lived less well than they did in the 1960s. In a sense, the continent moved backward in the later decades of the twentieth century. In the early 1960s its nations were widely considered more advanced than East Asian nations, but between the early 1960s and the end of the 1990s, Africa, because of its many wars, endemic corruption, and myopic vision, retreated in real economic terms[37] while East Asia's economic output increased fourfold. Africa's share of world trade has steadily declined to less than 2 percent while its share of external investment is insignificant. Indeed, according to a UN report, capital flows to sub-Saharan African countries dropped from 11.5 percent of their gross national product in the 1970s to 10.6 percent in the 1990s. Private capital flows, over the same period, fell from 4.3 percent to 1.5 percent. For North Africa, the trend was more dramatic. Capital inflows dropped from 13 percent of GNP to 3.2 percent during the same period.[38] At the same time, during the 1980s and the 1990s, the continent spent twice as much as the rest of the Third World countries on arms purchases. Life expectancy at birth remains low throughout the continent.

The most persistent and devastating of Africa's postcolonial wars were supported by the superpowers through shipments of heavy weapons and military training. This study examines three of such conflicts—Ethiopia-Somalia, Western Sahara, and Angola—the last two of which continued after the end of the Cold War in order to illustrate the dimensions of U.S. role in postcolonial conflicts in Africa.

What Is to Be Done?

War is an economic and social disaster for the affected country. None of Africa's political, economic, and social needs—economic development, promotion of democracy and respect for human rights, provision of education and basic health care services, and a solution to the HIV/AIDS pandemic—can be adequately addressed in the absence of public order, security, and peace. On the one hand, Africa's premier organization, the Organization of African Unity (OAU) (now African Union), has lacked the capacity to foster this triple sine qua non for its troubled member states. On the other hand, the response of the international community to the widespread conflicts in Africa has been tepid and incoherent. Because the conflicts do not significantly threaten their own security or economic interests, the major industrialized powers have also been lukewarm in their response to Africa's predicament, committing only scant resources that have been insufficient to reverse the trend. Effective intervention by the major powers and the international community—the United Nations—has been constrained by another factor: The enormity and scale of the conflicts, including the size of the territories involved, such as the DRC and Sudan, and the logistical problems, preclude the kind of intervention by the United States and its NATO allies organized in Bosnia and Kosovo for an indefinite period of time. Even though this is a major problem, the international community can make a difference by increasing its commitment, especially to the smaller countries like Sierra Leone, Rwanda, and Somalia, where it had chosen to intervene.

A number of proposals have been suggested for addressing such problems as bad governance and the epidemic of violent conflicts in contemporary Africa. One suggestion is that African countries whose governments have failed should be recolonized. This assumes that the European colonization of Africa conferred redeeming benefits when, indeed, its legacy is among the causes of the continent's current problems. No postcolonial African state would voluntarily submit itself to recolonization. This suggestion is, therefore, out of the question. As it is presently constituted, the UN is not sufficiently equipped to assume such a responsibility, and hardly would any member state be entrusted by the rest of the members with such a responsibility. The 1993 attempt to recolonize Somalia, to build a new state in that failed and war-ravaged area, was a colossal failure. Together with the widely publicized killings of U.S. and other peacekeeping troops by Somalia militia, the failure bred Afro-pessimism, especially in the United States. Furthermore, it hardened attitudes among American policymakers and the public about the efficacy and costs of U.S.

participation in UN peacekeeping missions in Africa and was responsible for a strong U.S. reluctance to support UN engagement in the genocidal strife that erupted in Rwanda in 1994.

Another proposal suggests the retraining and reequipment of the armed forces, including the police. It is necessary to instill in the armed forces the virtues of civilian control of the military, but retraining and reequipping them will not resolve the problem of bad governance and violent conflict. It did not do so in the DRC after the Congo crisis of 1960–1964. The armed forces have frequently used bad governance and corruption as a rationale for their violent overthrow of civilian governments. The police force tends to support the government in power, which actually may be the source of the violent conflict. And there is no reason to assume that the police force itself is free of corruption.

In 1995 Warren Christopher, U.S. secretary of state, proposed an African Crisis Response Force to promote and ensure stability and prevent incipient crises from escalating into violent conflicts. He proposed this in the aftermath of (1) the loss of eighteen U.S. soldiers participating in UN multilateral peace building, formerly Operation Restore Hope, in Somalia in 1993 and (2) the genocide in Rwanda in 1994. The idea was that the United States would help train African soldiers to enable them to nip in the bud violent conflicts in their states. This, it was hoped, would prevent the need for American soldiers to be used in conflicts in which no vital U.S. interests were at stake. A number of African states embraced the proposal, but others rejected the idea. (For a detailed discussion, see Chapter 9.)

The emphasis on the use of force is flawed by the fact that in two recent instances—Rwanda and Sierra Leone—UN attempts to use force did not succeed in resolving the conflicts. In the latter case, the UN was embarrassed when members of its forces were taken hostage by rebels.

Other approaches may be more practicable. Equitable allocation of each nation's wealth to all segments of its society as well as transparency and accountability in governing process are both reasonable goals. The agreement by African nations, announced on 14 February 2004 in Kigali, Rwanda, to monitor one another's performance on governance, democracy, human rights practices, and corruption, as part of the continent's rescue plan—the New Partnership for Africa's Development (NEPAD)—is a welcome step in the right direction.[39] The international community should join forces with African states in this task to address the twin problems of poverty and the state as the source of wealth and power. It can prevent violent conflicts and save lives rather than stand aloof and try to repair the damage after conflicts. It can provide assistance for economic development and support a more equitable international economic order, especially in terms of prices African countries receive for the commodities they sell and prices of goods they buy. The funds for such support could be raised by reducing the huge amount (more than $850 billion) spent annually on military forces around the world.[40]

The major and more industrialized powers can assist in this task by providing more access for African products in their markets and by forgiving the debts crippling the economies of African states and impoverishing their people. They should do away with the global system of agricultural subsidies. One of the obvious ways for poor farmers in developing countries to lift themselves out of poverty is to sell their products abroad. But this they cannot do, mainly because the rich and more industrialized countries have rigged their markets, subsidizing their farmers so heavily that farmers in developing countries cannot compete. Reducing, if not totally eliminating, farm subsidies would do far more to help poor countries than large increases in direct foreign aid. It will put more money in the pockets of the poor; promote both greater social and political stability across the developing world, and provide a fairer distribution of the fruits of globalization. Furthermore, the billions of dollars spent by donors on refugees and internally displaced persons and on postwar reconstruction could be devoted to the elimination of poverty and unemployment.

Thus, the adage "an ounce of prevention is worth a pound of cure" should be applied to minimize the incidence of conflicts in Africa. There were early warnings of impending crises in Somalia and Rwanda, but African states and the international community failed to act decisively as the conflicts escalated. Decisive measures must be taken to translate knowledge of such impending crises into preventive action. Local, subregional, and regional bodies and, finally, the international community should respond as a crisis escalates. African states should seize the initiative for conflict prevention, management, or resolution on the continent as they work with local disputants to bring about conciliation. External forces, such as the great powers and international organizations, the UN specifically, can contribute to the process by providing support for the search for resolution and peace.

The international community and African states should enforce existing conventions prohibiting the use of child soldiers against those governments and rebel leaders in Africa who violate them. Such violators should be subjected to the measures used against war criminals in Bosnia and Kosovo. A breakthrough in efforts to end the use of child soldiers occurred on 21 January 2000, when six years of negotiations led to agreement on a new international treaty to prohibit the use of children as combatants. Technically an optional protocol to the Convention on the Rights of the Child (which by 2000 had been ratified by every government except the United States and Somalia), the treaty established "eighteen as the minimum age for direct participation in hostilities, for compulsory recruitment, and for any recruitment or use in hostilities by non-governmental armed groups."[41] In addition, it established a clear standard that any use of children in war was unacceptable, and provided a critical new basis for exerting public and political pressure against governments and armed groups that use children in armed conflict. The UN General Assembly unanimously adopted the protocol on 25 May 2000. By August 2002,109 countries had signed it, and 35 countries had ratified it.[42] For the good of humanity, the treaty should receive scrupulous enforcement.

The world community should not reward or fraternize with such exploiters of child soldiers as Charles Taylor, Foday Sankoh, and their like. It should ostracize authoritarian and corrupt African rulers who incite civil wars and ethnic hatred and plunge their people into poverty and despair. It should break the link between conflict and crime by arresting and punishing those who commit crime in order to wage war or to perpetuate it as a money-making venture. This is the spirit and intent of a 27 July 2000 U.S. draft resolution which asked the UN Security Council to establish a special court to try Fodah Sankoh and others accused of committing horrific atrocities in the ten years' war in Sierra Leone.[43] It is, therefore, a bold step that the UN-sponsored Special Court for Sierra Leone indicted Charles Taylor on 4 June 2003 for war crimes, crimes against humanity, and violations of international law. Arresting and putting him on trial for these crimes would set a tremendous precedent for Africa. Similarly, the world community should break the link between criminal warriors and legitimate businesses by punishing both parties. Conflicts can thus be shortened by forcing criminal warriors and rebel organizations to give up their sources of external finance. Finally, the international community should stem the flood of small arms and light weapons that are inundating African countries.

Among the underlying sources of conflict in Africa are underdevelopment and deprivation, overpopulation, environmental stress, refugee and migration flows, and the increasing erosion of the capacity of the state to administer its territory and provide basic services to the people. Conflict resolution in Africa will be successful only when the various underlying sources of violence are addressed and ameliorated and when citizens of African states perceive that justice and economic resources are administered and distributed fairly to all segments of the population.

Notes

1. Contemporary Conflicts in Africa: http://www.synapse.net/~acdi20.

2. Eric Young, "Warfare in Africa Since Independence," http://www.africana.com/tt212 htm (28 October 1999).

3. See James Woods, Cohen and Woods International, United States Institute of Peace, "Peace Keeping in Africa: Special Report," (26 March 2001). http://www.usip.org/oc/ newsroom/5r66no. html (03/27/2001).

4. Colum Lynch, "UN Panel Decries the 'Looting' of the Congo: Security Council Asked to Restrict Neighbors' Activities in War-Torn Congo," *The Washington Post* (17 April 2001), p. A. 18, wysiwyg://8/http:washingtonpost.com/wp-dyn/world/africa/A25493-2001April16. html; KarlVick, "Vital Ore Funds Congo's War: Combatants Profit From Col-Tan Trade," *The Washington Post* (19 March 2001), p. A01.

5. See "Africa and UN Peace Missions," *Africa Recovery*, Vol. 17, No. 3 (October 2003), p. 17.

6. Abdel-Fatu Musah and J. Kayode Fayemi, eds., *Mercenaries: An African Security Dilemma* (Sterling: Pluto Press, 2000).

7. Neil Cooper, "The Arms Trade and Militarized Actors in Internal Conflict," in Paul B. Rich (ed.), *Warlords in International Relations* (New York: St. Martin's, 1999), pp. 17–37.

8. *The Atlanta Journal Constitution*, "Lewis Leads Effort to Ban Use of Children in Warfare," http://www.africana.com/news/homepage/2000/06/08/C/30999902-0297-Home.htm.

9. "Regions in Conflict," *Scientific American* (June 2000), p. 51; John Tessitore and Susan Woolfson (eds.), *A Global Agenda: Issues Before the 54th General Assembly of the United Nations, 1999–2000 edition* (New York: UN Association of the United States of America, 2000), pp. 17–18.

10. Special Issues and Campaigns—Child Soldiers Campaign: http://www.hrw.org/wr2k1/ special/child.html.

11. "Special Report: Waging a New Kind of War," *Scientific American* (June 2000), pp. 47-65.

12. See Report of the Panel of Experts on Violations of Security Council Sanctions Against UNITA, http://www.un.org/News/dh/latest/angolareport_eng.htm.

13. Paul Collier et al., *Breaking the Conflict Trap: Civil War and Development Policy* (Washington, DC: World Bank and Oxford University Press, 2003); K.Y. Amoako, "The Economic Causes and Consequences of Civil Wars and Unrest in Africa," Address to OAU Council of Ministers in Algeria (8 July 1999), http://www.afbis.com/analysis/ Africa%20war.htm; "The Causes of Conflict and the Promotion of Durable Peace and Sustainable Development in Africa," *Report of the [UN] Secretary General,* http://www. un.org/ecosocdev/geninfo/afrec/sgreport/ report.htm (28 June 1998); Catherine Newbury, "Background to Genocide: Rwanda," *Issue: A Journal of African Opinion,* Vol. XXII, No. 2 (1995), pp. 12–18; F. U. Ohaegbulam, "Postcolonial Conflicts in Africa: The Case of Angola," *The Journal of African Policy Studies,* Vol. 3, Nos. 2 and 3 (1997), pp. 405–440.

14. "'A Continent in Crisis': Kofi Annan Reflects on Africa," [An Interview by Henry Louis Gates, Jr.] in *Naijanet* (19 June 2000).

15. Kofi Annan, *The Causes of Conflict and the Promotion of Durable Peace and Sustainable Development in Africa* (New York: United Nations, 21 April 1998), p. 3, http://www. un.org/ecosocdev/geninfo/afrec/segreport/report.htm.

16. Adebayo Adedeji (ed.), *Comprehending and Mastering African Conflicts: The Search for Sustainable Peace and Good Governance* (New York: Zed, 1999), p. 7.

17. "Oil and War in the Sudan," http://www.nytimes.com/2001/01/13/opinion/13SAT3.html.

18. "The Causes of Conflict and the Promotion of Durable Peace and Sustainable Development in Africa," *Report of the UN Secretary-General,* http://www.un.org/ecosodev/geninfo/afrec/ sgreport/report.htm.

19. *Report of the UN Secretary-General.*

20. *Report of the UN Secretary-General.*

21. Ian Fisher, "Playing by the Rule: From an Old-Fashioned War, a Very Modern Calamity," http://www.nytimes,com/library/review/06040ethiopia-eritrea-review.html.

22. Ian Fisher, "Ethiopians and Eritreans Sign Cease-Fire," *The New York Times* (19 June 2000), http://www.nytimes.com/library/world/africa/061900ethipia-eritrea.html.

23. Douglas Farah, "Liberia Reportedly Arming Guerrillas," *The Washington Post* (18 June 2000), p. A21, wysiwyg://35http://www.washingtonpost.com/wp-dyn/world/africa/A14038-2000 Jun17.html.

24. "Key Events in Sierra Leone's Conflict," *The New York Times,* http://www.nytimes.com/ library/world/africa/sierra-leone-chrono.html.

25. *Africa Confidential,* "Chronology of Sierra Leone: How Diamonds Fuelled the Conflict," http://www.africa-confidential.com/special.html.

26. U.S. Department of State, *Background Notes: Sierra Leone* (Washington, DC: Bureau of Public Affairs, 1994).

27. For a sketch of Sankoh's life, see Howard W. Fench, "African Rebel with Room Service," http://www.nytimes.com/library/world/africa062396sierra-leone-sankoh.html.

28. Tessitore and Woolfson (eds.), *A Global Agenda: Issues Before the 54th General Assembly of the United Nations, 1999–2000 edition*, p. 16.

29. See Ryan Lizza, "Sierra Leone, The Last Clinton Betrayal: Where Angels Fear to Tread," *New Republic* On Line http://www.tnr.com/072400/lizza072400.html; http://www.tnr.com/072400/2lizza072400.htm; http://www.tnr.com/072400/3lizza072400.html.

30. The UN refused to recognize the amnesty and noted that it did not apply to international crimes of genocide, crimes against humanity, and war crimes.

31. Norimitsu Onishi, "Freetown Journal: Survivors Sadly Say, Yes, Reward the Tormentors," http://www.nytimes.com/library/world/Africa/083099sierra-leone.html; Lizza, "Sierra Leone, The Last Clinton Betrayal," *New Republic* On Line.

32. UN, Department of Public Information, *Sierra Leone—UNAMSIL: Background*, http://www.un.org/Depts/dpko/unamsil/UnamsilB.html.

33. Barbara Crossette, "Singling Out Sierra Leone, UN Council Sets Gem Ban," http://www.nytimes.com/library/world/africa/070600sierra-leone.html; UPI, "Council Oks Sierra Leone Diamond Certification," http://www.africana.com/news/homepage/ 20...5/up/000-6113-sierra-leone-embargo-4.htm; *Africa Confidential*, "Special Reports: Chronology of Sierra Leone, How Diamonds Fuelled the Conflict," http://www.africa-confidential.com/special.html.

34. "Diamond Industry Acts to Halt Trade in Illicit Gems from Africa" Associated Press, wysiwyg://21/http://www.nytimes.com/libr...rid/africa/072000africa-diamonds-ap.html.

35. Nick Shaxson, "Fueling the War: Diamonds and Oil" (BBC News 11 January 2000); David Johnson, "Diamonds Fuel Africa's Ongoing Wars," http://www.africana.com/index_19991028htm (28 October 1999); Bureau of Intelligence and Research, "Arms and Conflict in Africa" (Washington, DC, July 1999); Joseph Kahn, "World Bank Blames Diamonds and Drugs for Many Wars," *The New York Times* (16 June 2000), http://www.nytimes.com/library/world/global/ 061600world-bank-diamonds.html.

36. Editorial, "Africa's Swelling Refugee Crisis," *The New York Times*, http://www.nytimes.com/yr/mo/day/editorial/17sat1.html.

37. Colin Legum, *Africa Since Independence* (Bloomington: Indiana University, 1999), pp. 30–31.

38. Reuters, "UN Report Says $20 Billion Needed for Africa Aid," *The New York Times* (27 July 2000), http://www.nytimes.com/reuters/international/international-africa-.html.

39. Reuters, "African Nations Plan to Monitor One Another," *New York Times* (15 February 2004), in: http://www nytimes.com/2004/02/15/international/africa/15AFRI.html.

40. "A Scourge of Small Arms," *Scientific American* (June 2000), p. 49.

41. UN, Optional Protocol to the Convention on the Rights of the Child on the involvement of children in armed conflict. Adopted and opened for signatures, ratification and accession by the General Assembly resolution A/RES/54/263 of 25 May 2000, entered into force on 12 February 2002. *Human Rights Watch World Report 2001*, http:///www.hrw.org/ campaigns/ cp/protocol.htm.

42. Human Rights Watch, "International Legal Standards Governing Child Soldiers," http:// www.hrw.org.camnaims/crp/int-law.htm.

43. Colum Lynch, "U.S. Urges War Crimes Court for Sierra Leone," *The Washington Post* (28 July 2000), p. A18, wysiwygi://23http://washingtonpost.com/wp-dyn/articles/A59014-2000 Jul27.html; Associated Press, "UN Plans to Create S. Leone Court," http://www.nytimes. com/aponline/i/AP-UN-Sierra-Leone.html.

CHAPTER 3
Origins of the U.S. Role
in African Conflicts

U.S. administrations, for obvious reasons, did not support a single war of national liberation in Africa. Historically, they had an aversion to revolution and instability and preferred a stable environment in which American nationals could safely pursue their global economic and other interests. As a consequence they were generally cautious about recognizing the legitimacy of nationalist groups that were determined to wrest self-determination and independence from imperial control. This was particularly the case in Africa where Western European powers, targets of the struggle for national liberation, were political and economic allies of the United States. The Harry Truman and Dwight Eisenhower administrations were concerned primarily with ensuring that Western Europe became a stable bulwark against Soviet expansion and believed that any criticism of colonial rule would alienate America's European allies—Britain, France, Belgium, and Portugal. Thus, those powers received U.S. sympathy and understanding, covert and indirect support despite the fact that at their summit meeting in Newfoundland in August 1941, President Franklin D. Roosevelt persuaded the British Prime Minister, Winston Churchill, to accept the provisions of the Atlantic Charter. In their joint declaration at the end of the summit, the two leaders agreed that after the end of the war all non-self-governing territories would be allowed "to choose the form of government under which they will live."

But after the war, as a satisfied power which believed that its political and economic system and values were threatened by communist and Soviet expansionism, the United States preferred to preserve the status quo wherever doing so served its national security interests. The apprehension that abrupt decolonization might lead to political disorder and create opportunities for communist penetration of Africa was so strong among U.S. leaders in the 1950s that they decided to subordinate the promotion of African freedom to this overriding concern. The concern was reinforced by the "necessity" to support America's NATO allies and their colonial policies. Therefore, invariably, U.S. administrations approved constitutional and peaceful transitions to independence in Africa, while they viewed with disfavor revolutionary struggles against various imperial overlords. African nationalists were therefore frequently warned that "premature independence could be retrogressive and dangerous."

For their part, European imperial powers in Africa saw the preoccupation of American leaders with communism and their perceived threat of Soviet expansion as a blessing in disguise for their imperial status quo. They exploited the concern by maneuvering American leaders into defending their imperial presence in Africa. Such maneuvering was evident in 1947 when the British informed the Truman administration that they could no longer afford to suppress the communist-led rebellion in Greece without American support. The Truman administration's response was U.S. aid of $400 million to Greece and Turkey under the Truman Doctrine.[1] President Truman's Undersecretary of State Dean Acheson explained to congressional leaders why the American commitment had to be global: "Like apples in a barrel infected by one rotten one, the corruption of Greece would infect Iran and all in the East. It would also carry infection to Africa through Asia Minor and Egypt to Europe."[2]

In North Africa, the necessity of defending the European democracies and the Mediterranean basin against Soviet forces overrode other political considerations in American policy towards the region during much of the 1950s. Consequently, high priority was assigned to U.S. military requirements, often at the expense of relations with emergent nationalist forces in the region. During the same period, U.S. administrators abandoned the principle of national self-determination when the question of Moroccan and Tunisian independence arose in the United Nations. They remained silent when Habib Bourguiba, leader of the Neo-Destour Party of Tunisia, was arrested and imprisoned by French authorities in 1951. The Department of State offered no objection when Sultan Sidi Mohammed Ben Youssef, leader of the Moroccan nationalist movement, was deposed by French protectorate authorities in August 1953 and banished into exile.

In the case of Guinea-Conakry in 1958, U.S. policy under the Eisenhower administration did not ostensibly serve those perceived interests—denial to the Soviet Union of a foothold in emerging Africa. In 1958, the political leader of Guinea, Sekou Toure, and his people had opted for independence from France in a referendum permitted France's colonies by Charles de Gaulle rather than membership in a Franco-African community as De Gaulle would have preferred. In offering them the plebiscite, De Gaulle had calculated that France's "overseas territories" were poor and weak, and none of them would make the risky choice of independence from a Franco-African community. When the

Guinean leader and his people demonstrably "preferred poverty in freedom to riches in slavery," De Gaulle severely punished Guinea for choosing independence.

Consequently, Guinea's political economy and educational system collapsed as De Gaulle withdrew the supporting infrastructure. To avoid displeasing De Gaulle, as it was also to avoid doing during the Algerian struggle for independence, the Eisenhower administration flatly refused to go to the aid of the desperate West African nation. The Soviet Union, America's ideological rival, moved in. It obtained thereby its second foothold in Africa (after Egypt in 1956). In the early 1960s, President John F. Kennedy, who as a senator had made a public appeal in 1957 for self-determination in Algeria, worked to correct the Eisenhower administration policy miscalculations.[3] His administration viewed with sympathy the Algerian liberation struggle. It promptly improved relations with Guinea. Consequently the West African nation became one of the earliest beneficiaries of the work of U.S. Peace Corps volunteers, a foreign aid program the administration had set up early in 1961. But in the case of nationalist movements in Guinea-Bissau, Cape Verde, Angola, and Mozambique seeking to liberate their countries from Portuguese colonial control, the Kennedy administration and all its successors, for geostrategic and ideological reasons, supported America's NATO ally, Portugal. After the collapse of Portuguese imperial control of those countries, the Gerald Ford administration chose to support a preferred faction in Angola in an ensuing struggle for succession in the former colony.

The Metamorphosis of the U.S. Role

United States' role in conflicts in postcolonial Africa had humanitarian, political, and strategic objectives. Its origins can be traced to a global foreign aid program American leaders initiated in the 1940s, the series of mutual security agreements the United States concluded with several nations, and its arms shipments to various regions of the world after the end of World War II. These programs, pacts, and shipments[4] were all part of the U.S. strategy of containing communism and the ideological expansion of the Soviet Union. Accordingly, from the early years of the Cold War to its end in 1989, the United States provided humanitarian, political, economic, and military assistance in order to reward friends, to woo skeptics and potential supporters, and to deny or punish nations that tended or pretended to be genuinely nonaligned but which maintained ties with the Soviet Union and its allies. In keeping with the mutual security agreements, the United States provided military assistance, including arms transfers to geopolitically relevant and less developed nations as a hedge against communist and Soviet expansion and as an anchor for its security interests and those of its allies. The Inter-American Treaty of Reciprocal Assistance or the Rio Treaty (1947), The North Atlantic Treaty Organization (1949), the ANZUS Treaty (1951) with Australia and New Zealand, the Southeast Asia Treaty Organization (1954), and the Central Treaty Organization formerly the Baghdad Pact (1959), were the major multilateral pacts. Those concluded with the Philippines, the Republic of Korea, and Taiwan typified bilateral ones.

U.S. intervention in Southeast Asia (1950–1975), Vietnam especially, was typical of the nation's efforts to deny a resource-rich, strategic region to communism and the entrenchment of Soviet ideology. For that reason, throughout the late 1940s and the early 1950s, the United States provided economic and military support to France in order to maintain French imperial control over Indochina. President Harry S. Truman viewed the French, the colonial power in the region, as deserving of American support against Vietnamese nationalists. France was perceived as an indispensable element in a possible solid anticommunist bloc in Southeast Asia. This was in accord with the prevailing American belief that national security was threatened by political change in regions fighting for political independence from Western European powers.

But Africa was not a focal part of the initial rivalry between the United States and the Soviet Union. During the late 1940s and the 1950s the Truman and Eisenhower administrations were preoccupied primarily with ensuring that Western Europe, especially, and Southeast Asia were stable bulwarks against communist and Soviet expansion. Consequently, with the exception of Liberia, no African country was directly involved in a bilateral or multilateral security treaty with either the United States or the Soviet Union. As one of the consequences of recommendations by Vice President Richard M. Nixon after his eight-country tour of Africa (February to March 1957), the United States signed a defense pact with Liberia—the traditional focus of U.S. interest in Africa—in 1959. The treaty committed the U.S. government to take appropriate steps if Liberia were threatened by an aggressor.

Other than that treaty with Liberia, before 1960 the African continent was overwhelmingly the preserve of European imperial powers and was not an area of world tension. The Western colonial powers were assisted through the European Recovery Program (the Marshall Plan) and their membership in NATO to hold their sway in the continent. France and Portugal used weapons supplied under the NATO umbrella to wage colonial wars in Algeria; Angola, Guinea, and Mozambique to protect the economic, strategic, and ideological interests of the West. However, six developments foreshadowed U.S. intervention in Africa and Cold War arms shipments to the region.

Developments Foreshadowing U.S. Intervention and Arms Shipments to Africa

One of the developments foreshadowing U.S. intervention and Cold War arms transfers to Africa was a consequence of the Korean War, 1950–1953. The good performance of the Ethiopian contingent in that East-West confrontation raised Ethiopia's priority in American defense planning.[5] That performance fitted well with the intention of the U.S. Secretary of State, Foster Dulles, to promote a southern tier of Middle East security, following the collapse of the Baghdad Pact in 1955. The Baghdad Pact had been intended to isolate the Soviet Union behind the northern tier of Turkey, Iraq, Pakistan, Jordan, Lebanon, and Syria. The good performance of the Ethiopian soldiers also fitted well with the wishes of Emperor Haile Selassie for a military strengthening and a counter to the undue influence in his empire of the British "liberators."

The second development flowed from a vital common interest of the United States and Emperor Haile Selassie, specifically Eritrea. Haile Selassie sought American support to strengthen his Ethiopian empire militarily and to acquire Eritrea, a former Italian colony.[6] Furthermore, acquisition of Eritrea would restore part of Ethiopia's ancient territory and provide it access to the sea. It could also help Ethiopia check a perceived growing threat of the Red Sea becoming an "Arab lake" as well as further consolidate the multiethnic empire.

America's strategic interest was to secure access to Kagnew, a former Italian military facility near Asmara, as a vital part of its global communications and intelligence network. As a result, the United States, which was the dominant influence in the UN in the 1950s, supported Ethiopia's UN-sponsored "federal" incorporation of Eritrea in 1952. On that occasion the U.S. Secretary of State, Foster Dulles, without mincing words, said:

> From the point of view of justice, the opinions of the Eritrean people must receive consideration. Nevertheless, the strategic interests of the United States in the Red Sea Basin and considerations of security and world peace make it necessary that the country has to be linked with our ally Ethiopia.[7]

In addition to its diplomatic and moral support for the incorporation of Eritrea, the United States provided Ethiopia with economic and military assistance of all kinds, including arms. In return, it was granted access to the facilities at Kagnew for twenty-five years.[8] The military assistance set a pattern that lasted until 1977, enabling Ethiopia, which consequently became the major recipient of American military aid in sub-Saharan Africa, to develop one of the continent's largest armies. Those armies were put to use in Ethiopia's thirty-one-year war against Eritrean rebels as well as Somalia's sixteen-year war of ethnic irredentism.

The Decline of British Influence after World War II

The third development that foreshadowed U.S. intervention and Cold War military transfers to Africa was the decline of British influence in Egypt and the Middle East generally. The decline occurred after a series of events: Britain's reduction of its presence in Ethiopia in the late 1940s, the overthrow of a British protégé, King Farouk of Egypt, by the military in 1952; the collapse of the Baghdad Pact in 1955; the withdrawal of 80,000 British troops from the Suez Canal Zone by June 1956; and the Suez Crisis of 1956. The effect of Britain's withdrawal from Ethiopia and the other areas was somewhat similar to that of its withdrawal from Greece and Turkey. The United States, according to Paul Henze, "assumed the British role as the primary concerned power in the afore-mentioned areas, though without consolidating alliance relationships of the kind that resulted from the Truman Doctrine in Greece and Turkey."[9] The American decision to assume that role derived from the persistent manner in which Emperor Haile Selassie systematically cultivated a relationship with the United States. More significantly, the decision derived from deliberate Soviet aggressiveness and refusal to cooperate in the restoration of representative governments in Eastern Europe in violation of agreements concluded at Yalta in 1945.[10] Such Soviet behavior solidified U.S. interest in a base near Asmara in Eritrea along the Red Sea, where it could establish a worldwide intelligence and radio communications network. Thus, American policy on the Horn of Africa was focused on keeping Haile Selassie in power and keeping the region relatively stable, secure, and free of communist and Soviet penetration.

The Suez Crisis, 1956

The Suez crisis was perhaps the most significant precursor of U.S. intervention and arms shipments to Africa. The crisis evolved from Soviet-approved Czech arms sales to Egypt, but its roots lay deeper in the intensity of Arab nationalism as represented by Gamal Abdel Nasser of Egypt, the economic grip on the Middle East by European powers, the whirlpools of Palestine, and the eddies of the collapsed Baghdad Pact. The Dwight D. Eisenhower administration had promised to provide the bulk of the funding for Nasser's planned hydroelectric dam at Aswan. The administration failed to keep its promise because, failing to obtain arms from the United States for Egypt's intensive rearmament program, Nasser had obtained them from the Soviet Union. Following the Eisenhower administration's decision, the World Bank and the British government, which were to contribute funds for the dam, also withdrew their offers. Therefore, Nasser felt compelled by the U.S. cancellation of the promise on 19 July 1956 to nationalize the Suez Canal Company on 26 July in order to finance the project.

All along, Egyptian leaders had complained that almost all of the shareholders, directors, and employees of the Suez Canal Company were non-Egyptians; that the shareholders took a large portion of the revenue derived from the company; and that only a paltry sum was left to improve the canal while the Company kept large reserves outside Egypt. Nasser's ulterior motive in taking the calculated measure to nationalize the Company was to satisfactorily address these concerns and to enhance the independence and prosperity of Egypt and the region. He was prepared to advance his own ends with Soviet assistance.

In response to Nasser's action, Britain and France, joint-owners of the Suez Canal Company with Israel, attacked Egypt. As a consequence, the U.S. government, which had not been informed in advance of the invasion, followed the lead of Moscow and issued an ultimatum to its allies to withdraw from Egyptian territory. This was in accord with the condemnation of the invasion by the United Nations as well as the sympathy of the emerging nations of the world for Egypt. The Eisenhower administration enforced the ultimatum with sanctions imposed on all the belligerents, including Egypt. It cut off economic aid to Egypt and froze the assets of both the Egyptian government and the Suez Canal Company in the United States. It prevented oil shipments to Britain and France and simultaneously denied loans to Britain, blocked its borrowing from the International Monetary Fund, and stopped American aid to Israel. With much reluctance and disappointment the American allies, especially Britain, which had controlled the Suez Canal from 1882 to the time of its seizure by Nasser in October 1956, complied with the ultimatum. Anthony Eden resigned as British prime minister as a consequence of the development. In the meantime, the Soviet Union proceeded to build the hydroelectric dam at Aswan.[11]

The Suez crisis concluded in this manner. The measures by the United States against Britain and France for using force in Suez split the Western alliance and took the edge off their condemnation of the Soviet move to crush the Hungarian rebellion early in November 1956. The Soviet Union obtained its first major strategic foothold in North Africa. Nasser, whose influence Britain and the United States had wanted to eliminate or reduce, emerged from the crisis as the preeminent leader of Arab and African nationalism. The Soviets were to remain the major arms supplier to Egypt until 1975. The crisis demonstrated a shift in the balance of power in the region away from Britain. That shift and the emergence of a Soviet-backed Egypt in the aftermath of the Suez crisis promoted a highly controversial U.S. aid package to Egypt's southern neighbor Sudan, which recently had gained its independence from Britain. The U.S. aid package to Sudan polarized Sudanese parties between the blandishments of the East and the West. The polarization ultimately contributed to a crisis in which General Ibrahim Abboud overthrew the government in 1958. Subsequently, the U.S. aid package was accepted by Abboud's military regime which in turn was warmly embraced by the Eisenhower administration as it kept Egypt and Soviet influence at bay.

The North Atlantic Treaty Organization

A fifth precursor of U.S. intervention and arms shipments to Africa was the military support the United States government provided Portugal as an imperial power in Africa as well as a member of the North Atlantic Treaty Organization. Although announced U.S. policy prohibited Portugal's use of NATO military equipment outside the North Atlantic zone, Portuguese authorities did not make the distinction the United States made between Africa and the North Atlantic area. Therefore, Portugal used the weapons it received from the United States for the defense of the North Atlantic region to maintain its imperial rule in Africa. Similarly, France, another member of NATO and also an imperial power in Africa, used U.S.-NATO designated weapons in its colonial war against Algerian nationalists.

When Portugal flatly refused to negotiate independence with African nationalists, and its NATO allies, especially the United States, for political and strategic reasons, refused or failed to persuade it to do so, national liberation movements successfully sought military assistance from the Soviet Union. The Eisenhower administration had declined a request for such assistance as early as 1956. This subsequently became part of the background to the war of political succession in Angola in which the U.S. and the Soviet Union supplied military weapons to the combatants. (See Chapter 7.)

The Intensification of Superpower Global Rivalry

The U.S. role in postcolonial conflicts in Africa was a product of the superpowers' global rivalry. Intensified superpower intrusion into Africa began in the 1960s when seventeen countries emerged to join ten others as politically independent nations. The august meddling by the superpowers was stimulated by ideological and geopolitical considerations as they sought to enlarge their network for better control of political events but left little or no room for responding positively to the needs and aspirations of Africa's emerging nations or for understanding their social realities. U.S. policy towards Guinea-Conakry, during 1958–1962 illustrates this strategy. The political economy, including the educational and judicial system, of the emergent West African nation had collapsed because the nationals had voted in a referendum for independence contrary to the wishes of Charles de Gaulle of France who had authorized the referendum in the first place. Apprehensive that it might offend America's economic, ideological, and political ally, whose policy had caused the collapse, the Eisenhower administration flatly refused to assist in the rescue of the new state.

The Congo Crisis (1960–1964) was the first major event to draw the superpowers into a political contest in sub-Saharan Africa. The United States had suffered a series of setbacks abroad immediately prior to the beginning of the crisis. The first of these setbacks was Castro's revolution in 1959. The others included increased communist insurgency in Laos; the cancellation of President Eisenhower's trip to Japan because of leftist riots in that Asian nation; and the U-2 incident involving the capture of U.S. spy pilot, Francis Gary Powers, and his high-altitude reconnaissance plane over Soviet territory while on an intelligence-gathering mission. Following the incident, a bitter confrontation between President Eisenhower and Nikita Khrushchev ensued at their summit meeting in Paris in May 1960. Khrushchev walked out of the meeting when Eisenhower refused to apologize for the U-2 incident, for which he failed to deny responsibility and had justified.

Occurring so close to these U.S. setbacks, the crisis in the Congo marked the first massive support by the superpowers for rival sides in a conflict in postcolonial Africa. Its resolution and aftermath provided an opportunity for cooperation between the United States and the DRC for at the least thirty-two years. The Congo is a large country, well endowed with natural resources. It is strategically located in the "heart" of Africa, sharing borders with nine states. Therefore, because of its strategic location and economic significance, the Eisenhower administration was uncompromisingly determined to ensure that it remained under the influence of the Western bloc of powers. (See Chapter 4.)

Elsewhere in Africa, U.S. policy during the Cold War was also overwhelmingly shaped by intense competition with the Soviet Union. U.S. administrators often found it easier to throw military weapons at Africa's postcolonial conflicts than to contribute to their peaceful resolution. Throughout the period 1950–1989 successive U.S. governments transferred more than $1.5 billion worth of weaponry to Africa. They poured military aid and training, covert weapons, and political and financial support into the continent as they prosecuted the war against communism.

For their part, various oppressive regimes in Africa and certain Third World nations took advantage of the Cold War to request arms either from the United States or the Soviet Union in order to bolster themselves against critics and insurgents. Notably, therefore, most of the African countries that engaged in violent conflicts over the past fifty years were recipients of U.S. weapons and military training. U.S. military weapons and training delivered to Africa in 1998 alone were worth more than $20 million.[12] In general, the military shipments to Africa enhanced the capabilities of combatants and made the conflicts more violent, intractable, and protracted with enormous negative consequences to the societies.

U.S. interest in the continent, in the words of Michael Clough, "fluctuated with changing estimates of the threat posed by real or imagined Soviet gains."[13] Invariably, weapons and military assistance were offered to a repressive government with one hand while the other was raised in the name of securing democracy and promoting stability. Autocratic and unpopular regimes which had corrupted their political system and mismanaged their economies in such places as Ethiopia, Kenya, Liberia, Somalia, and Sudan were chosen as the leading recipients of U.S. aid. Such choice was not based on the development prospects of the chosen countries or their opportunities for trade and investment but on the global geopolitical battle with the Soviet Union. However, the recipients of the largest U.S. arms shipments—Liberia, Ethiopia, Somalia, Sudan, and Zaire—"turned out to be the top basket cases in the 1990s in terms of violence, instability, and economic collapse" according to William D. Hartung and Bridget Moix.[14] U.S. military weapons transferred to such African regimes and Jonas Savimbi's Total Union for the Independence of Angola during the Cold War were still being used in African conflicts as the twenty-first century began. It is easy to conclude, therefore, that the post-1997 civil war which devastated the Congo's eastern region and which drew other central—Rwanda, Burundi, Uganda—and southern African countries—Zimbabwe, Namibia, Angola—into the fray is a prime example of the deadly legacy of U.S. arms sales policy to Africa during the Cold War.

Effects of U.S. Intervention and Cold War Arms Transfers to Africa

Intervention in African conflicts through Cold War arms shipments was part of America's strategy in global politics. The utilization of arms illustrated the primacy of geopolitical and strategic considerations over such African-centered values as local autonomy, economic development, and political democracy in the making and conduct of American policy towards the continent. The arms shipments were also part of U.S. domestic policy to promote employment and commercial exports, as the United States became the world's largest exporter of military weapons after the end of World War II.[15] This was so even during the administration of Jimmy Carter, which had asserted that arms shipments to Africa would be an exceptional instrument of foreign policy motivated by a significant actual or potential threat to a pro-Western state.

The shipments stimulated an arms race and superpower rivalry in Africa as the Soviets and their allies also employed weapons transfers as a means of expanding their influence in the continent. Indeed, a substantial portion, if not the bulk, of their aid to African nations was military. Thus, arms transfers, including those made by private arms traffickers with the approval or connivance of the superpowers, became a game played by the superpowers as a means of counterbalancing each other's efforts to promote economic, political, and strategic interests. As a consequence Africa became the largest arms market in the Third World after the Middle East. On the one hand this militarization of Africa fueled conflicts, caused extensive destruction, created a culture of violence, spread political and economic instability, and complicated peaceful change. On the other hand, it benefited the economies of the superpowers and enhanced their leverage over the recipients of the arms. In a number of cases the arms shipments helped to ensure the superpowers votes in the United Nations and the acquisition of rights or access to military bases and intelligence-gathering stations as in the case of the United States in Kagnew noted here, and the Soviet Union in Berbera, Somalia.

Generally, the arms shipments strengthened the inclination of a number of African states to increase their military expenditure. The belief that a prestigious and modern military establishment is a major attribute of national independence and a symbol of national development fostered the acquisition of more and more weapons from major arms suppliers. Given the fact that African states had no modern arms industry, their leaders had to import them. In addition, throughout the 1960s and the 1970s and later, civil conflicts in various parts of Africa— Zaire, Nigeria, Angola, Chad, Western Sahara, and the Horn—increased military expenditures, military personnel, and weapons procured from the superpowers and their allies.[16] For fledgling African states, facing the urgent challenge of economic and social development, these increases represented a blatant misuse of scarce resources.

Of course, neither U.S. nor Soviet arms transfers to Africa provoked the region's many postcolonial wars. But undoubtedly, as legacies of the Cold War, those transfers helped to create or aggravate the conditions which caused the escalation of the conflicts and inflicted devastating consequences on Africa and its peoples. Worse still, they prolonged the conflicts, made them more lethal, and increased political and economic instabilities in the region. Some of the conflicts continued to boil even after the end of the ideological rivalry. A case in point is the war in Angola which lasted from 1975 to 2002. Another is the situation in the Horn of Africa, which the Cold War made a vast receptacle for weaponry. For about three decades arms became the currency with which the United States and the Soviet Union bought bases and political influence in Ethiopia and Somalia, two strategically important countries whose antagonism to one another mirrored the mutual antagonism of their superpower patrons. In a unique reversal, the United States and the Soviet Union each started out arming one side and ended up allied with and supplying the other. In the process both superpowers incurred vast expenditures of public funds that never realistically served their respective security needs. Their Cold War arms shipments to the region ended up being a nightmarish tragedy for the citizens of the governments that received them. Until as recently as 2001 Ethiopia was embroiled in a border war with Eritrea. As of this writing Somalia, whose northern section declared itself independent in May 1991 as the Republic of Somaliland, is a failed state. As such, it is unable to maintain an administrative system, effectively control its entire territory, or provide basic public services, including law and order, and domestic security sufficient to allow normal life and economic activity to continue.

When the Cold War ended in 1989, the United States lost its propensity to intervene in African conflicts. In Liberia, one of the major recipients of U.S. military aid in the early 1980s, the George H.W. Bush administration refused to intervene in a hideous civil war that led to the death of President Samuel Doe in September 1990. Two months later, the defeat of another U.S. client, Hissene Habre, by rebel forces in Chad elicited no protest from U.S. officials. Similarly, official Washington had no response when civil war in Somalia resulted in the ouster of another Cold War client, Mohammed Siad Barre.

Notes

1. In articulating the need for Congressional authorization of the $400 million in aid to Greece and Turkey, Truman asserted: "Totalitarian regimes imposed upon free peoples; by direct or indirect aggression, undermine the foundations of international peace and hence the security of the United States." Hence, he believed that "it must be the policy of the United States to support free peoples who are resisting attempted subjugation by armed minorities or by outside pressures." This became the Truman Doctrine.

2. Dean Acheson, *Present at the Creation* (New York: Norton, 1969), p. 219. Also quoted in Richard D. Mahoney, *JFK: Ordeal in Africa* (New York: Oxford University, 1983), p. 11.

3. Waldemar A. Nielsen, *The Great Powers and Africa* (New York: Praeger, 1969), pp. 268–270; Immanuel Wallerstein, "Africa, the United States, and the World Economy: The Historical Bases of American Policy," in Frederick S. Arkhurst (ed.), *U.S. Policy Toward Africa* (New York: Praeger, 1975), pp. 11–32.

4. Arms shipments or transfers here mean the dispatch of weapons or related war materials from the superpowers, private parties within their territories, and their allies to countries of the Third World by sale or loan or as a gift.

5. Paul B. Henze, *The United States and the Horn of Africa: History and Current Challenge* (Santa Monica, CA: The Rand Corporation, 1990), pp. v, 11.

6. J. Bowyer Bell, *The Horn of Africa: Strategic Magnet in the Seventies* (New York: Crane, Russak and Co., Inc., 1973), pp. 14, 39.

7. Foster Dulles, quoted in Bereket H. Selassie, "The American Dilemma on the Horn," in Gerald Bender et al. (eds.), *African Crisis Areas and U.S. Foreign Policy* (Berkeley: University of California, 1985), p. 169.

8   The resulting American military base at Kagnew tracked space satellites, relayed military communications, and monitored radio broadcasts from Eastern Europe. Until its closure after 1974, when a new base was opened in the Indian Ocean island of Diego Garcia, the base at Kagnew quartered more than 3,200 U.S. military personnel (U.S. Security Agreements and Commitments Abroad, Ethiopia, Committee on Foreign Relations, U.S. Senate, Part 1 [1 June 1970], p. 1902).

9. Henze, *The United States and the Horn of Africa*, p. v.

10. At the Yalta Conference (4–11 February) U.S. President Franklin D. Roosevelt, British Prime Minister Winston Churchill, and Marshal Joseph Stalin of the Soviet Union agreed, among other things, that after World War II (which the Allied Powers expected to win) there would be free elections and constitutional safeguards of freedom in Eastern Europe, mostly areas, liberated by Russia. Stalin's violation of that agreement played a significant part in touching off the Cold War.

11. For details on U.S. policy on the crisis, see Keith Kyle, *Suez* (New York: St. Martin's Press, 1991); *Foreign Relations of the United States, 1955–1956*, Volume XVI: The Suez Crisis July 25–December 31, 1956 (Washington, DC: U.S. Government Printing Office, 1990; *The Suez Canal Problem, July 26–September 22, 1956* (Washington, DC: U.S. Government Printing Office, 1956), pp. 25–32; Robert R. Bowie, "Eisenhower, Dulles, and the Suez Crisis" in W. Roger Louis and Roger Owen (eds.), *Suez 1956: The Crisis and Its Consequences* (Oxford: Oxford University, 1991), pp. 189–214.

12. U.S. Department of Defense, *Foreign Military Sales, Foreign Military Construction Sales and Military Assistance Facts* (As of 30 September 1998); William Hartung and Bridget Moix, "Deadly Legacy: U.S. Arms to Africa and the Congo War," World Policy Institute, http://www.worldpolicy.org (11 January 2000).

13. Michael Clough, *Free at Last? U.S. Policy Toward Africa and the End of the Cold War* (New York: Council on Foreign Relations, 1992), p. 1.

14. Hartung and Moix, "Deadly Legacy: U.S. Arms to Africa and the Congo War."

15. Frederick S. Pearson, *The Global Spread of Arms: The Political Economy of International Security* (Boulder, CO: Westview, 1994), pp. 13, 20, 53; James Schlesinger, "The Quest for a Post-Cold War Foreign Policy," *Foreign Affairs*, Vol. 72, No. 1 (1992/1993), p. 23.

16. See United States Arms Control and Disarmament Agency, *World Military Expenditures* and Arms Transfers, 1969–1978, pp. 117; Earl Conteh-Morgan, "The Arming of Africa," *TransAfrica Forum*, Vol. 5, No. 4 (Summer 1988), pp. 29–40.

CHAPTER 4
U.S. Interventions in
Postcolonial Africa

As a consequence of the "continuing legacies of its cold war policies towards Africa, the United States has some responsibility for the cycles of violent conflicts and economic problems plaguing the continent."[1]

As documented in Chapter 2, the African continent has been the scene of colossal human tragedies, frightful suffering, and retarded economic and political development, all resulting mostly from a crisis of leadership and wars of national liberation, ethnic and civil wars, and interstate conflicts. The issues of conflict management and resolution are, therefore, significant and necessary prerequisites for creating an environment in which these experiences can be averted and political and economic development of the continent is enabled. Addressing these issues too can contribute towards the promotion of such broad objectives of U.S. foreign policy and interests in Africa as regional stability, trade and investment, furthering human rights and democracy, and eliminating circumstances and conditions which tend to provide safe havens for international terrorists and drug traffickers.

The anarchy that resulted from the collapse of Somalia as a nation state in 1991 triggered large-scale migration of populations, economic chaos, and mass violence. Similar unresolved conflicts constitute a potential danger as they foster the emergence of groups whose main aim is to wage war and empower leaders who depend on a climate of fear to justify their own rule. Failed states such as Somalia and Afghanistan may have served as breeding grounds and safe havens for anti-American extremists. Al Qaeda has been linked to the attacks on U.S. Army rangers in Somalia in October 1993 and on the U.S. embassies in Kenya and Tanzania in August 1998. Furthermore, it has been suggested that the terrorist network that the United States has been seeking to eradicate since 11 September 2001, and in fact earlier, is a product of the protracted conflicts in Afghanistan and Kashmir and on the West Bank and Gaza. The 11 September attacks on the United States might never have occurred had these violent conflicts been resolved. Thus, it is obvious that helping to settle protracted civil conflicts, especially those in which vital U.S. interests are involved, is not merely good for the world in general; it can also make the United States safer. It is therefore not surprising that in a June 2002 Chicago Council of Foreign Relations poll, civil wars in Africa were rated as more critical to U.S. national security interest than the military power of Russia or economic competition from Europe.

With the above issues in mind, this chapter surveys the policies of U.S. administrations—Democrat and Republican—on political and armed conflicts in Africa since the end of World War II. It identifies the various ways, including covert operations, diplomatic activities, and arms transfers to belligerents, in which the administrations may have contributed to the onset, escalation, or resolution of the conflicts.

The U.S. role in postcolonial situations of acute tension and/or armed conflicts in Africa has several dimensions. The role is significant in terms of what U.S. political administrations may have done to complicate, escalate and prolong the conflicts or to diffuse, manage, and resolve them. Generally, U.S. national security bureaucracies, especially the Department of State, the National Security Council, and the Central Intelligence Agency, have been the primary institutional forces driving U.S. African policies during noncrisis situations. Most frequently, the president and Congress play the leading role in the formulation and implementation of the policies mainly during crises that threaten either U.S. strategic interests or those of its allies in the region. That role remained significant throughout the first fifty years of the independence of many African states whether the acute tensions and/or armed conflicts were generated and precipitated by local indigenous factors or whether those factors interacted with or were provoked and fostered by external influences and conflicting interests and policies.

In Angola, throughout the period 1975–1991, the United States deeply committed itself to embattled clients through its surrogates—Joseph Mobutu of Zaire and the white minority government of the Republic of South Africa. Similarly, it worked with the governments of Sudan, Egypt, and Saudi Arabia to support a favored faction in the civil war in Chad in 1982/83. It shipped arms at one time or another to a number of African states, such as Ethiopia, Morocco, and Somalia, engaged in internal or interstate conflicts.

Two Specific U.S. Interventions in African Armed Conflicts

Although U.S. administrations did not support any war of national liberation, they became involved in a number of armed and or political conflicts in postcolonial Africa through a variety of overt or covert measures. Diplomatic and/or military support through armed shipments was provided to embattled clients or a preferred party or rebel movement involved in an armed conflict. Aligning the United States in this manner with various state or insurgent leaders escalated conflicts and protracted their duration as happened in Angola and Ethiopia. Another measure was to exert pressures on parties in conflict in order to push them to negotiate. Indirect or direct mediatory action and assistance in monitoring or implementing agreements are typical of other measures the administrations used.[2] In South Africa, Kenya, and Uganda, U.S. officials publicly protested against human rights violations in order to diffuse potential conflicts. U.S. officials applied additional pressures, including the closure of the U.S. embassy in Uganda; economic sanctions on South Africa, Rhodesia, and Uganda; temporary cessation of bilateral aid programs; and termination of programs by U.S. government agencies such as Export-Import Bank and the Overseas Private Investment Corporation (in Uganda under Idi Amin, Rhodesia under Ian Smith, and South Africa under the apartheid regime). In the case of clan warfare in Somalia, the United States carried out a humanitarian intervention under UN auspices in 1992. In addition, for the fiscal years 1992 to 1995, it provided $14 million for funding a variety of conflict management activities in Africa. This amount included $4.5 million in U.S. assistance to the Organization of African Unity (OAU) for conflict management for the fiscal years 1992 to 1994. For the fiscal year 1996, the Clinton administration requested $29.61 million for conflict resolution, peacekeeping, and military training in Africa. The requested figure included $5 million to assist the conflict resolution activities of the OAU.[3]

The Democratic Republic of the Congo

The U.S. government intervened extensively in a series of internal conflicts in the DRC from July 1960 to the collapse of Eurocommunism in 1989. The intervention began as an effort to support the UN Security Council's approved peacekeeping and humanitarian mission in the emergent republic in central Africa. The republic found itself in the throes of a civil war that severely threatened its territorial integrity and political existence barely two weeks after its independence on 30 June 1960. Katanga, the richest and most developed province, had seceded and was immediately military supported by the former colonial power, Belgium. Confronted by these grave events, Congolese authorities—Prime Minister Patrice Lumumba and President Joseph Kasavubu—appealed to the UN for assistance to protect the security and national territory of their country against Belgian "reoccupation" and civil war.

The United States provided much of the airlift and the logistics for the United Nations Operations in the Congo (ONUC). The Soviet Union provided a portion of the airlift and logistics, while other African and nonaligned nations contributed armed forces to the peacekeeping and humanitarian mission.

Soon, a disagreement arose between the political leaders of the Congo—the executive Prime Minister, Patrice Lumumba, and the ceremonial Head of State, Joseph Kasavubu—and the UN secretary-general, Dag Hammarsjköld, as a result of the secretary-general's narrow interpretation of the mandate of ONUC. According to Hammarsjköld, the mandate of ONUC was to maintain law and order in the Congo, not to undertake the political task of reintegrating the provinces which had proclaimed their secession. Impatient with the UN secretary-general's stance, Lumumba sought assistance from the Soviet Union to expel the Belgian troops and reintegrate Katanga. This appeal and the prospects of a Soviet presence in Central Africa incensed the Eisenhower administration. In the view of the administration, the Congo, under the radical nationalist Prime Minister Lumumba, had become the first part of south-central Africa to flirt with the idea of a drastic and an unacceptable political realignment.[4]

In the meantime, a constitutional crisis developed in the republic. President Kasavubu and Prime Minister Lumumba mutually dismissed each other, and Kasavubu prorogued the Congolese parliament. The dismissal of Lumumba originated within the Eisenhower administration, which also adroitly bribed the Congolese Foreign Minister, Justin Bomboko, to countersign the dismissal order.

It was at that stage that the U.S. effort to support the UN mission began to assume a different hue. The Eisenhower administration, together with America's Western European allies, Britain and France, began to support Kasavubu and called for more UN vigorous action against Lumumba and less restraint in dealing with the secession of Katanga. In keeping with this policy, the Eisenhower administration covertly orchestrated, through the CIA and the Belgian government, the ouster, arrest, and the assassination of Lumumba in 1961[5] and the eventual installation of Mobutu Sese Seko to a significant political position as the chief of staff of the Congolese National Army.[6] Thus, Mobutu wielded effective power and control in the Congo from 1961 to 1964. In 1964, under the UN Plan for the Congo, actually crafted by the Lyndon B. Johnson administration, the DRC held general elections. A candidate, the former Katanga secessionist leader, Moise Tshombe, chosen by the Johnson administration, emerged as prime minister. In November 1964, the Johnson administration organized a U.S./Belgian paratroop rescue mission in Stanley-ville (now Lumumbashi). In that city, supporters of the late Prime Minister, Patrice Lumumba, and opponents of the secessionist-leader-turned-Prime Minister of the Congo, Moise Tshombe, had seized foreign nationals, mostly Belgian and American, as hostages in order to extract political concessions from Tshombe. While the OAU, working through President Jomo Kenyatta of Kenya, sought a diplomatic solution to the hostage crisis, the U.S. government carried out the rescue operation during which some of the hostages, including an American medical missionary and about 2,000 Congolese nationals, were killed. The operation generated much criticism of the United States in the UN by African members.

In June 1965, Joseph Mobutu, who christened himself Mobutu Sese Seko, removed Tshombe (who was detested in much of Africa, especially after the 1964 U.S.-Belgian paratroop rescue mission) from office and made himself the chief executive of the Congo. Later, in November 1965, Mobutu ousted the ceremonial Head of State, Joseph Kasavubu, and assumed absolute power over the central African nation.

Over the years, from 1960 until the disintegration of the Soviet Union in 1991, successive U.S. political administrations supported Mobutu's oppressive and corrupt regime against rebels that sought to overthrow it violently. With the help of Belgian, French, and Moroccan troops the Carter administration thwarted two attempts, Shaba I in 1977 and Shaba II in 1978, by Zairean rebels operating from Angola. Despite the practical and moral questions raised by the U.S. support for the Congo tyrant, the persistent U.S. rationale for the policy was: "Mobutu or chaos." From the perspectives of U.S. administrators, support for Mobutu was a means to a noble goal—preventing communist and Soviet penetration of the heart of Africa.[7] Such an eventuality, the U.S. administrators feared, could have an unacceptable domino effect in central Africa and beyond. In the end, the United States achieved its immediate objectives without, however, promoting political stability and orderly development in the DRC.

For the United States, the crisis established the pattern of future interventions in the changing politics and series of conflicts in Africa for over fifty years, at least until Operation Restore Hope in Somalia (1992–1993). Elements of that pattern included, as Walton Brown expressed it, "the avoidance of direct military intervention and the reliance on covert/indirect forms of intervention; containment of the Soviet Union; the cultivation of pro-American leaders in Africa…the extension of military and economic aid to pro-Western, anti-Soviet actors in crisis after crisis."[8]

Mobutu, the installed client and CIA political creation, turned out to be authoritarian and corrupt. He held sway in Kinshasa to serve the political, economic, and strategic interests of the United States and its Western allies at the expense of political development and stability in central Africa.[9] Here is what President George H.W. Bush said about him at the White House on 29 June 1989:

> Zaire is among America's old friends—and its President—President Mobutu—one of our most valued friends…And so I was honored to invite President Mobutu to be the first African head of state to come to the United States for an official visit during my presidency.[10]

It was in this manner, therefore, that for thirty-two years (from 1965 when he ousted Prime Minister Moise Tshombe and President Kasavubu to his own ouster in 1997) and under the doctrine "Mobutu or chaos," the United States provided Mobutu political and military support which enabled him to become one of Africa's most brutal dictators. Despite persistent reports of widespread corruption and human rights abuses in his government, U.S. administrations "helped to build [his] arsenal with a fleet of C-130 transport aircraft and a steady supply of rifles, ammunition, trucks, jeeps, patrol boats, and communications equipment. By the time [he] was ousted in 1997, the United States had delivered more than $300 million (measured in constant 1998 dollars) in military hardware to [his] regime. Through the International Military Education and Training [IMET] program, the United States also trained 1,350 of Mobutu's soldiers at a cost of more than $100 million."[11] Ironically, in 1991 Congress had suspended economic assistance to Zaire, not because of Mobutu's poor human rights record, but because it had defaulted on payment of loans to cover its weapons purchases.[12]

Nigeria-Biafra War

At the outbreak of the Nigerian civil war (1967–1970), the U.S. Secretary of State, Dean Rusk, expressed the Eurocentric view that Nigeria was a British "baby": in other words, the British government had the primary responsibility for resolving the Nigerian conflict. Therefore, the U.S. administration of Lyndon B. Johnson was officially sympathetically neutral, but it actually supported British policy on the civil war. The administration formally supported the cause of Nigerian unity. Although it refused to recognize the secessionist Republic of Biafra, it imposed an embargo on the sale of military weapons to both sides of the conflict. Congressional and public sympathy for Biafra led to the embargo and prevented the adoption of a strictly pro-federal Nigeria posture. To the displeasure of the Nigerian government, both the Johnson administration and that of his successor, Richard M. Nixon, provided food and financial support to a pro-Biafran interdenominational relief group—Joint Church Aid. Even so both administrations maintained unwavering official commitment to a united Nigeria throughout the conflict despite Soviet intervention through sales of military weapons and provision of Egyptian pilots to Nigeria.[13]

U.S. Administrations and the Struggle Against White Minority Rule in Southern Africa

In southern Africa—Angola, Mozambique, Rhodesia (now Zimbabwe), the Republic of South Africa—where nationalists sought to end white minority domination, successive U.S. administrations, from Harry Truman to Gerald Ford, consistently supported political stability and the political status quo, which they believed to be in accord with their goal of containing the spread of communism and Soviet ideology. Therefore, they maintained good relations with the minority regimes in the region. Simultaneously, they expressed in general terms American abhorrence of apartheid and colonialism. In the 1960s the John F. Kennedy and Lyndon B. Johnson administrations expressed their disapproval of both Portuguese colonial rule in Angola and Mozambique and white minority domination in South Africa and Rhodesia. They supported various limited UN measures against all the regimes, but at the same time they diplomatically supported the regimes in and outside the United Nations and other international forums. For example, in October 1974, the United States vetoed a UN Security Council resolution which sought to expel South Africa from the United Nations because of its apartheid policies, which were viewed by several members as a threat to international peace and security. However, in 1975, the Ford administration halted shipments of uranium to the republic until the government signed the Nuclear Nonproliferation Treaty (which the apartheid regime never signed).

The administrations condoned Portugal's use of U.S. weapons specifically supplied for the purposes the North Atlantic Treaty Organization in its colonial wars against nationalists in western and southern Africa. In addition, they shared strategic intelligence with the white minority regimes to the detriment of insurgent African nationalists. Frequently, they provided those white minority regimes material support in the form of military training and sold them weapons and dual-purpose equipment which they used against the nationalists. In no case did any of the administrations seek to project directly American power or influence into the southern Africa region in order to influence or alter the situation of minority and colonial domination there.

When he assumed office in 1969, President Richard M. Nixon and his adviser on national security, Henry Kissinger, ordered a review of U.S. policy towards southern Africa, which was then a source of world tension and a subject of considerable debate in the United Nations. The policy review, National Security Study Memorandum-39 (NSSM-39), recommended five policy options, the second of which Kissinger modified and made the basis of U.S. policy towards the region. Specifically, the modified option argued that the white minority regimes were in southern Africa to stay. It was only through them that positive change could come to the region. The nationalists seeking to overthrow them were believed to be incapable of doing so and would only bring chaos to the region and allow an opportunity for Soviet expansion there. The pragmatic choice was, therefore, to support the white minority rulers while proffering aid and counseling patience to the black nationalists and advocating evolutionary change in the entire region. Even though the administration could not demonstrate that opportunities for evolutionary growth towards full political participation by the black majority did, in fact, exist, an arms embargo that the John F. Kennedy administration had imposed on South Africa in 1961 was partially lifted. Also, the administration actually opposed UN resolutions condemning apartheid and Portuguese colonialism.

Increased U.S. military assistance to Portugal was one of the outcomes of Option II. Sales of dual-purpose equipment and aircraft, including helicopters, to Portugal for use in Mozambique and Angola, increased during the period 1969–72 to $14 million from a total of $150,000 during 1963–68. The increase was accompanied by speeded-up military training for the Portuguese armed forces, and renewal of the lease for a base in the Azores which the United States had obtained from Portugal. Proceeds from the renewal enhanced Portugal's military capabilities in Africa.

Support of the white minority regimes was reinforced by the Nixon Doctrine, an outcome of the prevailing mood in the nation, which was involved in an unpopular war in Vietnam and was experiencing civil disturbances at home. The popular sentiment was that America had become overextended overseas and was undercommitted at home. By the Doctrine, Nixon assured the nation and informed the world that the United States had neither the resources nor the inclination to play the role of policeman of the world. The United States, Nixon said, would provide assistance to any friendly nation whose survival was perceived to be vital to U.S. security, but that nation would have to fight its own wars. The United States would similarly, he added, rely on and provide military assistance to regional powers to protect U.S. interests in their region. Such assistance and more were provided to the white minority rulers in southern Africa.

In keeping with this policy, the Nixon administration conspicuously refrained from preventing the U.S. Congress from passing an amendment—the Byrd Amendment—to the Military Appropriations Act (1970) which violated U.S. obligations to the UN regarding the action of white minority nationalists in the British colony of Rhodesia. Led by Ian Smith, the white minority nationalists had unilaterally proclaimed the colony independent in November 1965 against the British policy of granting independence only after a constitution guaranteeing majority rule in the territory had been adopted. Britain opted to end the rebellion by seeking multilateral coercive action under the auspices of the UN. Consequently, the UN Security Council imposed selected sanctions on the rebellious colony. UN members were to refrain from importing chrome ore and tobacco—major foreign exchange earners for Rhodesia—from Rhodesia and from exporting petroleum to it. President Johnson had imposed the sanctions by executive order in 1968. It was these sanctions that the Byrd Amendment violated. The Nixon administration made no effort whatsoever to prevent the passage of that amendment. Rather, after its passage, it allowed the importation of Rhodesian chrome ore in violation of its own commitment to enforce the UN sanctions against the rebellious British colony.

The Nixon approach to the rebellion, continued by his successor, Gerald Ford, boosted the intransigence of the white minority nationalists and ensured a protracted war of national liberation in the British colony.

In 1976 the Ford administration cosmetically modified its approach to southern Africa as it sought to limit the adverse effects of the collapse of Portuguese colonial rule on its perceived interests and those of its allies in the region. Now the United States and its European allies no longer had hegemonic sway over the important mineral-rich region. The Soviet Union and its allies were able to establish their presence in the region and to contest with increased fervor and effect the dominance of the Western powers. Soviet naval forces in the region, in addition to Soviet ability to airlift Cuban troops and deliver in a timely manner critically needed weapons to Angola, contributed to the successful intervention there. Ford's Secretary of State, Henry Kissinger, saw that success as upsetting the balance of power in the region. To counter further Soviet inroads, Kissinger made the administration's first comprehensive policy speech on southern Africa in April 1976 and undertook shuttle diplomacy in the region. Specifically, he intended to use U.S. influence to end the ongoing guerrilla war by Zimbabwe nationalists and to replace Ian Smith's white minority regime with a moderate, pro-West black majority government. Kissinger pioneered an Anglo-American plan for a resolution of the Rhodesian conflict that proposed a black prime minister for Rhodesia but left much effective power—legislative, police, and judiciary—under the control of white nationalists. It was, therefore, rejected by the black majority. Thus, the plan was never implemented and ended as political casualty of Ford's electoral defeat by Jimmy Carter in November 1976.

In Rhodesia, unlike his predecessors, Carter dealt with the black nationalists honestly and positively, a behavior which had a salutary effect on the conflict there. Upon taking office in January 1977, Carter pressured the Senate to repeal the Byrd Amendment, which the House of Representatives had already repealed prior to his inauguration. In addition, he brought pressure to bear on both the Rhodesian rebel leader, Ian Smith, and his supporters and on the British government of Margaret Thatcher, resulting in the Lancaster House Conference in London in 1979. At the conference U.S. diplomats supported the British mediator, Foreign Secretary Lord Peter Carrington. They promised financial grants for agriculture and education to an independent Zimbabwe. The thorny issues of the conflict, especially the land problem, were ironed out and the modalities of the Constitution and elections to lead the country to independence were agreed to and implemented by all the parties. Accordingly, Rhodesia became independent as Zimbabwe, under majority rule, in April 1980.[14]

Regarding the three other crisis areas in southern Africa—Angola, Namibia, and South Africa—Carter administration policy did not differ significantly from that of the Ford administration although the administration initially sought to bring about a major transformation of U.S. policy towards the region. Like President Ford, Carter linked U.S. formal diplomatic recognition of the government of Angola with the withdrawal of Cuban expeditionary forces from

Angolan territory. He did this even though in his confirmation hearing, Andrew Young, his ambassador-designate to the United Nations, had stated before the Senate Foreign Relations subcommittee that Cuban troops were a force for stability in Angola. The Carter administration also sought congressional support for the National Union for the Total Independence of Angola (UNITA).

The administration played a more activist role in Namibia, a UN trust territory that had been mandated to South Africa in 1919 by the League of Nations after the defeat of Germany in World War I. But on 27 October 1966, a UN General Assembly Resolution 2145 revoked South Africa's mandate because of its poor administration and automatically converted its presence in the territory from a legal administration into an illegal occupation. A nationalist organization, South West African People's Organization (SWAPO), recognized by the UN as the authentic representative of the people of the territory, waged a guerrilla armed struggle to liberate the territory from South Africa's occupation.

Under the auspices of the UN Security Council, the Carter administration's Ambassador to the UN, Donald McHenry, and the British Foreign Secretary, David Owen, led the Security Council's Western Contact Group of five nations—the United States, Britain, Canada, France, and West Germany—in conducting negotiations with South Africa, SWAPO, and Angola to lead the territory to independence. The negotiations produced an agreement which became the basis of UN Security Council Resolution 435 in 1978.[15] According to the resolution, the UN was to supervise elections to lead to the establishment of a Constituent Assembly and eventually Namibia's independence. Although the elections were delayed by South Africa's bad faith and the policy of Carter's successor, Ronald Reagan, the resolution ultimately remained the basis of effecting Namibia's independence in 1990.

After the Carter administration had worked out the modalities for independence under UN auspices, the succeeding Reagan administration successfully linked the withdrawal of Cuban expeditionary forces in Angola with the independence of Namibia. In 1985 Reagan prevailed on Congress to repeal the Clark Amendment to the Military Appropriations Act of 1976, which had forbidden U.S. assistance to any of the factions in the Angolan civil war. From the repeal of the amendment in 1985 to the collapse of Eurocommunism in 1989, the Reagan and Bush administrations provided the Jonas Savimbi-led UNITA with financial, military, and moral support in its war against the Popular Movement for the Liberation of Angola (MPLA) government.

President Carter's initial approach to apartheid, the major source of conflict in South Africa, differed significantly from that of his predecessors. His administration believed that South Africa's policy of apartheid and its political and social practices posed the real danger in South Africa and so were an invitation to Soviet meddling. Thus, the administration attempted to distance the U.S. government from the apartheid regime. It publicly expressed support for political and social change in South Africa and informed the white rulers of the republic that they could not count on U.S. support in any crisis that resulted from their policy of apartheid. This posture drove a wedge between the U.S. government and the apartheid regime in Pretoria but symbolically aligned America with the goals of African nationalists. However, the administration did not express any support for the African National Congress (ANC) and other nationalist movements seeking to end white minority rule in South Africa. Rather, it discouraged revolutionary change in the republic and called for moderate reforms.

Two years into the administration in 1979, matters external to Africa altered its foreign policy approach. The first was the persistent tension between Carter's Secretary of State, Cyrus Vance, and the national security adviser, Zbigniew Brzezinski. Their differing approaches to foreign policy led to conflicting advice to President Carter. Brzezinski was a globalist who advised a continuation of the emphasis by Carter's predecessors on American-Soviet relations. That emphasis required a linkage between Soviet behavior in all areas of America's strategic interest and American foreign policy towards the Soviet Union and those particular areas. Cyrus Vance, a regionalist, sought to de-emphasize geopolitical theorizing and East-West competition in Africa. He stressed dealing with the realities in Africa, which would reduce, if it did not preclude, Soviet intervention. As he put it, "our best course is to solve the problems which create opportunities for external intervention."[16] Such an approach, he advocated, would make U.S. African policy affirmative and active rather than negative and reactive to Soviet behavior and initiatives.

Other events external to Africa that constrained Carter's policy towards southern Africa were the overthrow of the Shah of Iran, the seizure of American diplomats in Iran as hostages, and the Soviet invasion and occupation of Afghanistan, which escalated U.S. fear of Soviet expansion to the oil-rich Persian Gulf. Carter's critics believed that these events had damaged U.S. influence and credibility in the world and called for more, not less, cooperation with the white minority regimes in southern Africa. In addition, the Carter administration's southern Africa policy confronted a series of domestic constraints. Large majorities of the American electorate opposed both apartheid and any U.S. support for nationalist movements in southern Africa. Conservative forces regarded any signs of support for the nationalists as a sellout of the white minority regime. Further, conservatives in Congress, assisted by South Africa's lobbying and propaganda activities in the United States, opposed Carter's policy of assisting South Africa's northern neighbors, the "Frontline States." American business interests in South Africa opposed economic pressures on the minority regime to ensure the flow of raw materials and cheap labor for their companies and investment in the region. The collective effect of the external events and domestic forces was that ultimately the Carter administration maintained the basic traditions of U.S. policy in southern Africa.

President Carter's successor, Ronald Reagan, reinvigorated those basic traditions. President Reagan criticized the Carter administration as being "insensitive" to U.S. security interests and to America's position of power within the global system. Its southern Africa policy, he added, placed the interests of Africans above those of the United States and thus failed to check Soviet geopolitical gains and advances in southern Africa. As a consequence of these views, the Reagan administration began to support oppressive regimes in and outside southern Africa, so long as those regimes—King Hassan of Morocco, Mobutu of Zaire, Siad Barre of Somalia—professed to be anticommunist. Furthermore, it fully restored and embellished U.S. relations with the apartheid regime in Pretoria. It resurrected the Nixon administration's Option II of the National Security Study Memorandum-39 through the policy of "Constructive Engagement" with South Africa,[17] which sought to promote change by working with the white power structure and taking into account the fears of South Africa's white population. It supported evolutionary or white-controlled change and rejected the use of coercive measures to promote change in the Republic. Thus, the policy sought a more "constructive" relationship with the South African government and disavowed public criticism of the regime as well as multilateral diplomatic overtures that could coerce or put it on the defensive. In 1981 South Africa was defended at the UN for its incursions into Angola and Mozambique just as it was to be defended in March 1982 and in December 1983. In 1981 Mozambique expelled four U.S. embassy personnel in Maputo for spying for the CIA and providing intelligence to South Africa for a raid on ANC facilities in its territory. Exasperated by this collaboration with the South African government, in the United States, TransAfrica, the Congressional Black Caucus, and liberal Democrats and Republicans exerted enormous pressure on the Reagan administration to abandon its policy of constructive engagement.

This Reagan policy, following the Nixon administration's policy of supporting white nationalists who, it assumed, were in southern Africa to stay, reflected the intermingling of racial and ideological tendencies that characterized the Nixon, Ford, and Reagan administrations in southern Africa. The merging of these two tendencies fostered an implicit alliance and strategic ties between the administrations and the white minority regimes in southern Africa while conceding the political and moral high ground to the Soviet bloc. Therefore, South Africa, especially, became more intransigent on the issue of apartheid and more openly aggressive towards its neighbors. It was to address this behavior and the white minority domination of South Africa's majority population that the U.S. Congress enacted the Comprehensive Anti-apartheid Sanctions Act in 1986. President Reagan vetoed the bill, but Congress overrode his veto with overwhelming majorities (311–83 in the House of Representatives and 78–21 in the Senate).[18] President Reagan was, therefore, compelled to impose the sanctions. The U.S. measure contributed to genuine political reform and multiracial government in South Africa. It also influenced South Africa's thinking on the urgency of reaching an agreement with its regional adversaries—Angola and SWAPO in Namibia. President Reagan's Assistant Secretary of State for Africa, Chester Crocker, was able to exert such influence not only by implementing the comprehensive anti-apartheid sanctions and bypassing the South African government to support anti-apartheid groups but also by refusing to protest the increase in the number of Cuban troops in Angola in 1987.

After the end of the Cold War and the release of Nelson Mandela from jail in February 1990, the United States continued to adjust its policy towards South Africa. That was essential because the United States had substantial political and strategic interests in seeing South Africa become a peaceful, strong, and multiracial democracy. American policy, therefore, was adjusted in such a way that the George H.W. Bush administration was able to play a constructive role in South Africa's transition to a multiracial democracy. It offered informal diplomatic support and economic incentives to President Frederick W. de Klerk and his National Party and to Nelson Mandela and the ANC that facilitated the difficult process of the peaceful transition.[19] It also encouraged South Africans to return to the bargaining table when their negotiations at the Convention for a Democratic South Africa (CODESA) were suspended in the summer of 1992. Through this supporting role the Bush administration established a foundation for a solid and cooperative relationship with the Republic of South Africa that continued during the succeeding Clinton administration. President Clinton met with de Klerk and Mandela, provided South Africa economic assistance, and encouraged U.S. private investment in the country. The United States Agency for International Development (USAID) was thus enabled to provide training in conflict resolution for South Africa.

U.S. Diplomatic Initiatives in Conflict Resolution

In a number of cases the U.S. government became actively involved in diplomatic negotiation towards resolution of conflicts in postcolonial Africa. It did so in such conflicts as the Suez Canal crisis of October 1956. (See Chapter 3.) As we know, the United States spearheaded the negotiations on Namibia by the Western Contact Group which culminated in UN Security Council (UNSC) Resolution 435 on Namibia in 1978. Similarly, its initiatives in international negotiations on the protracted conflicts in Angola and Namibia resulted in the signing of the Angola-Namibia Agreements in December 1988 that led, among other actions,[20] to the phased withdrawal of Cuban troops from Angola and the implementation of UNSC Resolution 435. The Angola-Namibia agreements were facilitated in no small way by the realistic policies of Mikhail Gorbachev, which included the reorientation of Soviet policy towards Africa. However, in spite of its role in negotiating those agreements and its financial contributions to the peace process, including humanitarian peacekeeping and relief and rehabilitation, the United States continued to support Savimbi until 1993.

In Mozambique, where it had signaled its support of Pretoria's involvement in the conflict between the government and a rebel group—Mozambique National Resistance Movement (RENAMO)—the Reagan administration brokered the Nkomati Accord—a nonaggression and good neighbor pact—in March 1984 between Mozambique and the Republic of South Africa.[21] The South African government had been training and equipping RENAMO, labeled by President Reagan as a group of "freedom fighters," for fighting against the Marxist-oriented government of Samora Marcel. South Africa had accused the Samora Marcel government of allowing Mozambique to be used by South African nationalist rebels—the ANC. In the accord, the South African government pledged to terminate its support of RENAMO and to support tourism in Mozambique. Mozambique agreed to curtail ANC's use of its territory as a base of operations against South Africa. Mozambique did indeed close ANC bases in its territory, but South Africa openly continued to support RENAMO and was never publicly rebuked by the Reagan administration. Instead, the administration joined the South African government in violating the spirit of the accord as well as the Lusaka Agreement,[22] which it had brokered in February 1984 between Angola and South Africa. It did so by obtaining the repeal of the Clark Amendment, arming UNITA rebels with Stinger missiles, and supporting RENAMO. By late 1984, U.S. non-food aid to Mozambique, which had been banned by Congress in 1977, resumed to surpass $60 million in 1985.

In addition to the above instances, U.S. officials intervened directly as mediators at various points in the conflict in Sudan. They spoke out against human rights violations by the government, while some members of the U.S. Senate opposed the extension of more World Bank or International Monetary Fund loans to Sudan as long as the government continued to oppress the Nuba people of southern Sudan. As members of the Senate exerted this pressure, the George H.W. Bush administration took measures to protect the distribution of relief supplies to victims of the civil war and to facilitate the peace process. When the administration had little success in negotiating a Sudanese government-insurgents peace accord (1992–1993), it resorted to quiet support to the Abuja (Nigeria) peace process (1992–1993) mediated by Nigerian officials on behalf of the OAU.

After the flight of Mengistu Haile Mariam from Ethiopia in May 1991, the Bush administration, and later Clinton's, became actively involved in mediating among the various factions in the Ethiopian civil war. Earlier in 1989, the Bush administration had worked indirectly in support of a mediating role by former President Jimmy Carter. At the request of the caretaker government and its opponents—the Eritrean Peoples Liberation Front, the Ethiopian People's Revolutionary Democratic Front (EPRDF), and the Oromo Liberation Front—the Bush administration's Assistant Secretary of State for African affairs, Herman Cohen, convened a meeting of the factions in London on 27 May 1991 to agree on a cease-fire and a transition to a new government. When this effort failed and the caretaker government appeared unable to control its forces, Cohen publicly asked the EPRDF to take over Addis Ababa in order to spare the capital from destruction and further tension and uncertainty. Eventually, with the diplomatic assistance of the United States, a transition government under Meles Zenawi emerged at that stage of the civil war. The Clinton administration continued the U.S. diplomatic role, which contributed to bring about the independence of Eritrea in 1993.

With the windup of U.S.-Soviet confrontations in Africa, the United States began to engage increasingly in behind-the-scenes diplomatic activities with prominent local antagonists as well as through regional, continental, and global organizations. The administrations worked indirectly in support of a mediating role by America's Western European allies. Portugal, and Italy and the Catholic community of Sant Egidio were supported in such a role, respectively, in negotiations in Angola and Mozambique. As official observers, U.S. legal and military experts worked closely with the Italian mediators and the Mozambican parties in conflict to identify steps towards a settlement. Alongside Britain, France, Portugal, and the United Nations, the United States was an official observer to the Rome negotiations in 1992. Later in the year those negotiations culminated in an agreement between the Mozambican government and its major opponent, RENAMO, and in a subsequent and successful UN-monitored elections on 27–28 October 1994. U.S. administrations also supported UN peacekeeping operations in Sierra Leone, Angola, and Namibia as well as UN monitoring in South Africa. In fiscal year 2000, the United States contributed more than $128 million to the United Nations Assistance Mission in Sierra Leone (UNAMSIL). The figure rose to $190 million in fiscal year 2001. The Clinton administration worked closely with Britain in the latter's lead role in restoring peace in Sierra Leone. It also provided technical counsel and limited material and financial support to the peacekeeping efforts of the Economic Community of West African States, through its monitoring group (ECOMOG), as a regional actor in the civil wars in both Liberia and Sierra Leone.

Part of U.S. policy in West Africa, in addition to these efforts, was to contain the spread of war by the Charles Taylor government in Liberia. The United States supported, through legislation, sanctions on diamond exports and arms sales and a travel ban on Liberian government officials, UN efforts to break the link between the Taylor regime, and the sale of conflict diamonds.

In Rwanda, the United States provided technical advice and supplies to the OAU and the French government in their mediation activities. In dealing with the conflict in Burundi, the Clinton administration supported the Arusha peace process, initiated by President Julius Nyerere of Tanzania and continued by the President of South Africa, Nelson Mandela. Howard Wolpe, former U.S. congressman who served as its special envoy in the process, engaged in several meetings and discussions with regional leaders and representatives of concerned European governments and institutions. In 2000 President Clinton assisted in a ceremony in Arusha, where a limited peace agreement which did not include the principal armed groups was signed. In 1999 his administration had appointed a special envoy, Harry Johnston, to work with America's European allies, specifically Norway and Italy, to support a peace process in Sudan's protracted civil war under the auspices of the Intergovernmental Authority on

Development (IGAD). The succeeding George W. Bush administration continued the effort by appointing former Senator John Danforth as a special envoy and by providing $60 million in humanitarian assistance to needy persons in both northern and southern Sudan. It also pledged to contribute to an international effort to reach a negotiated just settlement of the conflict by an even-handed approach, inducements, and pressures upon both the government in Khartoum and the southern opposition. The measures reflected the administration's positive response to the appeals of a group of Evangelical Christians on behalf of suffering southern Sudanese Christians.[23]

Over a period of two years, 2001–2003, Senator Danforth worked with Assistant Secretary of State for African Affairs, Walter Kansteiner, and other officials of the Bush administration to support Kenya's mediation of the conflict under the auspices of IGAD. Consequent negotiations between the government and the Sudanese People's Liberation Movement/Army (SPLM/A) led to an internationally monitored cease-fire and the signing of Machakos Protocol on 20 July 2002. The protocol signed in Kenya resolved critical issues of state, religion and the right of southern Sudan to self-determination. In October 2002 the two sides recommitted themselves to cooperate in providing unhindered humanitarian access to all areas of Sudan and to a cessation of hostilities. Further agreement at Naivasha, Kenya, in September 2003 resolved thorny security issues and paved the way towards a final and comprehensive settlement by the end of the year. President Bush invited Sudan's President Bashir and John Garung, leader of the SPLM/A, to the White House once that final agreement was signed.[24] However, he made it clear that Sudan would remain isolated, with sanctions in place and limited diplomatic relations, until there was peace.

U.S. Humanitarian Intervention in Somalia

In 1992, under UN auspices, the United States carried out a humanitarian intervention—Operation Restore Hope—in Somalia, where state collapse and clan warfare had caused so much insecurity, starvation, and suffering. Without exception, it helped to rehabilitate the refugees and people displaced internally by the conflicts. As discussed in Chapter 3, the humanitarian mission, initiated by President George H.W. Bush and inherited by President Bill Clinton, was not a major military or diplomatic success for both presidents. Nor did it restore a stable government in Somalia. Rather, clan wars resumed while Northern Somaliland persisted in its secessionist rebellion. Because of the domestic fallout from the operation, among other reasons, the U.S. government obstructed UN attempts in 1994 to intervene in Rwanda to prevent the Hutu massacre of an estimated 800,000 Tutsi and their Hutu sympathizers. This action was in no way in accord with the projected policy towards Africa which Clinton had articulated during his 1992 campaign. At that time Clinton asserted that the United States, under his administration, would support measures to strengthen UN peacekeeping capabilities and pay its fair share of the cost of the organization's peacekeeping operations. He had gone further to suggest the need to explore new ideas for UN preventive diplomacy, including the idea of creating a UN Rapid Deployment Force that could be used for purposes beyond traditional peacekeeping for humanitarian purposes. Without such measures, the world, Clinton stressed, would witness an unending series of humanitarian crises such as those in Somalia and Mozambique. Among other things, he added:

> If we are to lead a global alliance for democracy, we must be willing to work as hard in Africa as we are working in other parts of the world. That means putting the same kind of energy into helping South Africans overcome the legacy of apartheid as we do into helping the peoples of the former Soviet Union overcome the legacy of communism. It means opposing political oppression across Africa as firmly as we oppose political oppression in Asia and the Middle East. And it means providing support to the victims of war in Liberia and Somalia as we are providing support to the victims of war in the former Yugoslavia.[25]

In spite of these Clinton campaign utterances in 1992 and U.S. diplomatic initiatives, indirect support, and humanitarian intervention in Somalia, the capacity of U.S. administrations for conflict management in Africa was undermined by a number of forces. For example, upon assuming the presidency in January 1993, Bill Clinton committed his administration, first and foremost, to domestic issues, especially to growing the economy and enhancing U.S. global economic competitiveness. The administration, therefore, tended towards risk-averse strategies regarding the other conflicts (for example, ethnic cleansing in Bosnia and restoration of an elected civilian government to office in Haiti) it had inherited. The administration decided on maximum caution and backed away from the pattern of behavior Clinton had promised during the 1992 campaign. Follow-up of the Bush administration's humanitarian intervention in Somalia proved to be disastrous. Hence in Rwanda, there was no high-level sustained U.S.-international leadership on both political and humanitarian issues. The military was strictly ordered "not to become involved, even indirectly, in operations that could evolve into or be seen as peacekeeping or political, to limit its action to narrow technical humanitarian tasks that could be assumed by civilians."[26] The administration went further at the international level to prevent UN intervention to avert genocide in the troubled central African nation.

To palliate its conscience for its role in obstructing UN intervention in Rwanda in 1994, in contrast to its role in Bosnia, the Clinton administration, among other reasons, initiated a program—African Crisis Response Initiative (ACRI)—of training and equipping African militaries to intervene in internal African conflicts so as to obviate the need for intervention by the international community under UN auspices.[27] ACRI promoted the doctrine that African nations, not the United States, were primarily responsible for resolving African conflicts. This, it was stressed, would minimize the risk and cost of America's close involvement in many an intractable conflict in Africa. In keeping with this doctrine, the Clinton administration supported the military efforts of Rwanda, which enabled Laurent Desiré Kabila to violently end the authoritarian rule of Mobutu Sese Seko in Zaire in 1997. Similarly, it encouraged Isaias Afwerki of Eritrea, Meles Zenawi of Ethiopia, Paul Kagame of Rwanda, and Yoweri Musoveni of Uganda to undermine the Islamic fundamentalist regime in Sudan that was engaged in a civil war against the southern Sudanese. All in all, the Clinton administration was more reactive than active in promoting conflict resolution.

The Clinton administration's capacity for conflict management in Africa was further inhibited by the decline of U.S. bilateral influence on the continent. To illustrate, the Africa Bureau of the U.S. Department of State lost a deputy assistant secretary of state position and sixty officer positions. Throughout the 1990s, the bureau and U.S. embassies in Africa were unable to staff important mid-career positions. Several mid- and senior-level officers migrated out of the bureau. Consequently large stretches of Africa, including Sudan, eastern Congo, northern Nigeria, Angola, and Somalia, lacked on-site diplomatic personnel. Several U.S. embassies in Africa, such as those in Abuja (Nigeria), Abidjan (Côte d'Ivoire), and Harare (Zimbabwe) operated at substandard strength. Cutbacks in intelligence resources and the closure of more than a dozen USAID missions further reduced U.S. capacities for conflict management.[28]

Another factor that affected U.S. role in conflict resolution in Africa during the Clinton administration was the administration's identification of four African heads of state—specifically Meles Zenawi of Ethiopia, Isaias Afwerki of Eritrea, Yoweri Musoveni of Uganda, and Paul Kagame of Rwanda—as "new leaders." The administration praised them and accorded these leaders special status. Its close identification with them tended to fuse their interests with those of the United States and so effectively compromised the administration's role in African conflict resolution. On the other hand, the administration's hostility towards other leaders such as Laurent Kabila and the national Islamic Front government in Sudan limited contacts, access, and tactical maneuverability with them. Finally, the involvement in African conflict resolution during the Clinton administration was yet another reflection of the end of the Cold War and also, in part, a function of shrinking U.S. resources and a contemporary spirit of "Afro-pessimism," the prevailing belief that the United States could do little to alter perceived deteriorating political and economic conditions in Africa.

Notes

1. William D. Hartung and Bridget Moix, "Deadly Legacy: U.S. Arms to Africa and the Congo War" (World Policy Institute, 11 January 2000), http://www.iansa.org/documents/ research/ 2000/wpi_uscongo.htm.

2. Donald Rothchild, "The United States and Conflict Management in Africa," in John W. Harbeson and Donald Rothchild (eds.), *Africa in World Politics: Post-Cold War Challenges,* 2nd edition (Boulder, CO: Westview, 1995), pp. 209–233; Donald Rothchild, "U.S. Role in Managing African Conflicts," in David R. Smock and Chester A. Crocker (eds.), *African Conflict Resolution: The U.S. Role in Peacemaking* (Washington, DC: United States Institute of Peace, 1995), pp. 39–55; George H.W. Bush, "The U.S. and Africa: The Republican Record," *Africa Report,* Vol. 37, No. 5 (September/October 1992), pp. 13–18.

3. Herman J. Cohen, "African Capabilities for Managing Conflict: The Role of the United States," in David R. Smock and Chester A. Crocker (eds.), *African Conflict Resolution: The U.S. Role in Peacekeeping* (Washington, DC: United States Institute of Peace, 1995), p. 88.

4. Immanuel Wallerstein, "Africa, The United States, and the World Economy: The Historical Bases of American Policy" in Frederick S. Arkhurst (ed.), *U.S. Policy Toward Africa* (New York: Praeger, 1975), pp. 11–37.

5. Ludo De Witte, *The Assassination of Lumumba,* translated by Ann Wright and Renée Fenby (New York: Verso, 2001); François Misser (Reuter), "Belgium to Probe Role in Lumumba Murder" (21 January 2000), posted in Naijanet (31 January 2000); Madeleine G. Kalb, *The Congo Cables: The Cold War in Africa—From Eisenhower to Kennedy* (New York: Macmillan, 1982), pp. 46–70, 128–196; F. U. Ohaegbulam, *Nigeria and the UN Mission to the Democratic Republic of the Congo* (Tampa: University Presses of Florida, 1982), pp. 38–39, 48.

6. See Kalb, *The Congo Cables;* Ohaegbulam, *Nigeria and UN's Mission to the Democratic Republic of the Congo,* Chapter 2, pp. 20–52; U. S. Senate, *Alleged Assassination Plots Involving Foreign Leaders: An Interim Report of the Senate Committee to Study Government Operations with Respect to Intelligence Activities* (Washington, DC: U.S.

Government Printing Office, 1975). See Michael G. Schatzberg, *Mobutu or Chaos? The United States and Zaire, 1960–1990* (Lanham, MD: University Press of America, 1991).

7. See Schatzberg, *Mobutu or Chaos?*

8. Walton L. Brown, "American Policy Toward Africa," in Kul B. Rai et al. (eds.), *America in the 21ˢᵗ Century: Challenges and Opportunities in Foreign Policy* (Upper Saddle River, NJ: Prentice Hall, 1997), p. 228.

9. Sean Kelly, *America's Tyrant: The CIA and Mobutu of Zaire*   (Washington, DC: The American University, 1993); Schatzberg, *Mobutu or Chaos?*

10. Quoted in Kelly, *America's Tyrant.*

11. Hartung and Moix, "Deadly Legacy."

12. U.S. Department of Defense, *Foreign Military Sales, Foreign Military Construction Sales and Military Facts* (30 September 1998); Human Rights Watch, "Clinton Administration and Human Rights in Africa" (March 1998).

13. For details see John J. Stremlau,   *The International Politics of the Nigerian Civil War, 1967–1970* (Princeton, NJ: Princeton University, 1977), pp. 280–294.

14. Michael Clough, "From Rhodesia to Zambia," in M. Clough (ed.), *Changing Realities in Southern Africa* (Berkeley, California: Institute of International Studies, 1982), pp. 1–60.

15. The resolution called for the independence of Namibia through free and fair elections; established a United Nations Transition Assistance Group (UNTAG); endorsed a special representative of the UN secretary-general for the latter purpose; and urged the cooperation of the South Africa's government and South West African People's Organization (SWAPO).

16. Cyrus Vance, "U.S. Policy Toward Africa," *African Directions* (Fall 1977), p. 47. See also Anthony Lake, "Africa in Global Perspective," *Africa Report* (February 1978), p. 44.

17. See Chester A. Crocker, "South Africa: Strategy for Change," *Foreign Affairs*, Vol. 59, No 2 (Winter 1980/1981), pp. 323–351; Chester A. Crocker, "Africa Policy in the 1980s." *Washington Quarterly*, Vol. 3, No. 3 (1980), pp. 72–86; Chester A. Crocker, "Regional Strategy for Southern Africa," *Current Policy*, No. 38, Bureau of Public Affairs, U.S. Department of State (29 August 1981); F. Ugboaja Ohaegbulam, "The U.S. Congress and the Reagan Administration's Policy of Constructive Engagement with South Africa," *New Political Science,* Number 27 (Winter 1993), pp. 105–128.

18. See Ohaegbulam, "The U.S. Congress and the Reagan Administration's Foreign Policy of Constructive Engagement with South Africa."

19. See Princeton N. Lyman, *Partner to History: The U.S. Role in South Africa's Transition to Democracy* (Washington, D.C.: United States Institute of Peace, 2002).

20. Also by the Angola-Namibia Agreements South Africa was to withdraw from Angolan territory; Angola was to restrain SWAPO guerrillas from operating from its territory against South Africa-"occupied" Namibia; and the United States was to withdraw its support of South Africa's troops in Namibia.

21. For details of the Accord and U.S. role see Martin Lowenkopf, "Mozambique: The Nkomati Accord," in Michael Clough (ed.), *Reassessing the Soviet Challenges in Africa: Policy Papers in International Affairs,* No. 25 (Berkeley, CA: Institute of International Studies, 1986), pp. 48–68; Appendix, pp. 91–96.

22. The Lusaka Agreement (February 1984) called for the disengagement of South African and Angolan forces from southern Angola and the establishment of a joint South African-Angolan team to supervise the withdrawal of South African forces from Angolan territory; and required Angola to restrain SWAPO guerrillas from attacking Namibia. For details see Pauline Baker, *The United States and South Africa: The Reagan Years* (New York: Ford Foundation/Foreign Policy Association, 1989), pp. 18–20.

23. Elisabeth Bumiller, "Evangelicals Sway White House on Human Rights Issues Abroad," *The New York Times* (26 October 2003), http://www.nytimes.com/2003/10/26/politics/26 RELI.html.

24. Colin L. Powell, "An Opportunity for Peace in Sudan," Statement Released by Secretary of State Colin L. Powell on 28 October 2003; also see Colin L. Powell, Op-ed, *Los Angeles Times* (28 October 2003).

25. Bill Clinton, "The Democratic Agenda," *Africa Report*, Vol. 37, No. 5 (September/ October 1992), pp. 18–20. The quotation is from p. 19.

26. Robert B. Oakley, "A Diplomatic Perspective in African Conflict Resolution," in Smock and Crocker (eds.), *African Conflict Resolution: The U.S. Role in Peacemaking*, p. 71.

27. F. U. Ohaegbulam, "The Clinton Administration's African Crisis Response Initiative: An Examination of a Post-Cold War United States Africa Policy," *The New England Journal of History*, Vol. 68, No. 3 (Spring 2002), pp. 33–51.

28. J. Stephen Morrison and Jennifer G. Cooke (eds.), *Africa Policy in the Clinton Years: Critical Choices for the Bush Administration* (Washington, DC: CSIS, 2000), p. 41.

CHAPTER 5
U.S. Role in Conflicts in the
Horn of Africa

The Horn of Africa, including Ethiopia, Eritrea, Djibouti, Somalia, and Sudan, is a major geopolitical region of the world. Overlapping the Indian Ocean and the Middle East, the region has been the scene of several intrastate and interstate wars since 1956. Each of the countries in the region, except Djibouti, has at one time or another been embroiled in a civil war. Sudan has had two: 1956–1972, and from 1983 to date. After several years of an irredentist war against Ethiopia, Somalia was convulsed by clan warfare. The internal warfare turned it into a collapsed state, unable to perform the basic functions of a state. The Ethiopian state/empire, whose ruling elites refused to share power with other nationalities, confronted two major internal struggles. The first, beginning in 1961, was the Eritrean liberation struggle. Eritrean nationalists accused Emperor Haile Selassie of flagrantly violating the terms of the UN-sponsored federal incorporation of Eritrea into Ethiopia and fought for more than thirty years for their separate identity as a nation. Added to that liberation struggle, after the overthrow of Emperor Haile Selassie, was the struggle for national self-determination by two national groups within Ethiopia—the Tigreans of northern Ethiopia and the Oromo in south and southwest Ethiopia. Further, Ethiopia and Somalia fought each other intermittently from 1962 to 1978 over the Ogaden Province of Ethiopia, which was largely populated by the Ogaden Somali. Later, Ethiopia and Eritrea, to which the former had conceded independence in 1993 after several years of civil war, warred against each other from 1999 to 2001.

Apart from being the site of protracted sociopolitical upheavals, culminating in a large-scale and successful Soviet-Cuban military intervention (1977–1978) in support of the Ethiopian government, the Horn is near the Persian Gulf and Western Asia, a region of special importance to United States' economic interests and global strategy. The United States and its Western European and Japanese allies import, respectively, about 15 percent, 60 percent, and 90 percent of their crude oil from the Persian Gulf. A slump in the production of the economies of these allies, resulting from their greater dependence on Gulf

Map 5.1 Horn of Africa

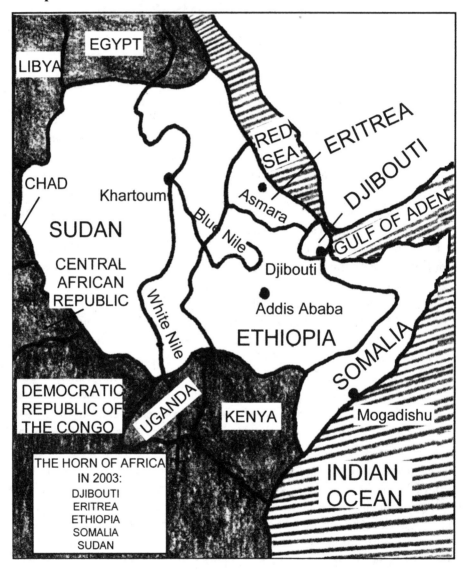

oil would inevitably affect U.S. economic output levels as well. Hence, historically, American leaders have considered the entire area—the Gulf and the Horn—particularly sensitive. Furthermore, American allies in the Gulf, especially Iran, under the Shah, Saudi Arabia, and Kuwait, were fragile monarchies, ruling without the consent of their people and with enormous corruption and inequality of wealth. One of these allies, Iran, was the site of a revolution in January 1980 that brought about the overthrow of the Shah, Mohammad Reza Pahlavi, by the Ayatola Khomeini's Islamic fundamentalists. More humiliating, it was the site of the seizure and holding of American diplomats as hostages in Tehran for more than one year. An additional cause of concern for the United States was the large-scale Soviet military occupation of Afghanistan in December 1979. This development provoked the Carter Doctrine (January 1980) and the consequent establishment of U.S. Rapid Deployment Force (RDF) with bases in Diego Garcia in the Indian Ocean, Berbera in Somalia, and Mombasa in Kenya.

Historically, the Horn of Africa assumed a geopolitical and strategic importance to the United States from the onset of World War II when fascist Italy occupied three of its components—Ethiopia, Eritrea, and Somaliland. Because of its strategic location near the oil-rich Persian Gulf and, perhaps more importantly, developments within the region and among its component states, the region became a major area of intense competition between the United States and the Soviet Union during the Cold War. Each superpower acquired a military presence in the region. Although for most of that period the United States provided Ethiopia with technical and military support, including arms, while the Soviet Union similarly supported Somalia, historical and indigenous forces had primacy over U.S.-Soviet ideological competition in the region. The two superpowers intervened in the region on behalf of one or more indigenous antagonists in order to advance their own geopolitical and strategic interests. Their ideological rivalry gave the states of the region, especially Ethiopia and Somalia, some leverage through which they obtained substantial economic and military assistance from both rivals.

The Ogaden war, 1977–1978, produced a realignment of forces in the region. It transformed Somalia into a U.S. ally and Ethiopia—long a close friend of the United States—into a Soviet ally. The U.S. interest in Somalia climaxed in 1980 with the signing of a Somali-United States military agreement. U.S.-led multilateral intervention in the country, discussed below, was terminated in 1994, but a few years later, at the turn of the twenty-first century, the war on global terrorism heightened U.S. interest in the Horn. Al Qaeda terrorist cells in Somalia and Yemen had mounted attacks against U.S. troops in Somalia, embassies in Kenya, and Tanzania and bombed the U.S.S. Cole in Yemen's harbor. In response to these developments, the 11 September 2001 attacks on the New York World Trade Center and the Pentagon, and the subsequent war in Afghanistan, the George W. Bush administration began to turn the Horn into a U.S. military hub, using Djibouti as a launching pad. The move was primarily undertaken in order to put American forces in a position to strike Al Qaeda refugee havens in Yemen and East Africa and to train American forces in desert warfare.[1] In this chapter we focus mainly on U.S. role in two of the conflicts in the region: the Ethiopia-Somalia conflict and the clan wars in Somalia.

U.S. Role in the Ethiopia-Somalia Conflict

The dynamics of the U.S. role in the Ethiopia-Somalia conflict (1962–1978) contrast vividly with those of the cluster of its goals and objectives and the outcome of its role in an earlier conflict, 1934–1941 involving Ethiopia and fascist Italy, then the imperial overlord of Ethiopia's neighbors—Eritrea and Italian Somaliland. What was U.S. role in each conflict? What accounts for the contrasting U.S. policies towards the two conflicts and their differing outcomes? To address these questions, we sketch U.S. policy in the earlier conflict in order to appreciate the circumstances and dynamics of the policy rationale, the goals and objectives sought, and the outcome of the role. Next, we examine similar dynamics, goals and objectives, and outcome of the policy in the second and more protracted conflict.

U.S. Neutrality in the Italo-Ethiopian Conflict, 1934–1941

Both Italy and Ethiopia had signed a treaty—the Kellogg-Briand Pact (1928)—initiated by the American Secretary of State, Frank B. Kellogg, and a French Foreign Minister, Aristide Briand. By the treaty both countries and sixty-four other signatories, including the United States, undertook to settle their disputes by peaceful negotiation and thus to renounce war as an instrument of national policy. But in pursuit of imperial glory, economic opportunity, and overseas settlement territory for unemployed nationals who were unable to emigrate to the United States or to other European nations, Benito Mussolini utilized an incident between Ethiopian and Italian soldiers at Wal Wal in 1934 to provoke a war of imperial conquest against Ethiopia. Accordingly, fascist Italy attacked the Ethiopian empire in October 1935, conquered, and occupied it from 1936 to 1941.[2]

The immediate action of the United States on the eve of the Italian invasion of Ethiopia was to pass a neutrality act. In August 1935, just before fascist Italy unleashed its war of imperial conquest on Ethiopia, Congress passed the first of the interwar Neutrality Acts. The Neutrality Act of 1935 required that the president, after proclaiming the existence of a state of war, should prohibit all arms shipments to belligerents and could prohibit American citizens to travel on belligerent vessels except at their own risk. The act benefited Italy, the aggressor, rather than Ethiopia, the victim of its aggression, which could not purchase weapons to defend itself. The legislation also reduced any bargaining power the administration of Franklin D. Roosevelt had with Benito Mussolini and prevented it from using such trump cards as sending military supplies to Ethiopia. The neutrality law of 1935 was followed up by another one in February 1936 which forbade loans to belligerents.

The policy of neutrality on the Italo-Ethiopian conflict was a product of official American response to both external forces and internal circumstances and realities. The policy was designed to isolate America from European politics and troubles and to keep the country focused on domestic economic problems, particularly the Great Depression and the nationwide frustrations that resulted from U.S. participation in World War I. Developments in Europe at the time appeared to be reminiscent of those that had led to the first global war. The findings of a Senate Committee chaired by Senator Gerald Nye of North Dakota into the causes of American intervention into that war and the aftermath of that intervention created a climate of disillusionment in the United States. The committee, which began its work in 1934, reported in 1936 that investment bankers and munitions manufacturers had dragged the United States into the war in order to maximize their profits and protect their investments. In addition, the European nations had defaulted in paying their war-related debts to the United States. This rankled as every aspect of American life was ravaged by the Great Depression (1929–1934), causing international affairs to take a back seat to attempts to restore the economic health of the nation. Some who saw collusion by sinister U.S. forces with Europeans to drag the United States into an unwanted war sought to prevent a repetition as the Italo-Ethiopian crisis loomed on the horizon. In an act of 11 August 1935, Congress took measures to ensure that just before Mussolini attacked Ethiopia in October 1935. Hence the policy of neutrality on the Italo-Ethiopian conflict.

In keeping with this policy President Franklin D. Roosevelt and his Secretary of State, Cordell Hull, flatly refused to invoke the Kellogg-Briand Pact when requested to do so by Emperor Haile Selassie of Ethiopia. As noted previously,

Italy, Ethiopia, and sixty-four other nations, including the United States, had signed this pact at the initiative of the United States and France. The U.S. administration asked Haile Selassie to appeal to the League of Nations, of which the United States did not belong. When the issue was submitted to the League of Nations in Geneva, the Roosevelt administration also refused to collaborate with the League in its attempts to resolve the conflict. Cordell Hull was afraid that, given the isolationist sentiment in the nation, any collaboration with the League would damage President Roosevelt's national recovery program—the New Deal.[3] He was also reluctant to involve the United States in a collaboration with the League as long as Britain and France, afraid they would drive Mussolini into the embrace of Adolf Hitler, were themselves appeasing the Italian leader and were unwilling to confront Italy without American participation. The appeasement of Mussolini was due to the fact that after World War I, Britain's ability to exercise world leadership was severely strained. The United States, which could have assumed that role, refused to do so. One outcome of American aloofness and the appeasement of Mussolini by Britain and France was the Italian conquest and occupation of Ethiopia from 1936 to 1941. In effect, the event marked the first steps towards World War II. The United States forfeited the influence it could have wielded not only over the outcome of the Italian invasion of Ethiopia but also over German rearmament and annexation of the Sudetenland from Czechoslovakia. The United States was dragged into the ensuing war in December 1941 after the Japanese attack on Pearl Harbor (7 December 1941). It emerged from the war as a superpower with global interests, including those in Ethiopia and the entire Horn of Africa.

The Dynamics of the U.S. Role in the Ethiopia-Somalia Conflict

These were the circumstances and the outcome of U.S. policy on the war between a European nation and an African empire. The United States administration saw the conflict in Eurocentric term and so assigned Europe primacy. Global circumstances at the time of the Ethiopia-Somalia war were completely different from those that obtained during the war between Ethiopia and fascist Italy. The world had become bipolar in a drive for global domination, politically and ideologically, by the respective leaders of the two blocs. Seeing its national security interests after World War II in global terms, the United States assumed the mantle of world leadership and the role of a defender of the Western world and its values against perceived threats from communism and the Soviet Union. Neither country saw Africa realistically in terms of the needs of the continent and its nations but saw it only from the prism of the global rivalry in which emergent African nations became pawns. These were the circumstances that influenced U.S. policy choices and role in the Ethiopia-Somalia conflict.

The outcome of the interaction was both problematic and complex. The conflict became very prolonged. The superpowers changed sides in their support for the two African nations: the Soviet Union switched from supporting Somalia to supporting Ethiopia, and the United States first supported Ethiopia, then Somalia. Neither of the combatants, pawns in the ideological struggle, remained what it had been prior to the onset of the war. Both had received massive arms transfers from the United States and the Soviet Union and had experienced internal convulsions. By 1993 Ethiopia lost Eritrea, which it had annexed with apparent nods from both the United Nations and the United States. By the same year Somalia had become a collapsed state, with no legitimate government, requiring the assistance of the United States and the international community as represented by the United Nations for the precarious survival of its nationals.

Armed conflict between Ethiopia and Somalia began when the rulers of emergent Republic of Somalia decided to reunite all the Somali people who had been split into five separate political territories by European imperial powers. Perhaps the most homogeneous of precolonial African nationality groups, with a common language, a common religion, a common culture, and common understanding of themselves as a political community, the Somali were initially divided by three European powers into British Somaliland, French Somaliland, and Italian Somaliland. Part of the Horn of Africa, Somaliland was perceived to be so geopolitically significant and strategic that the rival European imperial powers were unwilling to leave it entirely in the control of only one of them. Subsequent boundary adjustments made by imperial Britain and Ethiopia gave Ogaden, populated mainly by Somali nomads, to Ethiopia. Similar adjustments between Britain and Italy included Somali people in the northeast province of British East Africa, Kenya. In this manner, the Somali were balkanized into five political territories.

After their independence in June and July 1960, formerly British Somaliland and Italian Somaliland united (1 July 1960) as the Republic of Somalia. Leaders of the new republic mounted a five-point star on a flag of what they envisioned would be a "Greater Somalia." The five-point star represented the northern and southern regions of the united republic as well as the "unredeemed" Somali in the Ogaden province of Ethiopia, the northeastern province of Kenya, and the French Somaliland (later the French territory of the Afars and Issas, now Djibouti). It was to bring about this Greater Somalia, embracing the five regions—the united and the unredeemed Somali—that Somali rulers soon after their independence adopted an irredentist policy towards the Ogaden province of Ethiopia, the northeast province of Kenya and the French territory of Afars and Issas (Djibouti). Mohammed Siad Barre, who had become president of Somalia in 1969 through a military coup d'etat, devoted most of his efforts towards reintegrating the Ogaden and Djibouti into Somalia. The French, at the behest of Emperor Haile Selassie, had remained in effective control of their colony of Djibouti until 1977, preventing thereby an extension of Somalia's irredentist war to the territory.

The two foremost targets of Somali irredentism were viewed by Ethiopia as vital to its national security. Djibouti was one target although it was still under French control until 1977. It has a sizable Ethiopian population—the Afars. Through a railroad it provides Ethiopia transportation and access to the sea. Two other outlets—Assab and Massawa—were in rebel territory, Eritrea, by the time Somalia launched its irredentist policy. Hence, Haile Selassie pressured France to remain in control of Djibouti. The other target, Ogaden province, was larger and, potentially, richer. It is known to have deposits of oil and natural gas. It was there that Somalia, shortly after independence, initiated a border war against Ethiopia. The war continued off and on from the 1960s to 1977 and 1978.

In waging the wars the belligerents sought and received military assistance from the superpowers: Ethiopia from the United States and Somalia from the Soviet Union. The geopolitical significance of the Horn—its proximity to the Middle East and its importance for international shipping and worldwide defense as well as the contending interests of the superpowers—dictated the provision of such military assistance. As noted, U.S. officials wanted to preserve regional security and stability in the Horn of Africa and the Middle East. They believed that the entire area was of such great importance to the economic well-being of the industrialized world that it should have logistical facilities which would permit the United States to maintain a credible presence.[4] The facilities at Kagnew and military relations with Ethiopia were designed for this purpose. Therefore, prior to 1977, the United States supported Ethiopia. Hence, it turned down Somali requests for military assistance in the early 1960s as a potential threat to Ethiopia's security interests. This position was reinforced by the formation of the OAU in 1963 and the organization's Cairo Resolution in 1964 by which members agreed to respect the inviolability of the colonial boundaries they inherited at independence. In light of U.S. policy, Somalia turned to the Soviet Union for aid. It began to send its air force pilots to the Soviet Union for training by 1965. Ties between the two countries were further strengthened by

1969. By that time Mohammed Siad Barre had seized power and sought to double the size of Somalia's armed forces. Barre devoted his energies to prosecuting the war that had been going on intermittently since 1960.

Continued instability in the Horn, arising from events in Ethiopia and Somalia's persisting irredentist policy, combined with the wider geographic importance of the area to cause further concern. Because of the general situation in the region and, above all, the increased naval presence of the Soviet Union in the Indian Ocean after the October 1962 Cuban missile crisis, U.S. officials began to perceive the possibility of a Soviet-American confrontation in the Horn. This necessitated continued U.S. military and economic aid to Ethiopia until its Marxist-oriented military rulers who had deposed Emperor Haile Selassie in 1974 turned to the Soviet Union in 1977. This ended the formal relationship between the United States and Ethiopia. With the termination of that formal relationship, the government of Somalia began to distance itself from its long relationship with the Soviet Union, with which it had signed a Treaty of Friendship in 1974. That relationship was effectively damaged when the Soviets began to build formal and closer ties with Ethiopia's Marxist-oriented military regime led by Mengistu Haile Mariam. Concomitant with the damaged relations, the government of Mohammed Siad Barre began to make overtures to the United States for closer ties. In order to maintain its influence in the Horn of Africa, the United States responded favorably to those overtures during the Carter administration. The subsequent U.S. presence in Somalia was an appendage of U.S. interests in the Gulf and Indian Ocean. It was designed to protect those larger interests.

U.S. Cold War Arms Shipments to the Ethiopia-Somalia Wars

U.S. military assistance to Ethiopia began after 22 May 1953 when the two nations signed two treaties covering U.S. use of military facilities in Ethiopia and provision of military assistance to Ethiopian armed forces. Valid for a period of twenty-five years, the treaties, on the one hand, provided Ethiopia military assistance for its internal security requirements and limited international security obligations. On the other hand, they guaranteed the United States unlimited access to military installations by surface, sea, and air and overflight privileges over all of Ethiopia.[5] In addition, the treaties granted the United States control of a communications base at Kagnew in Asmara, the capital of Eritrea. Central to America's global communications system, at least up until 1976, the Kagnew communications base monitored Soviet activities and gathered intelligence for the United States in Africa, the Indian Ocean, and the Middle East.

The agreement did not constitute a mutual defense pact as Ethiopia was a member of the Nonaligned Movement comprising a group of nations which preferred to pursue an independent foreign policy rather than to conclude a military pact with either of the East/West ideological blocs. Because of that membership and his own caution about overdependence on a single foreign country, Haile Selassie chose to diversify his military relationship, including advanced training of military officers. However, the 1953 agreements brought Ethiopia a steady flow of U.S. economic and military aid until 1977. For the period 1946–1977, the economic assistance amounted to $395.4 million. For the period 1953–1977, the military assistance was $287.3 million.[6] In 1976, two years after the military overthrow of Haile Selassie, Ethiopia bought $100 million worth of arms supplies from the United States. These amounts seem small, but in the 1970s they were a huge amount, about half of the total U.S. military assistance to all African states.[7] During the period 1953–1977, the United States trained more than 3,500 Ethiopian military personnel in the United States. In addition, U.S. administrations maintained counterinsurgency teams in Ethiopia from 1964 to 1977 and assisted the African nation in opposing Eritrean liberation movements.

Although it was widely regarded until 1977 as the United States' favorite, Ethiopia, on a per-capita basis, received substantially less U.S. (and Western) aid than other countries—Sudan and Somalia—of the Horn.[8] Total arms shipments to Ethiopia (1961–1974) from the United States and its allies amounted to $151 million, while those to Somalia from the Soviet bloc during the same period amounted to $210 million.[9] When compared specifically with Soviet military assistance to Somalia during the period 1961–1977, U.S. military aid to Ethiopia during the same period was very modest.

The modest increase in aid which occurred in the mid-1960s was prompted by two developments. One was the increase in the flow of Soviet military aid to Somalia during the period.[10] The Soviets exploited Somali ambitions to create a Greater Somalia by force. In the mid-1960s, they began to arm the country beyond its needs and requirements. Thus, Somalia became, by far, the most militarized of the countries of the Horn and the one that devoted the largest percentage of its own GNP to military expenditures.

The second development was that in 1962 the Soviets began to help Somalia construct port facilities at Berbera overlooking the Red Sea. In 1972, three years after the facilities at Berbera were completed, the Soviets opened naval support networks, including two communication satellites, at Berbera and the air base at Harghessa. In 1977, three years after it signed a Treaty of Friendship and Mutual Assistance with Somalia in July 1974 (following revolutionary developments in Ethiopia in that year), the Soviet Union granted $300 million in military assistance to Somalia. This sum alone was more than the United States had provided Ethiopia during the entire period of twenty-five years, 1953–1977. The Soviets went further. They established a missile storage and handling facility at Berbera and placed 2,000 of their personnel, including 300 military advisors, in Somalia.

Added to these developments, events in Ethiopia pointed in the direction of a disintegrating empire. There was widespread internal rebellion by the Tigreans and the Oromo; an ongoing Eritrean war of secession which began in 1962 and continued in spite of a U.S. supply of counterinsurgency training and on-the-ground advisers to Ethiopia. Furthermore, in 1974 a revolution touched off by social unrest caused the overthrow of Haile Selassie by a fractious military. Mengistu Haile Mariam, the emergent Marxist-oriented leader of the military regime, became openly hostile to the United States and desired a military relationship with the Soviet Union. The Mengistu factor caused U.S. officials to reduce military assistance to Ethiopia. They did so notwithstanding the perceived strategic value of Ethiopia as a potential staging ground for the projection of American military power into the Middle East and the Persian Gulf. In the meantime, Mengistu signed a military aid agreement with Moscow on 14 December 1976. Implementation of the agreement was linked to Ethiopia's severing of military links with the United States. Accordingly, Mengistu terminated such ties in 1977. He used as his pretext the Department of State's annual human rights reports, which had documented human rights violations within Ethiopia.

Soviet military aid began to arrive in Ethiopia in September 1977. The Soviets had hoped that their policy to assist Ethiopia would not alienate Somalia. They had also proposed a federation of countries of the Horn. President Siad Barre of Somalia rejected the idea out of hand. Meanwhile, in view of these circumstances, the Carter administration began to move closer to Somalia in an effort to dislodge the Soviets. Accordingly, the administration and its Western allies wooed Somalia away from the Soviet Union. They encouraged such Western friends as Egypt, Saudi Arabia, and Sudan, apprehensive themselves of the growing Soviet presence in the Horn, to funnel aid to Somalia. Given these overtures and his perception that direct U.S. military aid was forthcoming,[11] Siad Barre ordered Somali regular forces to join the Western

Somalia Liberation Front in July 1977 to attack Ethiopia's Ogaden province. The invading forces established a temporary control over virtually all of the Ogaden except Harrar and Diredawa, which they could not capture.

Switching clients, the Soviet Union went to Ethiopia's rescue with a billion dollars' worth of weapons and 20,000 Cuban troops. Such massive Soviet and Cuban intervention helped to turn the tide against the invaders as Ethiopian forces counterattacked. President Siad was thus forced to withdraw his troops from Ethiopian territory in March 1978. Soviet assistance to Ethiopia continued to the tune of $12 billion by 1989, encouraging Mengistu to assist dissidents and insurgency within Somalia against Siad Barre.

The government of Jimmy Carter, which had earlier in June 1977 denied a request by Siad for military aid, condemned the Soviet-Cuban intervention. In July the administration reaffirmed the policy of neutrality in the Ogaden conflict but warned the Soviet-backed Cuban and Ethiopian troops not to invade Somali territory. The major goal was twofold: to prevent the overthrow of the Siad Barre government in favor of one more closely aligned with Ethiopia and the Soviet Union and to "keep the Soviets from becoming arbiters of Horn politics, advancing their interests in the Indian Ocean, and consolidating a position of dominance in Ethiopia."[12] Furthermore, as a consequence of the Soviet-Cuban intervention in the Ogaden war, President Carter's adviser on national security affairs, Zbigniew Brzezinski, asserted that the process of détente with the Soviet Union had become buried in the sands of the Ogaden. Henceforth, the Carter administration revived the Nixon-Kissinger-Ford policy towards the Soviet Union, linking U.S.-Soviet relations with Soviet behavior, especially in regions of strategic interest to the United States. Accordingly, in January 1978, the Carter administration sent a naval task force to the Indian Ocean and the Red Sea.

The aftermath of these events and measures was that Somalia abrogated its July 1974 Treaty of Friendship and Cooperation with the Soviet Union. The measure expelled the Soviet Union from its base and other facilities in Berbera. These would later become part of the facilities the United States acquired for its Rapid Deployment Task Force (RDF) established after the enunciation of the Carter Doctrine[13] in January 1980 in response to the 1979 Soviet invasion of Afghanistan. Specifically, the doctrine committed the United States to use military means to defend American interests in the oil-rich Persian Gulf. This pledge and the establishment of RDF greatly increased the strategic significance of Kenya and Somalia as way stations for U.S. troops and supplies en route to the Persian Gulf. During the same year Somalia received its first military assistance from the United States although it had benefited from U.S. economic assistance from the time it became independent in 1960. From that year to the end of the Cold War in 1989, the United States became the major supplier of military weapons to Somalia. By then Somalia had received $234.9 million in military assistance and $39 million through the security-oriented Economic Support Fund. In addition, it received $800,000 in 1990 for military education and training.

Ronald Reagan, perhaps the most ideological post-World War II president, succeeded Carter in January 1981 and enthusiastically embraced Siad Barre. He hoped to build up Somalia "as a bastion of strength from which to defend 'Free World' interests in Southwest Asia."[14] Anxieties over stability in the Persian Gulf during the Iran-Iraq war underlined this interest. However, Reagan did very little for Somalia after 1985. Among other factors, this was a function of the emergence of Mikhail Gorbachev in March 1985 as the new Soviet leader, an event that heralded the beginning of a new era in U.S.-Soviet relations. The realities of its economic and social problems together with the frustrations of costly military involvement in Afghanistan, Angola, and Ethiopia compelled Gorbachev to change the Soviet Union's course. Steadily, he initiated a new thinking and a reappraisal of both Soviet domestic policies and the Soviet Union's role in the world.[15] Gorbachev persuaded himself that it was critical for the Soviet Union to reconcile its differences with the Western capitalist powers in order to be able to reverse the deterioration of its economy and maintain its position as a major world power. Consequently, he adopted a policy of openness, *glasnost*; of restructuring of the Soviet economy and society, *perestroika*; and of retrenchment from Soviet overcommitment overseas. Furthermore, Gorbachev repudiated the Soviet Union's ideological commitment to encourage revolution and to assist national liberation movements seeking to overthrow capitalism.[16]

For its part, after its bellicose anticommunist statements, arms buildup, and support for alleged freedom fighters, the Reagan administration began to tone down its anti-Soviet rhetoric. The need to assuage domestic as well as European critics of its Cold War rhetoric, to reduce the risk of regional conflicts, and to reciprocate Gorbachev's new thinking pointed to a policy of dialogue and cooperation with the Soviet Union in seeking some solution to the conflicts within Africa. Gorbachev himself signaled the willingness of the Soviet Union to work with the United States to do so. It was within this political climate that in 1988 Ethiopia and Somalia signed a peace accord. Both agreed to reestablish diplomatic relations and to withdraw their troops from the Ogaden.

After the mid-1980s, Congress severely limited and then cut off military aid entirely to Somalia by the end of the decade as a result of increased calls in Congress for disengagement and press reports and charges of human rights violations against Mohammad Siad Barre's government. Somalia's problems were further exacerbated during the late 1980s when it was deserted by America's Western allies. The European Union cut off aid in 1989 as it sought to pressure Siad Barre to liberalize his country's political system.

This was the general situation which George H.W. Bush inherited when he became president in January 1989. The Cold War ended later that year with the collapse of communism in Eastern Europe, the fall of the Berlin Wall, and the reunification of Germany. The Soviet Union disintegrated in December 1991. These developments ended the flow of arms and military weapons from the superpowers to the Horn. However, armed conflicts continued within Ethiopia and Somalia thanks to the residue of Cold War arms shipments. Internal opponents of the regimes in both countries wanted to remove them. The Eritrean People's Liberation Front (EPLF) continued to fight Ethiopia for independence. Economic conditions drastically deteriorated in both countries. Famine and influx of refugees from war-torn rural areas contributed to a general breakdown of law and order, especially in Somalia. Neither the United States nor Russia had any compelling residual Cold War interests to assist in alleviating these problems. This reality attested to the truth of a West African proverb: "Whether elephants fight or make love, after them the grass is never the same."

Political and economic order in the Horn of Africa did not improve.[17] Instead, the region degenerated further into chaos in the 1990s, worsening the desperate economic circumstances of most of the region's citizens. In Ethiopia, the EPLF intensified the struggle for independence while the Tigrean People's Liberation Front and the Oromo Liberation Front sought to terminate Mengistu's fifteen-year rule.

Under the auspices of Jimmy Carter, abortive negotiations were held in Ethiopia in 1990 between EPLF and Mengistu's regime to resolve the Eritrean war. During a Washington summit in June 1990, President Bush successfully drew Mikhail Gorbachev onto a common ground regarding measures to alleviate famine in northern Ethiopia at the time. This raised a false hope that the Soviet Union might be willing to play a genuinely constructive role in a peace process in Ethiopia. Early in 1991, following Carter's lead, the Bush administration decided to serve as a peace broker between the Ethiopian government and EPLF, but for Mengistu it was too late. His regime collapsed in May of the same year. He fled into South Africa, from where he was a few years later to escape to Zimbabwe. His internal foes, led by the Tigrean People's Liberation Front, formed a coalition government in Ethiopia. The Bush administration facilitated that outcome and helped to negotiate the agreements that culminated in the independence of Eritrea under UN auspices in April 1993.

The United States and Clan Wars in Somalia in the 1990s

In Somalia, Siad Barre was discredited in the eyes of the Somalis because of the loss to Ethiopia in the 1978 war. This fall in public esteem added to the discrimination and violence by his regime against clans and communities other than his own, fueled three main insurgencies. However, external support, mainly from the United States, Saudi Arabia, and Libya, convinced Siad Barre that he could defeat his opponents by force, and so he saw no need to negotiate or respond to their needs and demands. The result was that the clan-based insurgencies—the Somali Salvation Democratic Front of the southern Darod clan, the United Somali Congress of the Hawiye clan of central Somalia, and the Somali Democratic Movement of the Ogadenis of the border with Ethiopia—joined forces to oust him from power in January 1991. This was accomplished amid economic destruction, predatory militias diverting food aid from emergency relief operations, and waves of human casualties estimated at 350,000 killed and 500,000 forced into refuge excluding those displaced inside the country. The clans and their warlords continued to fight each other and so were unable to form a viable or effective government. In May 1991 Northern Somalia declared itself the independent Republic of Somaliland while the rest of Somalia remained engulfed in civil war.

Attempts by the UN Security Council to broker a cease-fire among the warring clans were resisted by the United States on the grounds that the UN was already overburdened with peacekeeping operations. An eventual force of UN Pakistani peacekeepers achieved little progress mainly because of the intransigence of General Mohammed Farah Aidid, a leader of one of the warring clans, who earlier had rejected plans to deploy UN peacekeepers. Thousands of Somalis died of disease and starvation as the war continued unabated. Threats to hundreds of thousands more grew daily. Humanitarian assistance could not be delivered as armed gangs and militias freely attacked UN facilities, relief convoys, and distribution centers, stealing trucks, fuel, and food supplies. An official of the U.S. Agency for International Development (USAID) portrayed the situation graphically:

Food imported for relief effort became a prized plunder of merchants, unemployed people, and gangs of young men. Militia leaders used stolen food to amass wealth for purchasing weapons and keeping followers loyal. Merchants would actually request the local militia or bands of thieves to steal more food as their stocks diminished each day....The country's entire political and economic systems essentially revolved around plundered food.[18]

Also, on 9 December 1992, the International Committee of the Red Cross reported that as many as 95 percent of Somalis were suffering from some degree of malnutrition and more than 70 percent from severe malnutrition. It added that more than 400,000 people had perished. For their part, the news media provided additional graphic reports of suffering and famished men, women, and children in Somalia. These reports marked the prelude to Operation Restore Hope, initiated by the George H.W. Bush administration under UN auspices.

Operation Restore Hope

Initially, the George H.W. Bush administration pursued a policy of inaction regarding the entire situation in Somalia despite a plea by his Assistant Secretary of State for African affairs, Herman Cohen, for preventive diplomacy to avert the total collapse of the state. Also, there had been some congressional pressure for action after a number of visits to Somalia by members of Congress. The administration acted later under UN auspices to launch Operation Restore Hope in December 1992. This it did only in response to intense media coverage of the tragedy and after Bush had lost the November 1992 presidential election. The driving force that pushed him to act was a report by newscaster Tom Brokow on NBC television showing starving, diseased, and dying Somali men, women, and children. He wanted to alleviate the suffering of Somali civilians but also desired to leave office on a high note after his defeat at the polls in the November 1992 presidential elections.

President Bush had been leery of intervening in such a situation at the same time that he was resisting pressures to intervene to stop ethnic cleansing in Bosnia. He chose to deploy 30,000 U.S. troops to Somalia under UN auspices because the situation there was considered less of a risk to the lives of American soldiers. His deployment of troops to Somalia was a radical departure from traditional U.S. Africa policy. For the first time U.S. soldiers were deployed in a large number in an African crisis. And for the first time also the United Nations embarked on a mission in a country without legitimate authorities.

The U.S.-led intervention was in accord with Bush's New World Order strategy, which required a world community of states to cooperate under U.S.

leadership and UN auspices as had been done in Operation Desert Shield (which ousted Iraq from Kuwait) to stem aggression and alleviate suffering around the world. Indeed, by November 1992, more than twelve nations had agreed in principle to dispatch armed units to Somalia to safeguard the distribution of food and medical supplies to the people. To facilitate matters, General Farah Aidid, who had earlier opposed the deployment of UN peacekeepers, expressed his willingness to accept the U.S.-led multilateral humanitarian mission. He had recently suffered setbacks on the battlefield. Apprehensive of defeat and a loss of his bid for national primacy, he accepted the mission as an opportunity to recoup his political and military position.

Bush emphasized that the objective of Operation Restore Hope was limited and specific: To create secure conditions which would permit the feeding of the starving Somali people and allow the transfer of the security function to a UN peacekeeping force. He attached the following conditions to the mission: The forces would be large enough to discharge the humanitarian objective without unduly endangering American lives; they would remain under U.S. control; they would be part of a larger multilateral effort; they would be supported by a UN Security Council resolution approving the use of all "necessary means" to accomplish the mission. Such a resolution—UN Security Council Resolution 794 (3 December 1992)—authorizing the use of all necessary force to create a secure environment for the delivery of famine relief was drafted in the Pentagon in consultation with the UN Secretary-General Boutros Boutros-Ghali and adopted by the Security Council.[19] President-elect Clinton strongly endorsed the Bush undertaking. However, he would fall victim to an American lack of will to see the problems of Somalia through, a hint of which was provided in Bush's conception of the mission.

Indeed, the Bush administration's construction of the mandate of the mission—relief of starvation—was narrow. The fundamental issues underlying the Somalia starvation emergency were political. The Bush administration established no political agenda to address the fundamental issues. It did not only fail to discern the essential political dynamics of Somalia, it also failed to define what it hoped Somalia would look like after the end of the operation.

In spite of these shortcomings in the conception of the mission, by late spring 1993 Operation Restore Hope, comprising about 30,000 U.S. troops and supported by 14,000 others from other UN member states, had succeeded in opening Mogadishu warehouses and the highways into the interior of Somalia for food distribution. Humanitarian assistance flowed regularly to critical areas of the country as the Bush administration came to an end. The operation ended the famine, and an estimated 100,000 people were saved by the mission. Several schools and shops were reopened. Members of the Somali police force were returned to the streets. Mediation efforts progressed, with the major factions agreeing to a conference on national reconciliation in mid-March 1993. In May, the United States handed over formal control of the operation to the UN although it continued to determine the nature of the operation. Admiral Jonathan Howe, a U.S. citizen, assumed the role of the UN secretary-general's special representative to Somalia and accordingly took charge of the operation. Most U.S. troops were withdrawn; the lightly armed troops that remained were placed under the command of a U.S. Special Forces officer, Major General William Garrison, who was temporarily stationed in Mogadishu..

The Sequel to Operation Restore Hope

President Bush's successor, Bill Clinton, supported the UN Security Council Resolution 814 requiring the UN to help rebuild Somalia's "national and regional institutions and civil administration" and thereby help remove the political causes of the famine that had provoked the Bush administration-led humanitarian intervention in 1992. That resolution and other major UN resolutions on Somalia had been drafted by the U.S. Department of Defense. Resolution 814 was necessary because temporarily preventing the warlords and their militia leaders from stealing food imported for relief of the masses of Somali people was in no way a solution to Somali clan warfare. There was a critical need to go beyond stopping the man-made famine to rebuild political institutions, create order, and restore political stability and security. However, the implementation of the resolution was fraught with dangers. Nation building would require disarming the most violent clan militias and restoring peace. This step was not taken. Achieving the goal would also require sufficient political reconciliation among the Somali leaders and clans to foster the establishment of a stable government, which could then rebuild Somalia's shattered economy and infrastructure. These tasks could not be achieved overnight. Like Bush's initial aim of alleviating suffering, they inevitably involved political changes, especially since the suffering had political causes. War was the cause of the breakdown of order in the African nation. Stopping it required settling the political questions—who would govern the state and how—over which it was being fought. In Somalia,

> famine relief turned into counter-insurgency. Having warded off starvation, the United States and the UN were drawn into measures to prevent famine from returning. That

meant trying to disarm the factions whose internecine wars had disrupted the food supply. Beyond that, it meant trying to construct a stable political order [essentially an apparatus of government, which in Somalia did not exist].[20]

That was not a small task. But avoiding it risked wasting the relative successes of Bush's Operation Restore Hope and the efforts the international community had already made in Somalia.

From this perspective, Clinton's support of the UN Security Council resolution to construct a stable political order was a realistic one. However, Clinton made little or no effort to explain the need for the task or to obtain popular support for it in the United States. Attempts to enforce the resolution culminated in a hunt for Mohammed Farah Aidid, one of Somalia's clan leaders, who wanted to use the famine and political chaos in the country to entrench himself in power. Hence, increasingly he saw the UN forces as obstructing his prospects of ruling the whole of Somalia. To achieve his political ambition his forces attacked and killed twenty-three UN Pakistani peacekeepers and wounded scores more. Earlier, the Pakistani forces in search of Aidid's militias had opened fire on a hostile Somali crowd, killing about 100 civilians.

On 3 October 1993 a clash ensued in which eighteen U.S. soldiers died in Mogadishu while hunting for Aidid, a man wanted by the UN Security Council. Additional casualties of the firefight included seventy-seven wounded American soldiers, an estimated 300 Aidid militiamen killed, and another 700 wounded.[21] The U.S. soldiers had lacked adequate heavy equipment and backup forces to defend themselves. The gruesome sight on television of the dragging of the corpse of one of the U.S. soldiers provoked widespread revulsion and a barrage of criticism of the Clinton administration from a large number of American political leaders. The Somalia mission, initially thought to be less risky, had become costly in human lives as well as lacking any clear endpoint. Neither the American people nor their representatives in Congress were willing to commit lives, resources, and time to the challenges of nation building in an African country which they perceived had no apparent strategic significance to U.S. security interests.

In response to the situation and especially to critics who charged that there were no clear American national security interests at stake in Somalia, President Clinton took three specific measures. He argued against a public demand for a hasty exit, pointing out the probable consequences of such a step. In a speech on 7 October 1993 Clinton said:

If we were to leave today, we know what would happen. Within months, Somali children again would be dying in the streets. Our own credibility with friends and allies would be severely damaged. Our leadership in world affairs would be undermined at the very time when people are looking to America to help promote peace and freedom in the post-Cold War world. And all around the world, aggressors, thugs, and terrorists will conclude that the best way to get U.S. to change our policies is to kill our people. It would be open season on Americans.

Second, Clinton rapidly dispatched to Somalia 5,000 additional troops with adequate firepower. This measure was designed to demonstrate U.S. resolve and the military might that could be deployed against Aidid and any others who might attempt to threaten American lives or security interests. It was also meant to reassure the American people that his administration was committed to protecting American troops carrying out government policy overseas. Finally, conscious of possible electoral consequences and congressional budget cuts, Clinton promised an orderly withdrawal of the troops. Congress had used its power of the purse to bring the operation to a halt. Shortly after the death of the American soldiers, it passed legislation prohibiting the use of any funds after 31 March 1994 for the operations of U.S. armed forces in Somalia unless the president requested an extension and received authority from Congress. Orderly withdrawal of the troops was accomplished by 31 March 1994.[22]

In the meantime, Aidid and his militias carried out no more hostile attacks on U.S. forces. Importantly also, a politically costly struggle with Congress was averted. Domestic political calculations—the fear of domestic political backlash—had triumphed. Thus, despite Clinton's arguments against a hasty exit, the Somalia operation was abandoned after a single bloody skirmish with Aidid's militias. The UN-sponsored project of constructing a stable political order in the African nation was also abandoned. No plan was developed to restore to normal Somalia's economy, which had come to revolve around the plunder of food aid. The UN took over the operation but did not have the resources or the ability to do the job. Its forces were unable to recover from the precipitous American withdrawal. However, the Clinton administration lent U.S. military equipment to the residual UN forces in Somalia. On 16 October 1994 it authorized the redeployment of U.S. troops to assist in the withdrawal of the remaining UN troops from Somalia. This was accomplished by the spring of 1995, terminating the UN Operations in the country. Before long, conflict among the clans resumed, and Somalia remained a failed state.

This development, together with the withdrawal of U.S. troops, did not mute or totally end political criticism of the Clinton administration's role in attempting to create a viable government in Somalia and elsewhere. As candidate for the presidency in 2000, George W. Bush repeatedly criticized the administration for its attempts at nation building in Somalia and Kosovo. But, a month after the 11 September 2001 terrorist attacks on the United States, his own administration openly acknowledged that its campaign to dislodge the Taliban from political authority would be (in fact, it has been) accompanied by deliberate efforts by the United States and its NATO allies to create a viable Afghan government and to rebuild the war-torn country.

The humanitarian intervention in Somalia produced other results.[23] It led directly to the Clinton administration's refusal to suppress genocide in Rwanda in April 1994. It contributed to heightened congressional opposition to U.S. participation in UN-sponsored multilateral peacekeeping and enforcement operations. A sequel to that opposition was a draft National Security Restoration Act which was never enacted into law. The proposed legislation, which sought not only to sharply restrict U.S. contributions to UN peacekeeping but also to prevent the participation of U.S. armed forces in UN multilateral peacekeeping missions, was averted by a policy directive—PDD-25—issued by President Clinton in April 1994. The directive clarified the circumstances and conditions under which U.S. armed forces would participate in UN peacekeeping and enforcement missions. A final consequence of the humanitarian intervention and the related congressional opposition to U.S. participation in UN multilateral peacekeeping missions was a plan initially articulated by Clinton's Secretary of State, Warren Christopher. Among other things, Christopher pledged that the United States would help Africa to build its capacity for preventive diplomacy and conflict resolution, so that the people of the continent can live free of the terror of war.[24]

The pledge gave birth to the Clinton administration's African Crisis Responsive Initiative (ACRI). After consultations with African states and its European allies, the United States began under ACRI to help African countries to train and equip their military forces in order to contain incipient crises in Africa and to forestall their escalation to the proportions of those in Somalia and Rwanda. (For more details on ACRI, see Chapter 9.)

Notes

1. For details see http://www.nytimes.com/2002/11/17/international/africa/17Horn.html.

2. For details of the conflict see John H. Spencer, *Ethiopia at Bay: A Personal Account of the Haile Selassie Years* (Algonac, MI: Reference Publications, 1987), Introduction and Chapters 1–5.

3. Cordell Hull, *The Memoirs of Cordell Hull,* vol. 1 (New York: Macmillan, 1940), pp. 418–433.

4. Peter Schwab, "Cold War on the Horn," *African Affairs*, Vol. 77, No. 306 (January 1978), pp. 6–9.

5. U.S. Department of State, *Treaties in Force...on 1 January 1975* (Washington, DC, 1975).

6. Paul B. Henze, *The United States and the Horn of Africa: History and Current Challenge* (Santa Monica, CA: The Rand Corporation, 1990), pp. 12–13.

7. Schwab, p. 12.

8. Henze, *The United States and the Horn of Africa*, p. 13.

9. Henze, *The United States and the Horn of Africa*, p. 16, Table 1.

10. Richard H. Deutsch, "Fueling the African Arms Race," *Africa Report* (March-April 1977), pp. 50–52.

11. Edmond J. Keller, "United States Foreign Policy on the Horn of Africa: Policymaking with Blinders," in Gerald J. Bender et al. (eds.), *African Crisis Areas and U.S. Foreign Policy* (Berkeley: University of California, 1985), p. 187; Henze, *The United States and the Horn of Africa*, pp. 25–27.

12. Henze, *The United States and the Horn of Africa*, p. 27.

13. The Doctrine states: "Any attempt by any outside force to gain control of the Persian Gulf region will be regarded as an assault on the vital interests of the United States of America, and such an assault will be repelled by any means necessary, including military force." (Jimmy Carter, State of the Union Address, 23 January 1980, *Weekly Compilations of Documents,* xvi [23 January 1980], pp. 194–200).

14. Henze, *The United States and the Horn of Africa*, p. 29.

15. For more details, see David Holloway, "Gorbachev's New Thinking," *Foreign Affairs,* Vol. 68, No. 1 (1989), pp. 66–81; Dimitri K. Simes, "Gorbachev: A New Foreign Policy," *Foreign Affairs*, Vol. 65, No. 3 (1987), pp. 477–500; Archie Brown, "Change in the Soviet Union," *Foreign Affairs*, Vol. 64, No. 5 (1986), pp. 1048–1064; Seweryn Bialer and Joan

Afferica, "The Genesis of Gorbachev's World," *Foreign Affairs,* Vol. 64, No. 3 (1986), pp. 605–644.

16. F. Ugboaja Ohaegbulam, *A Concise Introduction to American Foreign Policy* (New York: Peter Lang, 1999), p. 42.

17. John W. Harbeson, "The Horn of Africa: From Chaos, Political Renewal?" *Current History: A World Affairs Journal,* Vol. 90, No. 556 (May 1991), pp. 98; Ken Menkhaus and John Prendergast, "Conflict and Crisis in the Greater Horn of Africa," *Current History*, Vol. 98, No. 628 (May 1999), pp. 213-217.

18. Walter Clarke and Jeffrey Herbst, "Somalia and the Future of Humanitarian Intervention," *Foreign Affairs*, Vol. 75, No. 2 (March/April 1996), p. 74 .

19. Walter Clarke and Jeffrey Herbst (eds.), *Learning from Somalia: The Lessons of Armed Humanitarian Intervention* (Boulder, CO: Westview, 1997), p. 9; p. 18, n 19.

20. Michael Mandelbaum, "The Reluctance to Intervene," *Foreign Policy,* No. 95 (Summer 1994), p. 4.

21. Patrick J. Sloyan, "How the Warlord Outwitted Clinton's Spooks," *The Washington Post* (3 April 1994), p. A 29.

22. John R. Bolton, "Wrong Turn in Somalia," *Foreign Affairs*, Vol. 73, No. 1 (January/February 1994), pp. 56–66.

23. See Clarke and Herbst, "Somalia and the Future of Humanitarian Intervention," pp. 70–85.

24. Warren Christopher, "A New Relationship," *Africa Report* (July /August 1993), pp. 36–37.

CHAPTER 6
U.S. Role in the Western
Sahara Conflict, 1975–2003

In northwest Africa a conflict with broad regional and international repercussions has raged since 1975 between the Kingdom of Morocco and the Popular Front for the Liberation of Saquiet el-Hamra and Rio de Oro (Polisario) over sovereignty of the Western Sahara, formerly a Spanish colony. The conflict caused a rupture of diplomatic relations in the Maghrib, especially between Algeria and Morocco. At stake also was the overall balance of power in all of northwest Africa as well as the legitimacy of the Moroccan monarchy, which became directly intertwined with the conflict. The militarization of the region impeded its development and integration, distorted trade profiles, misdirected the productive structures of the economies, exacerbated financial problems, and caused massive suffering among the Sahrawi people and those of Morocco as well. In addition, the conflict created deep divisions within Africa's premier organization—the Organization of African Unity (OAU). On at least three occasions it threatened the demise of the organization. It also tarnished the credibility of the United Nations as an institution capable of making peace.

U.S. policy on the conflict remained consistent under five successive administrations, those of Gerald Ford, Jimmy Carter, Ronald Reagan, George H.W. Bush, and Bill Clinton. From the beginning of the conflict in 1975 to the present deadlocked UN-prescribed referendum in the territory, U.S. policy has been one of solid support for Morocco. This support was decisive in Morocco's initial attempt to secure control of the Western Sahara and has remained solid in spite of Morocco's destabilizing and precedent-setting behavior for African states and the whole world. The policy has not changed under Clinton's successor, George W. Bush. In fact, Colin Powell, Bush's secretary of state, said in a Moroccan television interview on 30 January 2002 that he fully supported the work and recommendations of former Secretary of State James Baker on the conflict.

For the United States the policy on the conflict raises ethical questions, especially regarding the nation's traditional values and principles, global leadership, and credibility. For example, the United States was providing

Morocco with arms and military training to wage an imperial war in a postimperial age in a territory where Morocco's dubious claim to sovereignty was still not formally recognized by Washington. On the one hand, the U.S. government voted in the UN Security Council to authorize a plebiscite in the Western Sahara, in which the people were to decide either to be a sovereign state or to become incorporated into the Kingdom of Morocco, but on the other hand, it cooperated with Morocco to obstruct the process of the referendum. Also, U.S. policy has produced repercussions for the international community as well as for the protection of human rights, political stability, and economic development in all of northwest Africa. A clear ramification of the Moroccan imperialist war and U.S. support for it was the Iraqi invasion and occupation of Kuwait in 1990. President George H.W. Bush, with multilateral action under UN auspices, reversed these actions in Operations Desert Storm and Desert Shield in 1991. The results of the Bush-led actions linger on for Iraq and the international community to this day as manifested by his son's defiance of the United Nations in his unilateral invasion and occupation of Iraq in 2003.

This chapter provides a succinct background to the origins and development of the conflict in the Western Sahara and the efforts made by the Organization of African Unity and the United Nations to resolve it. It focuses on the major obstacles to resolution, particularly the policy of the United States. Analysis shows that the greatest obstacle to the resolution of the conflict is not the intransigence of the Moroccan monarchy but the policy of the United States on the one hand and the weakness and ineffectiveness of the OAU and its member states on the other. The OAU (if its member states had been capable) could have intervened at the request of Polisario to defend a member state from Morocco's occupation.

Origins and Development of the Conflict

In the 1960s the UN pressured Spain to hasten the decolonization of the Western Sahara by means of a referendum to enable the inhabitants to exercise freely their right to national self-determination. This was in keeping with both Article 73 of the UN Charter and UN General Assembly Resolution 1514 (XV) adopted in December 1960. The latter states that all peoples have the right to self-determination and that by virtue of that right they may freely determine their political rights and freely pursue their economic, social, and cultural development. In 1967 Spain set up in the territory a Yemaa—a colonial legislative assembly—the majority of whose members held political views sympathetic to Spain.[1] In 1973 a group of Western Sahara nationalists organized

Polisario, which initiated guerrilla activities against the Spanish administration. In 1974 Spain agreed in principle to a 1973 request by the Yemaa to allow self-determination in the territory and proceeded to conduct a census of the territory to facilitate a 1974 referendum.

In the meantime, the Kingdom of Morocco and Mauritania rejected the idea of any expression of self-determination in the Spanish colony and asserted instead "historical" claims to sovereignty over the territory. Note that Morocco had made similar claims on a "historical" basis on Mauritania. It had waged a vigorous diplomatic campaign to deny that nation international recognition when it gained independence in 1960. In 1963, the Moroccan King, Hassan II, withdrew his kingdom from the nascent OAU because Mauritania was a member of that organization. Later in 1969 Morocco recognized Mauritania as an independent state and rejoined the OAU, accepting thereby the provisions of the Charter and the cardinal principles of the organization. One of those principles is that boundaries inherited at independence should be respected by all member states as sacrosanct and that no colonially established boundaries should be revised by armed force.

To deal with the claims of the two African countries, the UN sent a fact-finding mission in May 1975 to Western Sahara that found an overwhelming consensus in favor of independence and against integration with any neighboring country. Also, at the instance of the two African claimants who were seeking to prevent the referendum, the UN, by Resolution 3292 (XXIX), 13 December 1974, sought and obtained an advisory opinion from the International Court of Justice at the Hague on two questions.

1. "Was Western Sahara (Rio de Oro and Sakiet El Hamra) at the time of colonization by Spain a territory belonging to no one (terra nullius)?"
2. "What were the legal ties of this territory with the Kingdom of Morocco and the Mauritanian entity?"

In October 1975 the court advised that while there had been certain legal ties between some groups in the disputed territory and Morocco and between others and Mauritania, those ties did not constitute legal sovereignty. Regarding Morocco's claim, the Court explained that it found that "neither the internal nor the international acts relied upon by Morocco indicate the existence at the relevant period of either the existence or the international recognition of legal ties of territorial sovereignty between Western Sahara and the Moroccan State.

Map 6.1 Western Sahara

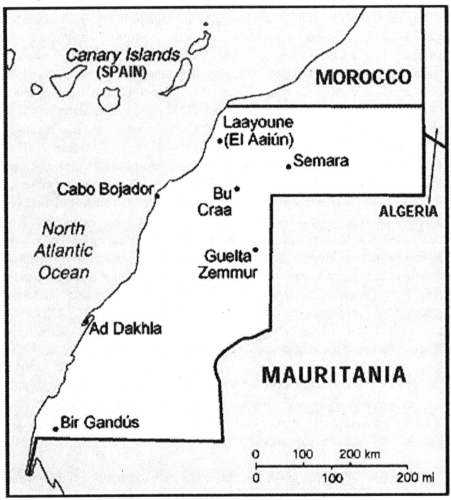

Adapted from CIA - *The World Factbook 2002*.

Even taking account of the specific structure of that State, they do not show that Morocco displayed any effective and exclusive State activity in Western Sahara." Similarly, regarding Mauritania, it concluded that "at the time of colonization by Spain there did not exist between the territory of Western Sahara and the Mauritanian entity any tie of sovereignty...or of simple inclusion in the same legal entity." The Court went on:

> The Court's conclusion is that the materials and information presented to it do not establish any tie of territorial sovereignty between the territory of Western Sahara and the Kingdom of Morocco or the Mauritanian entity. Thus the Court has not found legal ties of such a nature as might affect the application of resolution 1514 (XV) in the decoloniza- tion of Western Sahara, and, in particular, of the principle of self-determination through the free and genuine expression of the will of the peoples of the territory.[2]

The advice proved moot. Morocco ignored it. On 6 November 1975 when the leader of Spain, Francisco Franco, lay seriously ill, King Hassan II of Morocco organized a "Green March" by which he invaded Western Sahara with 350,000 unarmed Moroccan volunteers waving copies of the Koran. By the march Hassan sought to achieve two related goals: to divert the attention of the Moroccan masses from increasing economic hardships and price rises in Morocco towards an apparently more grandiose and prestigious recovery of "southern provinces" and past glory and to provide jobs for the large number of unemployed Moroccans. Eventually, many of these found work in the public service of Western Sahara.[3]

As the Green March was carried out, the Ford administration persuaded Spain, which was wrestling with an impending succession crisis, not to risk any conflict with Morocco over Western Sahara. As a consequence, on 14 November Spain, in defiance of the will of the inhabitants of the territory and international law, concluded with Morocco and Mauritania a tripartite agreement whereby administrative responsibility over Western Sahara was to be transferred to the two claimants. On 26 February 1976, Spain withdrew from the territory. Immediately, Morocco annexed the more populous and phosphate-rich northern two-thirds, while Mauritania grabbed the southern third, which has extensive fishing resources. While the Sahrawi nationalists primarily desired independence, Morocco and Mauritania sought essentially economic interests— control and exploitation of the mineral resources, the fishing resources, and the tourist potential of the Western Sahara.

Neither the OAU nor the UN recognized the partition and annexation. However, neither initiated any measures, such as economic sanctions, to reverse the partition and annexation. For its part, Polisario declared the territory independent on the same 26 February as the Saharan Arab Democratic Republic (SADR). It evacuated about 170,000 Sahrawis—largely children and elderly men and women—to Tindouf in northwest Algeria, where they were granted autonomy by the Algerian government. With the help of Algeria, which had held the position that a colonial territory was entitled to self-determination, it mounted a war of national liberation against the two occupying African nations. Libya provided support until 1984. Mauritania, the weaker of the two occupants, bore the brunt of the war, jeopardizing thereby its precarious unity and sovereignty. Military expenditures and losses arising from the campaign drove its government into bankruptcy and wrecked the country's economy. The armed forces overthrew the civilian government of Ould Daddah in 1978 and on 6 August negotiated an agreement in Algiers with Polisario, by which they renounced all claims to Western Sahara.

King Hassan became even more ambitious after the Polisario-Mauritania agreements. He immediately extended his kingdom's occupation of the former Spanish colony by annexing the southern third renounced by Mauritania. For Morocco, the war had become not just an expression of King Hassan's imperial ambition but also a geopolitical rivalry with Algeria, a successful outcome of which would shift the regional—northwest Africa—balance of power in Morocco's favor. In addition, Hassan II sought to use Western Sahara to divert attention from internal challenges to his regime—which, especially in the early 1970s, experienced serious political instability (failed coups and leftist plots in 1971–1973)—and to improve his internal standing as well as the economic prosperity of his kingdom from the phosphates and fisheries he intended to exploit in the territory. But as the war continued, Morocco managed to hold on to Western Sahara only at great expense. Polisario guerrillas inflicted heavy losses on it. Its occupation forces of about 100,000 troops consumed up to half the national budget, not including subventions it received by way of arms purchases paid for by Saudi Arabia.

Efforts towards a Resolution

To date, the OAU, now the African Union, and the United Nations have attempted unsuccessfully to find a resolution to the conflict. Initially the OAU assumed major responsibility for resolving the conflict as a regional problem. Morocco favored it as a mediator, but its member states were divided on the issue of supporting either Morocco or the Polisario. Two of the members—Algeria and Libya—were materially supporting the Polisario. The division inhibiting the organization's ability to deal with the conflict was aggravated by intense pressures exerted by Morocco and its Western allies—the United States and France in particular—on African states that had benefited from Morocco's past support. A meeting of the organization's Council of Ministers at Addis Ababa in February 1976 affirmed that recognition of the Polisario was to be decided individually by member states. At its July 1976 summit in Mauritius, the OAU upheld the right of Sahrawi people to self-determination and independence.

The organization attempted from 1978–1984 to mediate the conflict. In 1978 it set up an ad hoc committee of five heads of state (from Mali, Guinea, Nigeria, Côte d'Ivoire, and Tanzania) called "wise men" to investigate the conflict and to suggest a solution. It proposed a peace plan which called for

1. a 31 December 1980 cease-fire deadline,
2. a UN peacekeeping force in the disputed territory to supervise the observance of the cease–fire, and
3. a fair and general referendum in the territory under UN and OAU supervision to determine the wishes of the people on independence or incorporation into Morocco.

While Polisario accepted the peace plan, King Hassan rejected the idea of a cease-fire as well as that of an internationally supervised referendum with the option of independence on the ballot. He persistently held that the conflict was a purely bilateral one between his kingdom and Algeria and that only a summit meeting with the Algerian president could solve the conflict. Given his intransigence and the fact that twenty-six out of the fifty member states of the OAU had accorded SADR diplomatic recognition, Edem Kudjo, the secretary-general of the organization, without a formal vote of the full membership, officially seated SADR at the Council of Minsters Conference as the rightful authority in Western Sahara on 22 February 1982. This action provoked a boycott of subsequent OAU conferences by Morocco and twenty-one support-ing members, including a proposed August 1982 summit in Tripoli, Libya.

For a number of reasons, the proposed Libya summit was aborted.[4] After intense diplomatic efforts, the venue of the summit was changed to Addis Ababa, where it finally was held in June 1983. By consensus the summit adopted a resolution (104) naming Morocco and Polisario parties in a conflict and urging them to begin direct negotiations. Furthermore, the resolution called for a cease-fire, recommended the holding in December 1983 of the referendum the organization had called for, and reaffirmed the need for an OAU-UN peacekeeping force.

When it adamantly rejected direct negotiations with Polisario, Morocco exhausted the patience of the OAU majority, which consequently admitted SADR as the fifty-first member of the organization in 1984. Morocco immediately withdrew from the OAU with the words: "While we wait for wiser days, we will bid you farewell."[5] This was a tacit admission that Hassan's intensive diplomatic exertions to deny recognition to SADR had failed.

Upon Morocco's withdrawal from the OAU, the organization was no longer the credible, impartial, and honest broker King Hassan had anticipated. From then on, Morocco sought to exclude the organization from further role in resolving the conflict. Accordingly, responsibility for resolving the Western Sahara conflict shifted to the United Nations. However, the OAU continued to work with the world organization in designing a framework for a settlement of the conflict.[6] Its resolutions inspired most of the actions taken by the UN. Also, the relative unity of the African group in the UN encouraged and stimulated the Security Council resolutions and the initiatives of the secretary-general that pushed for the UN-stalled referendum in Western Sahara.

In 1988 there were signs that Algeria, the major supporter of Polisario's war effort, and Morocco were tired of the war as domestic problems had worsened for each because of the war. In May 1988 Algeria and Morocco restored the diplomatic relations which had broken off at the start of the war in 1976. Following this event, King Hassan reversed his stand on direct negotiations with leaders of Polisario. After a peace initiative by the UN and the OAU in August 1988, Polisario nationalists and Moroccan officials accepted the settlement proposals.[7] Two days of negotiations between King Hassan and leaders of the Front began on 3 January 1989 in Marrakesh. No immediate progress towards a resolution of the conflict or the holding of a referendum was announced after the talks. But a few weeks later King Hassan told a Spanish newspaper that he had invited Polisario leaders to listen to them as Moroccans and not to negotiate.

In the meantime, the war had become a major economic drain and more costly than any of the belligerents had expected. Polisario's diplomacy had won diplomatic recognition from more than seventy-five nations and admission into the OAU. However, the war had cost Morocco an estimated $350 million a year and an external debt burden of $25 billion, which collectively hamstrung its economic development. In addition, it had about four million jobless able-bodied nationals and a jobless rate of about 18 percent in the occupied Western Sahara,[8] a literacy rate below 50 percent, and discouraging health statistics. The longer the conflict lasts, the more of a threat it could pose to the stability of the Moroccan monarchy itself. It had already threatened the unity of the Maghrib, alienated Morocco from the OAU and many of its member states, and condemned the Moroccan government as an international outlaw in the eyes of many human rights organizations and those governments that had recognized SADR.

Given the situation, Polisario leaders and Morocco accepted a 1990 UN-brokered cease-fire and settlement plan and agreed to submit their dispute over Western Sahara to a popular vote on independence or integration with Morocco. In April 1991 the UN established a special peacekeeping force—the UN Mission for the Referendum in Western Sahara (MINURSO)[9]—to monitor a cease-fire and the confinement of Moroccan and Polisario troops to designated locations, verify the reduction of Moroccan troops in the territory, identify and register qualified voters, and organize and ensure a free and fair referendum and proclaim the results.[10] For the latter tasks, two commissions—Identification and Referendum—were set up, and the referendum was to take place in January 1992. The cease-fire accord took effect in September 1991. However, the two parties disagreed on the exact criteria for determining voter eligibility.[11] Polisario argued that only those people and their descendants who had been in Western Sahara at the time of the 1974 census by the Spanish colonial administrators should vote. This position was largely in accord with the 1988 UN settlement plan. On the other hand, fearing defeat under these terms, Morocco, which had been settling Western Sahara with its citizens since 1976, wanted to allow any person living within the territory at the time of the plebiscite to vote. In this manner, a voting list provided by the secretary-general in accordance with the 1988 settlement plan proved unacceptable to both Morocco and Polisario.[12]

In order to break the deadlock over voters' registration, the UN secretary-general, Kofi Annan, appointed former U.S. Secretary of State James Baker as his special envoy in March 1997. By September 1997, Baker brokered a series of agreements, called the Houston Agreements on voter identification, refugee repatriation, troop confinement, and a code of conduct. By that time, especially after the end of the Cold War, King Hassan had become increasingly aware of Morocco's declining usefulness to its Western friends as an intermediary in the Arab-Israeli negotiations. The levels of aid from Morocco's benefactors had also decreased while the social and economic situation in the country had continued to deteriorate. Prolonging the conflict further might imperil the stability of the regime itself. These may have been among the forces that caused the king to accept the agreements.

By the agreements, voting was to take place in early December 1999. Morocco and Polisario leaders agreed in April 1999 to expedite appeals for rejected voters once the identification process was completed and that appeals would be entertained only where new evidence could be introduced to establish a right to vote. However, Morocco reneged on this agreement once MINURSO had identified and registered 147,000 applicants. It filed blanket appeals for 79,000 rejected voters. This and a disagreement over the status of three specific ethnic groups, involving about 165,000 voters considered Sahrawis by Morocco but Moroccans by Polisario, prevented the referendum from taking place more than ten years after the UN established a mission to organize and supervise the process. By resolution 1309, the UN Security Council extended the mandate of MINURSO to 31 October 2000.

Because of the deadlock in the referendum process, Kofi Annan appeared to be looking for an alternate solution. In February 2000 he offered a bleak assessment of the referendum's future and expressed concerns about whether it would ever be held. He had also said that the UN "has no mechanism to impose on one of the parties...the result of the referendum."[13] This statement, interpreted by Morocco as meaning that the referendum was inapplicable, is inconsistent with the recent behavior of the UN in East Timor, where the Indonesian government was pressured to accept a referendum for independence. The statement, moreover, relegates MINURSO to powerlessness and irrelevance. In any case, in his report to the Security Council, Annan delayed the referendum for two more years. In April 2000, James Baker, proposed a settlement plan that would exclude the possibility of independence for Western Sahara. He called for negotiations on granting limited self-rule to the disputed territory. Such an approach, he said, would promote "a settlement or an arrangement that would promote peace and stability within the Maghreb."[14] Madrid, Paris, and Washington were believed to support such a plan. Observers saw the proposed Baker plan as a determination to revive the American initiative launched in 1998 to foster the integration of Morocco, Algeria, and Tunisia. But the proposal ran counter to the negotiations that culminated in the Houston Accords during which both Morocco and the Polisario were categorically unequivocal in their rejection of "an in-between category" of autonomy. They had insisted that "they didn't want to muddy the water. They wanted a clear up or down choice."[15]

In spite of their rejection of "an in-between category" of autonomy, Baker persisted in his plan. His refined plan postponed the referendum for a further period of five years, during which the Sahrawi would be allowed to elect an autonomous body with only limited authority.[16] Also, the postponed referendum voter list would be expanded from indigenous people to all residents, including settlers and soldiers Morocco had poured into the territory since it occupied it in November 1975. This is the Baker Plan, and what the Moroccan monarchy has always wanted—a UN measure that would convert its de facto rule to de jure, but which Polisario still rejects totally.

For its part, the Security Council, in two successive resolutions, supported the latest Baker proposal for a negotiated autonomy for Western Sahara within the Kingdom of Morocco.[17] In 2000, the situation looked entirely hopeless, even after the death of Hassan II, who had made Western Sahara the centerpiece of his foreign policy and of critical importance to the survival of his monarchy. After over thirteen years' efforts and the expenditure of more than $2.1 billion[18] to hold the referendum, grounded on international law and generally supported by the international community, the UN should have gone ahead with the referendum after the end of the appeals process. Hassan's son and successor King Mohammad should have been persuaded to allow the referendum to go forward and to let the chips fall where they may for the good of Morocco and regional stability in the Maghrib and Africa in general. But the refined Baker Plan, supported by the UN Secretary-General and three permanent members of the Security Council—the United States, Britain, and France—was a clear concession to Morocco at the expense of the basic principles that had informed UN actions on decolonization, international law, and UN resolutions. Polisario nationalists were intensely pressured by their major support Algeria, which the U.S. government had wooed into an increasing rapprochement, to accept the refined Baker Plan.

In November 2001, two oil companies—TotalFinalElf (Paris) and Kerr McGee (Houston, Texas)—signed deals with Morocco to prospect for oil off the southern and northern coasts of the disputed Western Sahara, respectively. In his tour of North Africa the following month, the French President, Jacques Chirac, joined the oil interests from his country and the United States in this calculated conspiracy to deprive the indigenous Sahrawi people of their right to determine their fate when he referred to Western Sahara as "the southern provinces of Morocco."[19]

An Assessment of UN Role on the Conflict

The UN has been ineffective in its dealing with the Western Sahara conflict. The organization failed to apply its own principles and those of international law to the decolonization of the Western Sahara. After embarking on the initial measures identified here, it tolerated the imperious manner in which Spain gave away the Western Sahara in 1975–1976 without any respect for the wishes of the indigenous inhabitants.

This tolerance represented a dramatic departure from a pattern of orderly decolonization through freely conducted elections or plebiscites in Africa and other regions of the world under the auspices of the United Nations. In such trust territories as British and French Togoland, British Northern and Southern Cameroons, Belgian-controlled Rwanda and Burundi, Western Samoa, and Papua-New Guinea, the UN supervised plebiscites in which the local population had the opportunity to choose its own national destiny. After the 1960 Declaration on Granting of Independence to Colonial Countries and Peoples, the organization exerted its influence in the self-determination process in such ordinary colonies as Equatorial Guinea and Cook Islands. The process resulted in independence for the former in 1968 and for the latter a "free association" with New Zealand in 1967. The UN exerted even greater influence in the process that culminated in the independence of Southwest Africa (Namibia) from South Africa in 1990.

In the case of the Western Sahara, the world organization abandoned that well-established pattern of orderly decolonization which it had advocated for the territory for more than a decade. The Security Council abdicated its responsibility to invoke Article 25 of the UN Charter in order to compel Morocco's compliance to UN decision to organize a referendum in the territory to ascertain the will of the people. The reluctance of the permanent members of the Security Council to enforce the UN mandate encouraged Morocco to sabotage the referendum and peace process at every turn. Hence, simply put, Morocco's strategy has been to delay the referendum it realizes it cannot win until the United Nations throws up its hands in frustration. The chief officers of the organization, especially Javier Perez de Cuellar and Boutros Boutros-Ghali, and their special envoys tended to support Morocco rather than seek an enforcement of UN resolutions and measures. Therefore, the Moroccan government persistently obstructed the activities of MINURSO. King Hassan convinced the Secretary-General Perez de Cuellar to accept thousands of ineligible Moroccans who could trace their ancestry to the Western Sahara as voters in the planned referendum. This act caused Perez de Cuellar's special representative on Western Sahara, Johannes Manz, to resign in protest.[20]

Perez de Cuellar's successor, Boutros-Ghali, was a personal friend of King Hassan and before assuming office as UN secretary-general had been a staunch defender of the Moroccan king's position on the Western Sahara in the OAU. As secretary-general, the peace process in the Western Sahara was for him not a priority. When he belatedly appointed a personal representative on the issue, the appointee was General Vernon Walters, the American who had close personal ties with King Hassan and had favored the king in his role on the November 1975 Madrid accords which divided the Western Sahara between Morocco and Mauritania. When the Polisario rejected General Walters, Boutros-Ghali selected another personal friend of King Hassan as his personal envoy on Western Sahara. This time it was Sahabzada Yaqub-Khan, formerly foreign minister of Pakistan, who shared with the United States and the secretary-general a real lack of enthusiasm and urgency regarding the Western Sahara situation.[21] Frank Ruddy, an American who served as deputy chairman of MINURSO, maintained that Boutros-Ghali's office failed to respond forcefully to Morocco's attempts to thwart the referendum process. The former U.S. diplomat revealed in an address at Georgetown University (16 February 2000) that Boutros-Ghali had personally intervened to prevent his sharing his experience in the Western Sahara with the UN Fourth Committee on decolonization.

The approach of Kofi Annan of Ghana is not much different from that of his predecessors.[22] The Sahrawis, who had high hopes for a settlement of the dispute when he assumed office as secretary-general of the UN in January 1997, are frustrated and disappointed that the referendum has not been conducted since he was elected to the office. They wondered why so much international interest was shown in Kosovo and East Timor and not in Western Sahara. The apparent double standard and any failure to resolve the Western Sahara situation would constitute a serious and long-lasting body blow to the Security Council as a credible force in upholding international law and resolving regional conflicts. The entire world witnessed when such a blow was even more dramatically dealt the organization in March 2003 when President George W. Bush defied the Council and launched a military attack on Iraq on the pretext of enforcing the Council's resolutions and ridding the country of its "alleged" weapons of mass destruction.

The approach of the UN chief secretaries to the conflict has been constrained, if not dictated, by the interests of the United States and France. These two powers have been secondary but decisive parties to the conflict. They have indirectly opposed the establishment of an independent Western Sahara state and have provided Morocco the diplomatic, military, and technological support which enabled it to maintain an effective control over the territory. Equally important, the two Western powers have essentially refrained from putting pressure on Morocco concerning the Western Sahara issue because they regard it as an ally in their design to maintain hegemony over the entire Northwest and West Africa. The European Union, within which France plays a leading role, lent its weight to Morocco's claim of sovereignty over Western Sahara by concluding fishing agreements on Western Saharan waters with the government of Morocco.

Major Obstacles to a Resolution

The policies of France, Saudi Arabia, and the United States, which provided enormous support for Morocco, constituted the major obstacle to resolving the conflict. For example, in 1975 the United States and France pressured the Spanish government, in its own's midst of a delicate transition to democratic rule, to capitulate to Morocco's invasion of Western Sahara. When Morocco totally ignored UN Security Council Resolution 380 calling on it to withdraw immediately from the territory, the United States and France prevented the UN from imposing sanctions to enforce the resolution. Furthermore, the two nations sent military advisers and weapons worth hundreds of millions of dollars in subsequent years to support Morocco's conquest and occupation of the territory. The United States and France also repeatedly used their power in the UN Security Council to block United Nations' enforcement of its mandate for a Sahrawi plebiscite. Those policies bring into a sharp focus the weakness of African states and, especially, the overwhelming influence the United States has over the United Nations. Of all the members of the United Nations, the United States is the most reluctant to endow the organization with sufficient capabilities to be effective, except on issues directly affecting American's geopolitical interests, narrowly defined. Its international primacy, coupled with its ability to shape the terms by which international relations take place, has made the UN and its leading secretaries a tool of U.S. foreign policy. This partly explains the UN's inability to assume a leadership role in international crises. We consider the U.S. policy the most significant obstacle to resolving the Western Sahara conflict and therefore devote considerable space to it.

U.S. Policy on the Conflict

U.S. policy on the Western Sahara conflict has been essentially consistent under five successive administrations of Gerald Ford, Jimmy Carter, Ronald Reagan, George H.W. Bush, and Bill Clinton. Clinton's successor, George W. Bush, is strengthening political and economic relations with Morocco. He is more likely than not to continue the policy of his predecessors. Indeed, from 2000 to 2003, America's Special Forces and the Army's 173rd Airborne Brigade conducted joint exercises with Moroccan troops. U.S. military officials indicate that they would like to expand and increase those contacts.[23]

From the beginning of the conflict in 1975 to the present deadlocked UN-prescribed referendum in the territory, the fundamental objective of the policy—the preservation of the throne of the king of Morocco as an ally of the West—has not changed. Thus, neglecting regional and other realities, the policy consistently sought to preserve the Moroccan monarchy rather than promote the basic interests of the United States and Morocco.[24] In spite of Congress' use of both its powers of the purse and investigation to influence U.S. policy on the conflict, the presidents maintained their resolute commitment to the king of Morocco. In doing so, they aided Morocco's refusal to negotiate seriously to end the war.[25]

Policy consistency notwithstanding, Congress differed with the administrations over how to resolve the Western Sahara conflict. Among other measures, relevant committees and subcommittees of the House and the Senate held hearings on proposed arms sales to Morocco.[26] Although they sympathized with Morocco as an American ally, the committee members strongly favored a negotiated settlement of the conflict. They recommended a concerted diplomatic initiative to find such a settlement. In 1982, the House Foreign Affairs Committee and its subcommittee on Africa voted to reject President Reagan's request for increased military aid to Morocco and imposed restrictions on his support for the conduct of the Sahara war. As indicated here, Congress' use of both its power of the purse and investigations to influence policy on the conflict did not significantly affect the resolute commitment to the king of Morocco by U.S. administrators. This further illustrates the present supremacy of the presidency over American foreign policy in spite of the constitutional designation of Congress and the executive branch as coequal managers of the policy.

In 1975 the U.S. government, supported by France, played a decisive role in pressuring the reluctant government of Spain to sign accords in Madrid in November transferring the administrative responsibility for the Western Sahara

128   *U.S. Policy in Postcolonial Africa*

to Morocco and Mauritania. It persuaded Spanish officials, in a delicate transition period as Franco lay dying, of the possibility of the overthrow of King Hassan II, a friend and strong American ally, if Spain failed to meet Morocco's territorial demands. The Spanish officials were convinced that a "radical political change across the Straits of Gibraltar would not serve Western interests, especially in a period of political uncertainty in the Iberian peninsula."[27] President Ford's Secretary of State, Henry Kissinger, Deputy Director of the CIA, General Vernon Walters, and Ambassador to the UN, Daniel Patrick Moynihan, were the major U.S. agents who worked to advance Morocco's ambitions in Western Sahara as the conflict was unfolding. Concerned with Soviet intrusion into Angola, Kissinger was apprehensive that the Western Sahara might be controlled by the left-leaning Polisario. He assumed, without proof, that Polisario would enhance Soviet political gains in Africa. He was therefore determined, he said, "not to allow another Angola on the East flank of the Atlantic Ocean."[28] To accomplish that objective, he dispatched General Walters to convince Spain of the need to meet King Hassan's territorial demands. Walters was required to link Spain's request for $1.5 billion in U.S. weapons and the renewal of the lease for U.S. air and navy bases in Spain on generous terms with Spain's cooperation with Morocco on Western Sahara.[29] Eventually, a five-year U.S.-Spanish treaty with terms favorable to Spain, was signed within two months of the conclusion of the tripartite Madrid accords of November 1975.[30] At the UN, Ambassador Moynihan was instructed to block efforts by Costa Rica, Sweden, and Spain to enforce a Security Council prohibition of Moroccan invasion. Accordingly, Moynihan worked with French representatives to prevent effective UN action. Later, he wrote in his memoirs:

> The United States wished things to turn out as they did, and worked to bring this about. The Department of State desired that the United Nations prove utterly ineffective in whatever measures it undertook. The task was given to me, and I carried it forward with no inconsiderable success.[31]

This prevention of effective UN action against the Moroccan seizure of Western Sahara starkly contrasted with American behavior fifteen years later when Iraq invaded and occupied Kuwait, which had been financially supporting Morocco's occupation of the Western Sahara. On that occasion President George H.W. Bush mobilized U.S. allies and members of the UN for multilateral actions—Operations Desert Storm and Desert Shield—against Iraq. Kuwait was liberated, Saudi Arabia was shielded, and sanctions were imposed on Iraq.

Contradictions permeated the entire American policy. There were official professions of neutrality on the substance and outcome of the conflict, of nonrecognition of Moroccan claim to sovereignty over Western Sahara and its subsequent annexation of the territory, of support for the principle of self-determination in Western Sahara and for a negotiated settlement under the auspices of the OAU rather than a military solution. However, despite these professions, contacts between U.S. diplomats and Polisario officials were prohibited until late 1979, when limited contact was initiated at the insistence of Congressional critics.[32] Also Morocco's administrative control over the territory, which the Ford administration helped to bring about through the pressure it had exerted on Spain, was recognized.

While the United States supported self-determination in Western Sahara, it maintained that independence is not the only appropriate outcome of an act of self-determination. The Reagan administration insisted that America's regional interests in northwest Africa would not be served by the emergence of a weak Saharan state. Such a state, it believed (without much evidence), would likely be dominated by Algeria, vote against the United States and its allies in the UN, and serve as a base and conduit of Libyan-Soviet interventionist activities in north and west Africa. Based on the opinion of their military experts, U.S. administrations believed that a military solution to the conflict was neither possible nor desirable, yet they supplied Morocco with weapons and training. This also was done in spite of a 1960 military agreement with Morocco which forbade the use of such arms outside Morocco's internationally recognized borders. The support for a negotiated settlement, under OAU auspices, was not reinforced by any pressure on Morocco to negotiate directly with the leaders of Polisario.

U.S. policy was predicated on a long-standing special relationship with Morocco that dates back to an extant 1787 treaty of friendship. Also critical were the strategic calculations that derived from two forces. First was the perceived increase in importance that Morocco, as one of the countries which broadly supported U.S. objectives around the world, assumed after the fall of the shah of Iran, the subsequent hostage crisis and terrorism in the country, and the Soviet invasion of Afghanistan. The second strategic calculation derived from the U.S. navy's interest in expanding NATO's operations into the east and south Atlantic to the southernmost limit of the military alliance's zone.[33] Strategically located in a corner of northwest Africa, bordering the Atlantic and the Mediterranean coasts and the Straits of Gibraltar, Morocco helps to meet this need. It permits ships of U.S. Sixth Fleet stationed in the Mediterranean to visit its ports and provides landing and refueling facilities for America's Rapid Deployment Force (RDF) established after Soviet invasion of Afghanistan (1979) for emergency intervention in the Persian Gulf. In addition, it maintains close cooperation with the United States in intelligence and communications. The king of Morocco was a moderate on the Arab-Israeli conflict. He secretly facilitated the Israeli-Egyptian peace negotiations of the late 1970s. On two occasions, in 1977 and 1978, he sent about 1,500 troops to Zaire to preserve Western interests in the central African nation's Shaba province.[34] Hence, U.S. administrators believed that American credibility as an ally required the nation to support a leader who had genuinely demonstrated his friendship with the West. Ultimately, therefore, the stability of the Hassan regime was the principal consideration which influenced U.S. policy on the conflict.[35]

Implementation of U.S. Policy

Military assistance, through arms sales and military training, to Morocco was the major avenue the United States used to implement its policy on the Western Sahara conflict. But before the start of the conflict, the United States was already a major arms supplier to Morocco, in keeping with a 1960 defense agreement by which the United States undertook to provide Morocco arms for defensive purposes. A stipulation in the agreement limited the use of such weapons to the defense of Morocco's internationally recognized borders.[36] In 1974–1975, just prior to and immediately after Morocco's "Green March" of November 1975 into the Western Sahara, the United States took steps that led to dramatic increases, from $8.2 million in 1974 to $242 million in 1975, in U.S. arms sales and military aid to Morocco.

Morocco continued to receive American arms throughout the tenure of the Gerald Ford administration. Between November 1975 and November 1976, Henry Kissinger authorized the transfer of thirty-six 106 mm recoilless guns, twenty F5 planes, six F5 A planes, and sixteen 155 mm mortars from Jordan to Morocco.[37] Additional weapons worth about $500 million were transferred directly to Morocco between 1975 and 1979.[38] But in 1977 President Carter imposed limited restrictions on U.S. arms sales because Morocco was using them in the Western Sahara in violation of the 1960 defense agreement and partly in keeping with his policy of reducing arms transfers to Africa generally. Also, Carter did not want Morocco's use of the weapons in the Western Sahara to damage U.S. relations with Algeria, a major oil and gas producer and commercial partner as well as an influential force in the nonaligned movement. Similar concerns had been expressed in a hearing by the House of Representatives subcommittees on Africa and International Organizations and in a letter by Senator Dick Clark of Iowa to President Carter. Morocco, however, continued to receive U.S. weapons and to ask for more. King Hassan was secretly permitted to buy American-made artillery from stocks already shipped to the shah of Iran.[39] Eventually, the Carter administration's limited arms curbs were lifted entirely by the end of 1979.

A variety of reasons account for the shift in the Carter administration's policy. The Polisario had carried the war into Morocco's internationally recognized territory; Morocco was facing a threat to its internal security as a result of the war and aggravated economic and social conditions; Saudi Arabia exerted considerable pressure for the sales and offered to provide for their financing. More importantly, concerns that arose in Washington about the stability of the Moroccan monarchy immediately after the fall of the shah of Iran in February 1979 and the subsequent Soviet invasion of Afghanistan prompted the administration to strengthen security ties with traditional U.S. allies in the Third World. At the same time, the resignation of Andrew Young as ambassador to the UN and later that of Secretary of State Cyrus Vance, left policy under the control of Zbigniew Brzezinski, who insisted on the need to support King Hassan.

Harold Saunders, Carter's assistant secretary of state, while acknowledging that the prospects in the field increasingly demonstrated the impossibility of a military solution to the conflict, explained the strategic rationale for the reversal of the U.S. arms sales policy and for the administration's plans to sell to Morocco an additional $232.5 million worth of aircraft in a hearing before the House Foreign Affairs subcommittee on Africa on 24 January 1980. According to him:

> ...We believe an outright victory over Morocco by Morocco's adversaries would constitute a serious setback to major U.S. interests. First and foremost, such a development would destabilize the region in general, and the political equilibrium in Morocco in particular. Beyond that, the United States cannot turn a blind eye to the fact that Morocco has historically been a good friend and, indeed, in a practical sense, an ally.[40]

The policy reversal, Saunders added, sought to offset Soviet arms in the arsenal of the Polisario, to avert a prolonged guerrilla war that could divide Morocco and substantially change its internal political complexion as a consequence of the economic drain and inability to win the war, and to enable Morocco to negotiate a solution to the dispute from a position of strength.

Concerned members of the subcommittee of the House Foreign Affairs Committee argued against the policy reversal. Stephen Solarz, chairman of the House subcommittee on Africa, writing in *Foreign Affairs* (Winter 1979/80), provided six reasons why the sale of offensive weapons to Morocco would have significantly negative consequences for U.S. foreign policy. Among others, Solarz vigorously argued that the arms sales policy would damage the nation's improved economic and political relations with Algeria, a more important economic partner of the United States than Morocco, and encourage the Soviets to become directly involved in the conflict. There was no way, he went on, that King Hassan could militarily drive the Polisario from the field. "But by encouraging the king to maintain the illusion that a military victory is possible, we are much more likely to prolong the war than to shorten it. And with Morocco spending a million dollars a day on a war it cannot win the king will be less able to deal with the festering problems within Morocco itself."[41] Thus, ultimately, the sale of U.S. offensive weapons, he opined, may do more to undermine the Moroccan monarchy than to shore it up.

The reversal of the arms sales policy was carried out in spite of Solarz's reasoned arguments, the opposition of the Department of State, and the skepticism of the CIA.[42] In January 1980 the Pentagon unveiled arms packages worth $232.5 million destined to Morocco, and in March another package worth $7 million was proposed.

Such was the legacy the Carter administration bequeathed to President Ronald Reagan on the Western Sahara conflict. Upon assuming the presidency in January 1981, Reagan officially endorsed King Hassan's claim to Western Sahara and pledged Morocco still more resolute support than his predecessor supplied. His purpose in all this was to demonstrate that strategically placed U.S. allies and close associates, like Morocco, could expect understanding and reliable support from America to meet their reasonable and legitimate needs.[43] Two months after his inauguration, President Reagan announced (2 March 1981) his decision to sell 108 advanced M-60 tanks to Morocco for $182 million. These, according to Morris Draper, assistant secretary of state for Near Eastern and South Asian affairs, were in addition to the delivery of the $232.5 million worth of counterinsurgency and fighter aircraft promised by the Carter administration. In the summer of 1981, ten observation planes designed to improve the Moroccan army's reconnaissance ability in the Western Sahara were delivered to Morocco.[44]

Draper explained that strategic considerations prompted the positive response to Moroccan requests for arms. Specifically, he stated:

Morocco is important to broad American interests and occupies a pivotal strategic area. We intend to maintain and reinforce our historically close relationship with reliability and consistency as our watchwords. Morocco has shared and has agreed with many of our foreign policy priorities and objectives.

Like the U.S. Morocco has been concerned over the challenges posed by the Soviets and their surrogates and client states. Morocco strongly opposed and criticized the Soviet invasion of Afghanistan. It voted for U.S. condemnation of the Soviet actions and sponsored similarly condemnatory resolution at the Islamic Summit Conference in Taif.

Morocco has been a responsible neighbor to many states in Africa. It sent troops to Zaire on two occasions to help the country deal with subversion generated by outsiders. Until 1963 Morocco was the home for American strategic bases. An American naval facility operated in Morocco up to 1978 when it was finally closed at our initiative. Morocco has consistently welcomed visits by American naval warships including those which are nuclear-powered.

While Morocco has been part of the Arab consensus critical of the Egyptian-Israeli peace treaty and the Camp David Accords, on the whole it has been a voice of reason and pragmatism in the world's councils, advising pragmatic policies as regards the Middle East issues and decrying sterile negativism.

For all these reasons, and others, we intend to carry out a relationship that assures Morocco that it will be able to count on the United States as a steadfast and reliable friend.[45]

Thus resolved, and believing that King Hassan could not "survive politically the erosion of his prestige and credibility that would result from a major reversal in the Saharan battlefield or in a free and fair referendum," the Reagan administration redoubled its military support for Morocco. In March 1981, it removed a requirement by the House Foreign Affairs Committee that Morocco should cooperate with international efforts to mediate the dispute as a condition for continued U.S. arms sales. It decided instead, that, while encouraging Morocco to seek a negotiated settlement to the conflict, the U.S. government would not make decisions on military sales "explicitly conditional on unilateral Moroccan attempts to show progress toward a peaceful negotiated settlement."[46] This position, it emphasized, recognized the reality that there were players other than Morocco in the Western Sahara conflict with a capacity to influence the outcome.

U.S. military support for Morocco received additional impetus from three events which occurred in October 1981. On 13 October the Polisario attacked Guelta Zemmour, decimating Morocco's 2,600-strong garrison in the Western Sahara and destroying five Moroccan aircraft worth about $100 million. The attack forced Morocco to abandon Guelta Zemmour and Bir Enzaren—two of its strongholds in the disputed territory. Three days after the Polisario attack, former U.S. President Richard Nixon visited King Hassan. His report to

President Reagan of the Moroccan situation contributed immensely to increased U.S. military assistance to Morocco. Another development was Colonel Muammar Qaddafi's activities in northern Africa and the uncertainties in the whole region following the assassination of President Anwar Sadat of Egypt on 6 October. During the same period it was alleged by official Washington that Qaddafi had sent would-be assassins to assassinate President Reagan and other high-ranking U.S. officials.

The upshot of these developments was a series of efforts to reassure King Hassan that he could count on the United States to restore the military balance in the war in his favor. Senior Reagan administration officials[47] met with him between November 1981 and April 1982 and discussed the Western Sahara conflict and Morocco's security needs. Consequently, the United States provided Hassan's armed forces with electronic equipment so that Moroccan planes would be able to evade Polisario's missiles and promised to train Moroccan commando units to stage behind-the-scenes offensive operations against Polisario guerrillas. Furthermore, U.S. officials began to cooperate with King Hassan to make Rabat, the Moroccan capital, the principal CIA base in North Africa for covert operations against radical states in the Maghrib and West Africa. From then the Reagan administration intensified its use of Morocco as a conduit for arms transfers to Jonas Savimbi's National Union for the Total Independence of Angola (UNITA) against the government of Angola.[48]

In May 1982, after extensive talks with the Reagan administration's Secretary of State Alexander Haig and King Hassan's visit to Washington, the United States and Morocco signed a six-year renewable military agreement designed to serve the global strategic interests of the United States on the one hand and to meet the military needs of Morocco on the other. Thereafter, U.S. military aid to Morocco increased threefold. Contingents of U.S. military instructors were sent to train Moroccan pilots and ground forces. At the same time the number of Moroccan military personnel training in the United States increased from 168 to 514. Plans to sell Morocco 381 Maverick air-to-ground missiles for $25 million were announced, and authorization was given to deliver to it eighteen Bell helicopters manufactured under license in Italy. A request was submitted to Congress for $154 million in military aid and $56 million in economic assistance to Morocco in fiscal year 1983.[49] In March 1983 Howard Wolpe, who had succeeded Stephen Solarz as chairman of the House subcommittee on Africa, asserted at a hearing (15 March 1983) by the subcommittee that he had evidence that the Reagan administration had provided Moroccan forces in the Western Sahara with airborne radar and technical assistance in locating and tracing Polisario's bases and movements.

It was in this manner that U.S. military support for Morocco between fiscal years 1975 and 1984 escalated to include $880 million in Foreign Military Sales agreements, $55 million in grants to finance the military sales, $352 million in credits, $84 million in licensed commercial arms exports, and $10 million in the provision of training.[50] By 1998 Morocco had received from the United States a total of $1 billion in military aid and $1.3 billion in economic assistance.[51]

President Reagan's military support for Morocco's war in the Western Sahara was complemented on the diplomatic level by the termination of all the contacts established with the Polisario by the Carter administration. Reagan claimed that the Front was not an indigenous movement of the people of Western Sahara but consisted entirely of Algerian, Libyan, and non-African mercenaries. The termination of official contacts with the Polisario was accompanied with diplomatic pressures the administration exerted on a number of African governments to deny SADR admission into the OAU.[52] In a secret document, termed *talking notes*, the administration sought to persuade selected African governments to oppose the admission of SADR to membership of the OAU. In addition, it took measures, including lobbying, to block effective action by the UN and to prevent the Western Sahara situation from being placed on the agenda of the Decolonization Committee. These measures and the administration's calculated efforts to enable Morocco achieve a military solution to the conflict failed to do so. They only emboldened King Hassan to remain as adamant as ever in his refusal to negotiate with the Polisario.

Developments occurring between 1988 and 1989 and overlapping the last year of the Reagan administration and the first of that of George H.W. Bush led to agreement in 1990 on a cease-fire arranged by the OAU and the UN. Specifically, Morocco was experiencing a growing fiscal crisis and associated security concerns with the monarchy. Algeria, Polisario's major supporter, fatigued by the war, reestablished diplomatic relations with Morocco in 1988. The international climate, resulting from the new policies of the Soviet leader, Mikhail Gorbachev, the end of the Cold War, and the cautious and pragmatic approach of the Bush administration to foreign policy, encouraged a global trend towards the resolution of regional conflicts. The U.S. government thus urged Morocco to negotiate. The result was Morocco's acceptance of the OAU-UN brokered settlement plan of 1990 and the subsequent cease-fire which went into effect in September 1991.

A few weeks after the cease-fire, President Bush used the occasion of the visit of King Hassan to the United States to declare U.S. support for the settlement plan. Given his administration's determination to reverse, through multilateral action under UN auspices, the 1991 Iraqi invasion and occupation of Kuwait, Bush could not strategically oppose or tolerate egregious violations of the peace plan. In the fall of 1991, the House of Representatives added its support to the peace plan and urged the UN Security Council to take vigorous action to ensure its enforcement. As the prospects for a settlement improved, the Bush administration quietly resumed contact with the officials of Polisario, which had been abandoned during the Reagan years. Although it failed to pressure Morocco to comply fully with the peace process, it refrained from undermining it.

The administration's support of the peace process was reduced in recognition of Morocco's modest support for the Bush-led UN coalition against Saddam Hussein of Iraq. In a demonstration of that reward for Morocco's role, the Bush administration prevented the Deputy Military Commander of MINURSO, Albert Zapanta, from testifying before a congressional hearing on the Western Sahara situation in February 1992, afraid that he would divulge Morocco's obstructions to the peace process as well as America's tepid support for it.[53] Morocco was thus enabled to take advantage of the Bush policy to delay the process of the referendum at every turn.

When he succeeded Bush as president in January 1993, Bill Clinton favored Morocco even more than Reagan and Bush had. His administration ensured that U.S. arms and assistance continued to flow to Morocco. It made no efforts whatsoever to restrain Morocco's delaying tactics. Rather, it sponsored but later withdrew, because Algeria protested vigorously, a Security Council resolution that sought to hold the referendum on the basis of a Moroccan voters' roll which was unacceptable to the Polisario. In 1995 U.S. Congress cut off all American contribution to MINURSO due to secrecy or lack of transparency and progress in handling the referendum process by the office of Secretary-General Boutros-Ghali. However, after the Houston Accords negotiated by Jim Baker as special envoy of Kofi Annan, it passed a resolution in October 1997 expressing support for a "free, fair, and transparent" referendum as agreed upon by the two parties and urged the Clinton administration to support the referendum process.

Consequences of U.S. Policy

Consistent U. S. support for the rulers of Morocco on the conflict in the Western Sahara contradicted a major U.S. aim, in the geopolitically significant

Northwest Africa, of promoting stability, economic growth, and democracy. Achieving this goal required U.S. support for regional cooperation and conflict resolution, not a destabilizing war catering to Morocco's expansionist ambitions while isolating Algeria, a country that has the greatest potential among the Maghribian countries to coordinate regional economic development. The limited resources of Morocco, the beneficiary of the policy, have been drained by the war. The cohesion of the OAU was diminished by Morocco's withdrawal from the organization because of the admission of SADR as a member.

During the Cold War, when the United States considered local conflicts to be primarily the result of America's geopolitical rivalry with the Soviet Union, U.S. administrations never perceived Morocco and the northwest Africa region as part of the vital security interests of the United States. Yet, the administrations acted as if Morocco were a U.S. ally against the Soviets and their northwest Africa surrogates and virtually ignored Algeria with which the United States has more substantial economic relations. The same attitude persists years after the U.S. obsession with a perceived Soviet threat had disappeared. U.S. support for Morocco's prosecution of the war in northwest Africa, which derived from this attitude, significantly increased the destructiveness of the war as well as the economic burden the war imposed on Morocco and Algeria. The support failed to enable Morocco to win the war or to shorten its duration. U.S. administrations, except that of Jimmy Carter in its initial stages, exercised no restraint whatsoever in supplying military weapons to Morocco. They supplied weapons despite their knowledge of the economic hardships such military transfers imposed on Morocco and the northwest Africa region generally.

The lack of restraint in transferring military weapons to Morocco and the unqualified commitment by the administrations to the Moroccan monarchy's security and political survival as a friend of the West diminished U.S. influence on the course Morocco has pursued in the Western Sahara. Because of unconditional promises by U.S. administrators, the late King Hassan and his son and successor demonstrated little or no willingness to allow the conduct of the UN-ordered referendum in the Western Sahara. Instead, the promises encouraged the king to persist in his unrealistic expectations of U.S. support for Morocco's military occupation of the Western Sahara or in the unlikely event of an attack by Algeria. At the same time the commitment to the security and survival of the Moroccan monarchy as a friend of the West cast the Moroccan monarchy in the role of the puppet of the West. To his critics this undermined the king's claims to Moroccan independence and nationalism, the essence of his quest in the Western Sahara. This constituted a potential crisis for the monarchy.

Should a crisis erupt, Washington, as in the case of the shah of Iran, may be utterly unable to save the Moroccan monarchy from the consequences of its imperial ambition. A similar U.S. policy that religiously supported Mobutu Sese Seko—"Mobutu or chaos"—as the sole source of political stability in Zaire and as worthy of U.S. blind support, turned out to be a colossal miscalculation that has continued to wreak havoc on the nationals of the central African nation to this day.

On the basis of his thirty years' diplomatic experience, Richard B. Parker argued that the United States had dangerously overidentified itself with Morocco,

> not so much in the level of its economic and military assistance programs, but in the pervasive perception in Washington that the [Moroccan monarch] is an Arab ally, and that he serves as a surrogate for the United States by protecting U.S. interests throughout Africa and the Middle East. Even if there were no war in the Western Sahara and no regional rivalry between Morocco and Algeria, this degree of identification with a local political leader is in error. It complicates U.S. relations with Algeria and could eventually undermine the security of [the monarchy], because Washington's commitment to [the] regime allows [its] domestic opponents to label [it] as a U.S. stooge.[54]

The unflinching U.S. support for Morocco in the conflict in the Western Sahara has been compatible neither with the interests of the United States nor its principles. Traditionally, the United States does not automatically recognize a government not based on the will of the people or a territorial transfer brought about by force in violation of the principle of self-determination. Yet in the Western Sahara situation, U.S. administrations invariably supported an illegality—a government that violated and continues to violate U.S. traditional principles. By their actions they abetted and supported the illegality of the Madrid accords of November 1975 by which Spain transferred the administration of the Western Sahara to Morocco and Mauritania. They did so in violation of international law as represented by UN Resolution 1514 (XV) on decolonization and the right of national self-determination as these relate to the Western Sahara. Also, their behavior made a mockery of United States' acceptance of the 16 October 1975 advisory opinion of the World Court dismissing the claims of sovereignty by Morocco and Mauritania over the Western Sahara. The profession by the administrations, on the one hand, that the United States seeks a just and fair resolution of the Western Sahara conflict under UN auspices, while, on the other, they obstruct UN efforts towards such resolution is glaringly hypocritical.

The assertion by the administrations that the United States has an overriding interest in the preservation of a pro-Western government in Morocco is a flawed rationale for U.S. policy on the conflict. There is no evidence whatsoever that Polisario nationalists could militarily force Morocco out of the Western Sahara or have any interest or plan to overthrow the monarchy at Rabat. Furthermore, the policy is in error because it fails to take into account the fact that the Moroccan monarchy's primary responsibility is to meet the needs of the Moroccan people and that it would not endure if that were not fulfilled. The United States has a permanent interest in maintaining its national security, not in a permanent monarchy in Morocco. Hence, a pragmatic policy would accept that the U.S. government should deal with a government in power in Morocco but would recognize that while governments may change, the United States' interest in a friendly Morocco might not.

From this perspective, what the Moroccan monarchy needed from the U.S. government was not arms to prosecute a protracted neo-imperialist war that drains its resources but rather a conservation program for those resources in addition to whatever economic and humanitarian assistance it could obtain in order to address festering social and economic problems within the kingdom. It is such problems, not the Western Sahara, that constitute the real threat to the survival of the Moroccan monarchy. Until the cease-fire of 1991, Morocco was spending $1.5 million a day to prosecute the war. Credits received from the United States, under the Foreign Military Sales program, for military purchases have to be paid with interest. Together with the costs of other military purchases from the United States and France, for example, such interest payments have reduced spending on economic development and social services and added to Morocco's debt. Thus, Morocco has been misdirecting the resources it needed to deal with the economic and social problems that afflict its citizens. In 1984 destabilizing riots arising from the social problems propelled the king to sign a dramatic treaty of union with Libya as a means of restoring the prestige of his monarchy. The event startled Washington but was hailed by Moroccan nationals.

The U.S. policy on the Western Sahara conflict undermines the nation's credibility, values, principles regarding international law, self-determination of peoples, and the promotion of human rights. The support for Morocco raises serious ethical questions:

1. of a double standard in U.S. leadership role in world affairs;
2. of why the United States mobilized UN members for multilateral sanctions (a) against Libya regarding the 1988 explosion of Pan Am Flight 103 over Lockerbie in which 270 people died but supports an imperialist war that has claimed many more lives; (b) against Iraq for the invasion and occupation of Kuwait but obstructs the implementation of the will of the United Nations on the Western Sahara conflict;
3. of why, without exception, the administrations of Ford, Carter, and Reagan openly and secretly sold military weapons to the Kingdom of Morocco when they were fully aware that the Kingdom violated the terms of those sales as agreed to in 1960;
4. of why the Reagan administration violated U.S. law—the Clark Amendment—when it used Morocco to transfer U.S. arms and aid to Jonas Savimbi's war in Angola.

U.S. administrations may not have had the influence or leverage to compel Morocco and Polisario to resolve the Western Sahara conflict, yet, they could have pondered these ethical issues. They could have denied or ended U.S. diplomatic, economic, and military assistance to Morocco to prosecute the war. They could have publicly reaffirmed the U.S. nominal position that the status of the Western Sahara has remained unresolved and that the United States does not recognize Moroccan sovereignty over the territory. They could have supported instead of obstructing UN efforts to organize a free and fair referendum in the Western Sahara. Finally, although U.S. administrations have espoused moralism or realism at one time or another as a guide to foreign policy, most administrations have tended to act pragmatically. Pragmatism has not been the guide of U.S. policy on the Western Sahara conflict. The policy has betrayed not only U.S. realism but also U.S. moral values and principles.

Notes

1.   The Yemaa was actually an imperial tool designed to "up-grade Western Sahara from the status of a simple colony to that of a 'respectable' overseas province of Spain." (See S. E. Orabator, "Irredentism as a Pretext: The Western Sahara Case 1960–1982," *Journal of the Historical Society of Nigeria*, Vol. XI, Nos. 1 & 2 [December 1981–June 1982], 168).

2.   International Court of Justice, Case Summaries, "Western Sahara: Advisory Opinion of 16 October 1975," http://www.icj.cij.org/icjwww/idecisions/isummaries/isasummary751016. html.

3. *Africa Confidential,* Vol. 19, No. 24 (1 December 1978), 5; Orabator, "Irredentism as a Pretext," p. 170.

4. See Azzedine Layachi, "The OAU and Western Sahara: A Case Study," in *The Organization of African Unity After Thirty Years*, Yassin El-Ayouty, ed. (Westport, CT: Praeger, 1994), p. 34.

5. William H. Lewis, "Morocco and the Western Sahara," *Current History,* Vol. 84, No. 902 (May 1985), p. 213.

6. "Security Council Approves UN Plan for Western Sahara; MINURSO to Supervise Elections," *UN Chronicle*, Vol. 27, No. 3 (September 1990), pp. 12–14.

7. United Nations, Department of Information, "Western Sahara—MINURSO: Background," http:// www.un.org/Depts/DPKO/Missions/minurso/minursoB.html.

8. Nizar al-Ali, "Development—Morocco; A High Price to Win over Western Sahara," Inter Press Service: World News, http://www.oneworld.org/ips2/dec/wshara-html.

9. This was by UN Security Council Resolution 690 (1991) of 29 April 1991 in accordance with the 30 August 1988 settlement proposal accepted by Morocco and the Polisario.

10. United Nations, Western Sahara—MINURSO Mandate, http://www.un.org/Depts/DP KO/Missions/minurso/minursoM.html.

11. According to the 1988 Settlement Plan, the voting was to be based on the Spanish census of 1974, updated by the Identification Commission. In updating the 1974 census the Commission was to take into account births, deaths, and movements of the Saharan population and consult with "tribal chiefs."

12. Nick Birnback, "Africa," in *A Global Agenda: Issues Before the 54ᵗʰ General Assembly of the United Nations,* John Tessitore and Susan Woolfson (eds.), (New.York: Rowman & Littlefield, 1999), p. 22; United Nations, Western Sahara—MINURSO Background, http://www.un. org/Depts/DPKO/Missions/minurso/minursoB.htm; Frank Ruddy, "The UN Mission for the Referendum in Western Sahara: Lofty Ideals and Gutter Realities," Address at Georgetown University (16 February 2000).

13. Zachariah Cherian Mampillyi, "The Last Colony: Western Sahara Fights On," wyswyg:// main.main.4/http://www.africana.com/index_20000412.htm; The Associated Press, "Baker Cuts Short North Africa Trip," *New York Times* (11 April 2000), http://www.nytimes. com/aponline/i/AP-Morocco-UN-Western-Sahara.html.

14. Quoted in Nizar Al-Aly, Inter Press Service: World News, "Politics—Maghreb—Sahara: New Ideas to Unlock a Settlement Plan," http://www.oneworld.org/ips2/mar00/16_24_109. html.

15. Honorable John Bolton, "Resolving the Western Sahara Conflict," Testimony before a 1998 Congressional Defense and Foreign Policy Forum held in Washington, DC by Defense Forum Foundation (28 March 1998).

16. Yahia H. Zoubir and Karima Benabdallah-Gambier, "Western Sahara Deadlock," *Middle East Report* 227 (Summer 2003), http://www.merip.org/mer/mer227/227_soubir.html; Toby Shelley "Behind the Baker Plan for Western Sahara," *Middle East Report* (1 August 2003), http:/www.merip.org/mero/mero080103.html.

17. UN Security Council Resolution 1309 (25 July 2000), first operative paragraph.

18. UN Security Council, *Report of the Secretary-General on the Situation Concerning Western Sahara*, S/2002/178 (19 February 2002); Zoubir and Benabdallah-Gambier, "Western Sahara Deadlock."

19. "Western Sahara: Polisario's Sinking Hopes," *The Economist* (8–14 December 2001), pp. 44–45.

20. Honorable John Bolton, "Resolving the Western Sahara Conflict," Testimony before a 1998 Congressional Defense and Foreign Policy Forum, held in Washington, DC by Defense Forum Foundation (28 March 1988); Stephen Zunes, "The United States and the Western Sahara Peace Process,"*Middle East Policy*, Vol. V, No. 4 (1988), p. 137; also endnote 32, 145–146; Ruddy, "The United Nations Mission for the Referendum in Western Sahara."

21. Ruddy, "The UN Mission for the Referendum in Western Sahara: Lofty Ideals and Gutter Realities"; Zunes, "The United States and the Western Sahara Peace Process," p. 139.

22. As UN Undersecretary in charge of the referendum process, he dismissed as "not serious" reports of Morocco's abuses and human rights violations in Western Sahara. Prior to assuming office as secretary-general, he was fully aware of U.S. diplomatic maneuvers, besides military assistance to Morocco, designed to prevent the application of the principle of self-determination in Western Sahara. Yet, he chose former senior American officials to serve as his representatives on the issues—James Baker, formerly U.S. Secretary of State as his personal envoy, John R. Bolton as Baker's deputy, and William Eagleton, formerly U.S. Assistant Secretary of State for International Organizations, as his special representative in Western Sahara. He is credited with originating the idea of abandoning the 1991 UN Settlement Plan when he appointed Baker his personal envoy in 1997. Marrack Goulding, a former UN undersecretary-general, has revealed that Annan had sent him to Houston in that year "to persuade James Baker III to accept an appointment as his Special Representative and try to negotiate a deal based on enhanced autonomy for Western Sahara within the Kingdom of Morocco" (Marrak Goulding, Peacemonger [London: John Murray, 2002], pp. 214-215).

23. "Pentagon Seeking New Access Pacts for Africa Bases," *The New York Times* International Section (5 July 2003).

24. Five weeks after Morocco's invasion and occupation of Western Sahara, Indonesia invaded and occupied the former Portuguese colony of East Timor. Fifteen years later Iraq invaded and occupied Kuwait. The United States played the leading role in the response by the

international community to that invasion.

25. Arms Sales in North Africa and the Conflict in the Western Sahara: An Assessment of U.S. Policy: Hearing before the Subcommittees on International Security and on Africa of the Committee of Foreign Affairs, House of Representatives, Ninety-Seventh Congress, First Session, 25 March 1981 (Washington, DC: U.S. Government Printing Office, 1981); Proposed Arms Sales to Morocco: Hearing before the Committee on Foreign Relations, United States Senate, Ninety-Sixth Congress, Second Session, 30 January 1980 (Washington, DC: U.S. Government Printing Office, 1980).

26. Arms Sales in North Africa and the Conflict in the Western Sahara: An Assessment of U.S. Policy: Hearing before the Subcommittees on International Security and on Africa of the Committee of Foreign Affairs, House of Representatives, Ninety-Seventh Congress, First Session, 25 March 1981 (Washington, DC: U.S. Government Printing Office, 1981); Proposed Arms Sales to Morocco: Hearing before the Committee on Foreign Relations, United States Senate, Ninety-Sixth Congress, Second Session, 30 January 1980 (Washington, DC: U.S. Government Printing Office, 1980).

27. Tony Hodges, *Western Sahara: The Roots of a Desert War* (Westport, CT: Lawrence Hill, 1983), p. 215.

28. Leo Kamil, *Fueling the Fire: U.S. Policy and the Western Sahara Conflict* (Trenton, NJ: The Red Sea, 1987), p. 10.

29. Tony Hodges, "At Odds with Self-Determination: The United States and Western Sahara," in *African* Crisis *Areas and U.S. Foreign Policy,* Gerald J. Bender et al. (eds.), (Berkeley: University of California, 1985), p. 264.

30. *Africa News* (2 November 1979).

31. Daniel Patrick Moynihan, *A Dangerous Place* (Boston: Little, Brown, 1978), p. 247; Ruddy, "The UN Mission for the Referendum in the Western Sahara."

32. The first of such contacts was made in December 1979. See Tony Hodges, "The Western Sahara: The Sixth Year of War," *Africa Contemporary Record,* 1980/81, pp. 91–92.

33. Claude Wright, "Journey to Marrakesh: U.S.- Moroccan Security Relations," *International Security*, Vol. 7, No. 4 (Spring 1983), pp. 170–171.

34. U.S. Policy and the Conflict in the Western Sahara, Hearings before the Subcommittees on Africa and on International Organizations of the Committee on Foreign Affairs, House of Representatives, Ninety-Sixth Congress, First Session 23/24 July 1979 (Washington, DC: U.S. Government Printing Office, 1979), p. 2; Crawford Young, "Zaire: The Unending Crisis," *Foreign Affairs,* Vol. 57, No. 1 (Fall 1978), pp. 169–185.

35. There were concerns among U.S. administrators that Hassan II might be humiliated, face domestic opposition, or even might be overthrown by the armed forces, which had twice attempted to do so in 1971 and 1972, if his Western Sahara venture failed, given the

enthusiasm and support it had generated for him among Moroccans.

36. The intention of this stipulation was "to prevent the use of U.S. arms against Israel." (John Damis, *Conflict in Northwest Africa: The Western Sahara Dispute* [Stanford, CA: Hoover Institution, 1983], p. 122).

37. "Kingdom of Morocco: Increasing Pressure to Abandon the War," *Africa Contemporary Record* (1979/80), pp. B84–85.

38. *Africa Confidential* (17 October 1979); *Africa Contemporary Record* (1979/80), p. B85.

39. Wright, "Journey to Marrakesh," p. 169.

40. Proposed Arms Sales to Morocco, Hearings before the Subcommittees on International Security Affairs and on Africa of the Committee on Foreign Affairs, House of Representatives, Ninety-Sixth Congress, Second Session, 24 and 29 January 1980 (Washington, DC: U.S. Government Printing Office, 1980), pp. 2–3.

41. Stephen J. Solarz, "Arms for Morocco," *Foreign Affairs*, Vol. 58, No. 2 (Winter 1979/80), pp. 286–292, 295.

42. Solarz, "Arms for Morocco," p. 278.

43. Bruce Oudes, "The United States and Africa: The Reagan Difference," *Africa Contemporary Record* (1981/82), pp. A154–162; Tony Hodges, "Western Sahara: The Maghreb Under Shadow of War," *Africa Contemporary Record* (1981/82), p. A80; "The Endless War," *Africa Report* (July/August 1982), p. 10.

44. *The Washington Post* (5 November 1981), in *AF Press Clips* 16, 45 (6 November 1981), 12.

45. Arms Sales in North Africa and the Conflict in the Western Sahara: An Assessment of U.S. Policy, Hearing (25 March 1981), pp. 3–4.

46. Arms Sales in North Africa and the Conflict in the Western Sahara: An Assessment of U.S. Policy, Hearing (25 March 1981), pp. 2–6.

47. The officials, among others, included Secretary of Defense, Casper Weinberger; Frank C. Carlucci, deputy secretary of defense; General Vernon Walters, Reagan's ambassador-at-large and formerly deputy director of the CIA; Francis West who headed a deputation of twenty-third Pentagon and State Department officials; U.S. Senator Charles Percy, Republican chairman of the Senate Foreign Relations Committee; Vice Admiral Bobby Irman, deputy director of the CIA; General James Williams, director of the Defense Intelligence Agency. (Edward Cody, "Morocco Seeks U.S. Aid in Sahara," *The Washington Post* [6 November 1981], in *AF Press Clips*, 16, 45 [6 November 1981], p. 12; *Africa Confidential* Vol. 23, No. 1 [6 January 1982], p. 9.)

48. "North Africa: Realignments," *Africa Confidential*, Vol. 32, No. 9 (28 April 1982), pp. 3–4; Wright, "Journey to Marrakesh," p. 173.

49. *Africa Report* (July/August 1982), p. 20.

50. Hodges, "Western Sahara," p. 270.

51. Zunes, "The United States and the Western Sahara Peace Process," p. 134.

52. *Africa Report* (July/August 1982), p. 11; *Africa Confidential* Vol. 23, No. 12 (9 June 1982), p. 4.

53. Zunes, "The United States and the Western Sahara Peace Process," p. 138; Barbara Crossette, "Congress Scrutinizes Peacekeeping Test Case," *The New York Times* (1 March 1992), p. 9.

54. Yahia H. Zoubir and Daniel Volman (eds.), *International Dimensions of the Western Sahara Conflict* (Westport, CT: Praeger, 1993), p. 97.

CHAPTER 7

U.S. Role in the Angola Conflict, 1975–2002

Few of Africa's intrastate conflicts have been of longer duration, produced greater bloodshed and mayhem, or attracted as many external actors—including the United States, the former Soviet Union, China, and South Africa—as the Angolan struggle for political succession. Rooted in the dynamics of Angolan society and historical experience, and exacerbated and prolonged by the Cold War, it was no small war, and neither side could easily win decisively. Its death toll approached two million. Its ramifications extended far beyond Angola. Lasting more than four decades, 1961–2002, the war originally had little specifically to do with the country's remarkable oil and diamond resources which, however, eventually fueled it. Instead, it derived from the nature of Portuguese colonialism, Portugal's failure to prepare for a stable transition to independence, the competition for political succession by rival nationalist movements with different ethnolinguistic bases, leaders without vision, bent on achieving absolute power at the expense of their rivals and competing external supporters. The war had neither a real social basis nor substantive ideological motives. For the first sixteen years, it was essentially a civil war by proxy that pitted a Soviet- and Cuban-backed government against rebels supported by the United States and the Republic of South Africa. From the end of the Cold War and the transition to majority rule in South Africa, when external support for the belligerents terminated, the war was no longer fueled by external strategic interests. Thereafter, it was driven by personal ambition, mutual suspicion and, above all, the prize of control of the state and the wealth to which it gave access, a common phenomenon especially in resource-rich postcolonial African countries.

This chapter provides a summary survey of the conflict.[1] It elucidates the causes of the conflict, the diplomatic efforts made to resolve it, and its effects and ramifications. Specifically, it details (1) how U.S. administrators, from Gerald Ford to George H.W. Bush, in their implacable ideological struggle with the Soviet Union, waged a proxy war in Angola; (2) how, at the same time, U.S. oil companies, protected by the armed forces of Cuba, a Soviet ally, exploited

Angola's mineral wealth, the rent from which financed the Angolan government war against rebels supported by U.S. administrations over a period of 16 years; (3) the stages and specifics of U.S. intervention in the conflict; and (4) the impact and consequences of such intervention.

Origins of the Conflict

Although the Angolan conflict had its own peculiar characteristic context and dynamics, its causes were typical of those of other conflicts in postcolonial Africa: the colonial legacy of politics of ethnic and regional security, the struggle for the control of the postcolonial state—the major source of wealth and development and upward social mobility—self-serving, corrupt, and inordinately ambitious leadership, and external intervention. One can see Angola—its heavy concentration of political and economic power in an executive president, its reliance on a highly personalized form of governance, the concentration of the overwhelming portion of its wealth in the hands of a small elite, the extreme poverty and suffering of its people, the dependence of most of its urban population on employment and incomes in the informal sector of the economy—in every region of Africa. For a generation of Angolans, violence, the rule of the gun, internal displacement, massive unemployment and underemployment, hunger, and hyperinflation became a way of life. The leaders of Angola, like others in various regions of Africa, condemned their followers to damnation, sacrificed their youth on the altar of power, and made their people's republic a country of inequalities, hunger, misery, and intimidation.

The Angolan conflict (1975–2002) began as a postcolonial struggle for political succession and evolved into a protracted civil war. It provided critical impetus to nationalist liberation movements in Rhodesia (now Zimbabwe), Namibia, and the Republic of South Africa, all southern African countries controlled for many years before independence by white minority regimes. Significantly, it constituted the first decisive battle to determine the course of southern Africa's political evolution. It manifested a lack of unity, not just among Angolan leaders but also among African states. Some African states became partisans of the conflict and conduits for arms that fueled the war. In addition, the conflict demonstrated not only the inability of the region's premier international organization—the Organization of African Unity (OAU)—to act with dispatch to prevent or reconcile warring factions in Africa but also the organization's "subordination to the interventionist designs of outside powers."[2] While Namibia, Zimbabwe, and the Republic of South Africa, whose liberation the Angolan conflict accelerated, became relatively peaceful, the Angolan conflict defied several attempts at a peaceful resolution. Angola bled not for reasons of interest or ideology but principally because of the weakness, folly, bad faith, and the inordinate political ambition of its rival leaders.

The roots of the conflict lay deep, first in Portugal's imperial policy and practice in Africa. Second, they lay in the struggle for control of state power among Angola's three national liberation movements immediately after Portugal was compelled to concede independence in the wake of a military overthrow of its civilian government in Lisbon in April 1974. The struggle became complicated by external forces—the dynamics of the Cold War and the security interests of South Africa's white minority government, which sought to perpetuate its rule in South Africa and Namibia as well as its hegemony in the whole of southern Africa. That interest was threatened by the collapse of the Portuguese colonial empire in southern Africa. The buffer zone that the empire had provided South Africa against black nationalism suddenly crumbled. In its place, Portugal's former colonial dependencies, Angola and Mozambique, began to allow their territories to be used as bases of operation against South Africa by forces that sought to overthrow its government. Angola allowed the Southwest African People's Liberation Organization (SWAPO) to establish training bases, supply routes, and logistical support bases and to mount guerrilla raids into Namibia, which, according to a 1966 UN General Assembly resolution, was illegally occupied by South Africa. This perceived threat to the security interest of the white minority government of South Africa expanded the scope and duration of the war.

The third root of the conflict was the ideological conflict for world hegemony between the United States and the Soviet Union which ended after the fall of Eurocommunism in 1989 and the subsequent disintegration of the Soviet Union in December 1991. Before the two related events, a major determinant of American foreign policy after World War II was the global containment of communism and Soviet Union's moves to spread its ideology. The notion of communist or Soviet expansionism, at least so far as Africa was concerned, was an American rationale for protecting a global status quo that benefited the United States and its Western allies. In terms of world politics, however, such apprehension could not be ignored, not just because the American administrations believed it and it was the basis of their action, but also because the Soviets themselves, indeed, had their own interests in Africa—the undermining or supplanting of Western influence in the continent. It was the clash of these two interests that, above any other force, escalated the Angolan war. We examine below, in some detail, each of the roots of the war.

We also consider why the conflict persisted after the end of the Cold War and the collapse of South Africa's apartheid regime, which had been apprehensive that an independent and stable Angola would constitute a threat to its security.

Portugal's Imperial Policy and Practice in Africa

Portugal regarded its territories—Angola, Cape Verde, Guinea-Bissau, São Tomé, Príncipe, and Mozambique—in Africa as its overseas provinces rather than as its colonies. Therefore, it never envisaged independence for them. The Portuguese believed that their presence in Africa was a work of civilization. They condemned virtually everything African, including cultural institutions, as primitive and barbaric. The African territories, therefore, were ruled directly from Lisbon. By this policy Africans were required to assimilate Portuguese cultural values, through Western education, conversion to Euro-Christianity, birth as *mestiços*, and abandonment of such traditional African practices as polygyny in order to become Portuguese citizens.

However, the Portuguese totally neglected the most important avenue of assimilation—formal education—for Africans. Ultimately, Portugal departed from its African empire with the worst literacy rate (less than 5 percent in both Angola and Mozambique) achieved by any European imperial power in Africa. Thus, very few Africans became Portuguese citizens prior to 1961, when that right was granted to all inhabitants of its African territories. Only a few of such citizens served as members of the Portuguese legislature. The few African *assimilados* who studied in Portugal found that the majority of the metropolitan Portuguese were less civilized than they were. This discovery intensified their resolve to rid their country of Portuguese rule altogether.

Throughout the years of its presence in Africa, Portugal was controlled by authoritarian regimes, especially those of Antonio Salazar and Marcello Caetano. Under these regimes, Angola suffered from uneven development of social forces and political awareness and from ethnic prejudices which were to haunt it after the end of Portuguese control. The colonial practices that sent Ovimbundu, Angola's largest ethnolinguistic group, and other conscript workers to labor on coffee plantations and in Portuguese-owned factories left a legacy of prejudice and mistrust between ethnic groups of the north and south. Portuguese colonial practices and legacy reinforced ethnic loyalties tapped by Angolan leaders in their struggle for power. In addition, Portuguese rulers insulated masses of Africans (with the exception of contract laborers in South African mines) from the outside world to prevent them from being "corrupted"

Map 7.1 Angola

Adapted from CIA - *The World Factbook 2002*.

by revolutionary ideas. Such an unrealistic policy could not stand the force of the revolutionary winds of change favoring national self-determination that blew across Africa in the wake of World War II.

While other imperial powers, notably Britain, France, and Belgium, bowed to such winds of change and negotiated the grant of independence to their colonies, Portugal flatly refused do so. Its authoritarian rulers committed themselves to resisting the forces of nationalism and insisted that Portugal had a "duty to safeguard a work which [they believed represented] a positive contribution to the progress of Humanity and Civilization."[3] Using a secret police force introduced in 1957, Portuguese imperial dictators rooted out critics of the colonial government and either imprisoned the educated and emergent nationalist leaders or forced them into exile. Foreign criticism of this policy and of the myth of a Portuguese civilizing mission in Africa was vehemently resented by Portuguese rulers as an unwarranted intervention in the internal affairs of Portugal. The consequence was a thirteen-year anticolonial war that pitted African national liberation movements against Portugal from 1961–1974. Portugal mounted its greatest military offensive to crush the nationalist forces in Angola, its richest colony in Africa. In that war Portugal was overtly and covertly supported by its NATO allies—the United States, Britain, France, and Germany—against the nationalist forces. The war was terminated after thirteen years by a military overthrow of the authoritarian regime of Marcello Caetano on 25 April 1974.

This revolutionary event marked the beginning of the end of the Portuguese colonial empire in Africa. By July 1975 all parts of the empire, except Angola, had become independent. After a chaotic political situation arose in Angola, Portuguese authorities refused to take any steps to control the disorder and fled the country on 11 November 1975 without a formal transfer of power. Consequently, Angola fell prey to a more destructive war, exacerbated by the United States, the Republic of South Africa, the Soviet Union, and Cuba, that lasted twenty-seven years.

The Struggle for Political Succession in Angola

The factions in the struggle for succession in Angola—the Popular Movement for the Liberation of Angola (MPLA), the National Front for the Liberation of Angola (FNLA), and the National Union for the Total Independence of Angola (UNITA)—were initially national liberation movements which sought to remove Portugal's imperial presence from their country. However, unlike the African Party for the Independence of Guinea and Cape Verde (West Africa) and the Front for the Liberation of Mozambique in southeastern Africa, they were unable to unify their forces and so unable to achieve much success against the Portuguese army. Two reasons account for that inability and failure. First, colonial Angola was a police state, a situation which made it almost impossible for the liberation movements, operating underground, to maintain and extend themselves effectively inside Angola. Portugal, enabled by this reality and its membership in NATO, mounted its greatest military offensive in Angola, the richest portion of its African colonial empire. It was able to receive military assistance and strategic intelligence from its NATO allies and the government of the Republic of South Africa which it used against the liberation movements.

The second reason for the failure to achieve some measure of success against the Portuguese colonial regime lay in the origins and composition of the three antagonistic liberation movements. Angolan society was already riddled with ethnic division before the anticolonial struggle was initiated. The three national liberation movements reflected ethnic identities and the differential access to the few educational and economic opportunities Portuguese colonial rule offered to Angolans.[4] The MPLA, the first to be organized, was a Marxist-oriented movement led by a relatively well-educated and racially mixed people (the *mestiços*) headed by Agostinho Neto. The movement drew its other members from the approximately 1.3 million Kimbundu-speaking people living in and around Angola's capital city, Luanda. In 1956 the MPLA leadership sought help from the U.S. government to win their independence from Portugal. The request was declined by the Dwight D. Eisenhower administration because of the Cold War, Portuguese membership in NATO, and U.S. bases at the Azores that were leased from Portugal. Consequently, the MPLA turned to the Soviet Union, which began to supply the movement with modest quantities of weapons to mount a guerrilla war of liberation. The initiative began in 1961.

When he succeeded President Eisenhower in 1961, John F. Kennedy did not allow his idealism about Africa to affect the prevailing official belief that the United States should deny the region to the Soviet bloc while strengthening its ties with the West. Rather, he decided to create a counterforce to the Marxist-oriented MPLA. This was the FNLA, led by Holden Roberto, a Bakongo nationalist and formerly deputy leader of the MPLA. The FNLA drew its membership from the Bakongo of northern Angola and used Zaire, where there were other Bakongo ethnics, as its base of operation. Observers saw the movement as "a rather safe, ineffective organization that [by U.S. design] could be supported without provoking serious Portuguese reprisals."[5]

In 1966, Jonas Savimbi, chief lieutenant of Roberto, organized his own movement, UNITA, charging that Roberto was a racist, divisive, and ineffective tool of the United States.[6] Savimbi's movement drew its membership from Angola's largest ethnolinguistic group, the 1.5 million Ovimbundu of Angola's central highlands, who had become hardened by their harsh experience as migrant laborers in Portuguese colonial plantations. The Kimbundu and the Bakongo regarded the Ovimbundu as the equivalent of scabs and country bumpkins, whose labor in the coffee plantations in northern Angola had facilitated Portuguese colonial exploitation of the region's best agricultural land. Savimbi received help initially from the People's Republic of China and from the Portuguese colonial government, which sought to use it against the MPLA. It received critical aid from the United States, the Republic of South Africa, and Zaire.

The three national liberation movements not only failed to avoid debilitating fratricidal disunity but only received sporadic and inadequate military assistance from their external supporters. They worked against each other, demonstrated a lack of vision, and none of them was ever able to defeat the Portuguese colonial regime.

In 1969 the newly inaugurated U.S. President, Richard M. Nixon, and his national security adviser, Henry Kissinger, ordered an interagency review of U.S. policy towards white minority-ruled southern Africa. As stated in Chapter 4, the review's highly nuanced Option II concluded that the white minority regimes were in southern Africa to stay and that any meaningful change to the region would have to come mainly through them. Further, it argued that it was impossible for the national liberation movements to gain the political rights they sought through violence, that they were ineffectual, neither realistic, nor supportable alternatives to colonial rule. They could only make the southern African region fertile for communist mischief-making. Henry Kissinger questioned "the depth and permanence" of the liberation movements' resolve (though not that of the Portuguese colonial regime) and ruled out their victory at any stage.[7] The decision, therefore, was to support the colonial regimes militarily and diplomatically while encouraging Africans with carrots in the form of foreign aid and urging them to reject revolutionary change in favor of more realistic evolutionary change.

In implementing this decision, the Nixon administration terminated U.S. assistance to the John F. Kennedy-CIA creation, FNLA. Instead, it recruited its leader, Holden Roberto, as a paid informant of the CIA. Thus, FNLA became moribund.

By the early 1970s, there were ample signs that Portugal's days as an imperial power in Africa were numbered. Demoralization and defection among the war-weary Portuguese military, economic stagnation and inflation, massive emigration of about 1.5 million Portuguese job seekers, and constant anti-Portuguese terrorism and sabotage were all clearly visible to perceptive political observers. In February 1974 General Antonio Spinola, a Portuguese military governor who had played no small part in Portugal's determination to suppress the African national liberation movements, published a book—*Portugal and the Future*—in which he called for fundamental change in Portugal's African policy. He argued that an exclusively military victory was untenable in the type of war Portugal was prosecuting in Africa. "The duty of the armed forces," he wrote, "is, therefore, limited to promoting and retaining for the necessary period of time—naturally not very long—the security conditions that enable the application of the political-social solutions that alone are capable of bringing an end to the conflict."[8]

The authoritarian regime of Marcello Caetano in Lisbon rejected General Spinola's timely call for a fundamental change in Portugal's African policy. Instead, Caetano dismissed General Spinola from office. Two months later, on 25 April 1974, Caetano's regime was overthrown by the military, and General Spinola was appointed the provisional president of Portugal.

The military coup set the stage for the decolonization of Portugal's African empire and heightened the interests and, subsequently, the activities of the external supporters of the national liberation movements in Angola.

Four months after the coup, Guinea-Bissau, which had liberated two-thirds of its territory from Portuguese colonial regime, was granted independence by the Portuguese military government on 10 September 1974. Under an interim arrangement the Mozambique Liberation Front (FRELIMO), which had also, prior to the coup in Lisbon, liberated one-third of its territory from Portuguese rule, began to govern Mozambique on 20 September 1974. On June 25 1975 the country was granted independence. Cape Verde became independent on 5 July 1975 and São Tomé and Príncipe on 12 July 1975.

The situation in Angola was entirely different. The territory's three liberation movements, based on different ethnolinguistic groups, had failed woefully to unify and to liberate any piece of territory from Portuguese control prior to April 1974. Following the Portuguese revolution of that month and separate cease-fires with the Portuguese military government, each of the three movements opened its headquarters in Luanda. Thereafter, each sought to position itself for the most favorable military location so as to seize political power. President Jomo Kenyatta of Kenya, serving as the chairman of the OAU, intervened to avert war among them. His efforts were followed by agreements reached by the Portuguese government and the three movements at Alvor in southern Portugal on 15 January 1975. At Alvor it was agreed that a transitional government of all three movements, assisted by a Portuguese high commissioner, was to prepare Angola for its independence on 11 November 1975. Attempts were made to reconcile the movements. But they soon were undermined by covert military intervention by the U.S. President, Gerald Ford, and his Secretary of State, Henry Kissinger. The situation thus deteriorated from a struggle for political succession into a civil war sustained by the two superpowers and their agents. Despite a series of diplomatic efforts to resolve it, the war continued until February 2002, when Savimbi was killed in combat with government troops. The war had raged for nearly twenty-seven years. The signing of a peace agreement on 21 November 2002 marked the definitive end of the conflict. However, a severely deteriorated infrastructure, land mines, banditry on the roads in the interior, and other legacies of the war continued to constrain life and safe movement throughout Angola.

The Ideological Struggle between the Superpowers

What catapulted the Angolan struggle for political succession into a major war was the geopolitical rivalry between the superpowers—the United States and the Soviet Union. The regional conflicts acquired larger significance and implications as they typically involved surrogates of the two rivals. In Washington the prevailing perception was that "a victory by a Soviet client state [or movement] meant a gain in power for Moscow and a corresponding defeat for the U.S.-led 'free world.'"[9] Thus, to perpetuate a status quo in southern Africa that favored the Western powers, the United States, under the Gerald Ford administration, collaborating with President Mobutu Sese Seko of Zaire and the white minority government of the Republic of South Africa, covertly supported an alliance of the FNLA and the UNITA against the Soviet- and Cuban-backed MPLA. The MPLA, which had already proclaimed itself the government of Angola (on 11 November 1975), won an indecisive victory in February 1976 against its rivals.

The MPLA victory was made possible by two forces. First, and more important, was an action of the U.S. Congress, which, determined to prevent the circumstances that led to the foreign policy debacle in Vietnam, attached an amendment to the Defense Appropriations Bill, 1976. Named after one of its major sponsors, Senator Dick Clark of Iowa, the amendment prohibited American assistance to any of the warring groups in Angola. The legislation stopped all U.S. material help to the FNLA-UNITA coalition. In addition, it forced the subsequent withdrawal of South African forces from Angolan territory. A second factor in the MPLA victory was the intervention of 15,000 Cuban troops, supported by massive shipment of Soviet military weapons.

The conflict, however, persisted after President Ford left office into the administrations of Jimmy Carter, Ronald Reagan, and George H.W. Bush. President Ford had flatly refused to recognize the MPLA government until the withdrawal of Cuban expeditionary forces from Angola. President Carter failed to reverse the Ford policy completely. President Reagan renewed American involvement in the continuing conflict by linking the independence of Namibia with the elimination of Cuban troops from Angola and by successfully persuading Congress in 1985 to repeal the Clark Amendment. In addition, upon his inauguration as president, he pledged critical political support to insurgents fighting against what he perceived as Soviet-supported, Marxist-oriented governments. Thus, throughout his administration, Angola became a test case of the "Reagan Doctrine" by which President Reagan pledged to roll back communist and Soviet-assisted governments around the world. The pledge redounded to the interest of the white minority rulers of South Africa, with whom Reagan was determined to strengthen diplomatic relations through his policy of "constructive engagement" with Pretoria.

The Reagan policy reescalated the conflict, increasing the scale of devastation and human suffering in Angola and causing the number of Cuban troops in the territory to be increased to about 50,000 by 8 August 1988. On that date a cease-fire in Angola and Namibia was agreed to by Angola, the Republic of South Africa, and Cuba with the assistance of U.S. diplomacy. Subsequent agreement signed by the three on 22 December 1988 did not directly address the ongoing conflict between the Soviet- and Cuban-backed MPLA government and U.S.-South Africa-supported UNITA rebels. Two weeks before his inauguration as President Reagan's successor in 1989, George Bush assured the UNITA leader, Savimbi, in a personal letter (6 January 1989) that his administration would continue to support him. Bush would provide his movement, he affirmed, "all appropriate and effective assistance" until the realization of a negotiated "national reconciliation."[10] Thus, the Angolan war continued. In the next section we address the series of diplomatic efforts made towards a political settlement of the conflict.

Diplomatic Efforts towards a Political Settlement

Diplomatic efforts to settle the Angolan conflict were protracted for a number of reasons.[11] Both the MPLA government and the UNITA rebels were rigid and unwilling to compromise their positions and to share power. Savimbi's ambition was to be the president of Angola regardless of the human and social costs. Until 1990 when it was compelled by economic and political realities to repudiate Marxism, the MPLA leadership rejected the concept of political pluralism. In addition, it regarded the politically astute Savimbi as a traitor who collaborated with Portuguese military officials in the early 1970s and with the South African military starting in 1975. Therefore, despite the pressures by the U.S. government to assure Savimbi a role in Angola's central government, it would have nothing of him in a government of national unity advocated by the U.S. government.[12] Hence, Savimbi and his future became a major stumbling block to political settlement of the conflict. In addition, the MPLA government failed, in the words of John Marcum, to "reach beyond its own traditional urban and northern strongholds to less-educated, rural and religious communities, whose support was essential to national unity."[13]

Furthermore, the Reagan administration's policy towards southern Africa rendered the process even more complicated. Reagan's policy of constructive engagement with the government of South Africa[14] provided that government enormous diplomatic support that helped to foster its assistance to UNITA rebels and the destabilization of its neighbors. The administration's linkage of the independence of Namibia with the withdrawal of Cuban troops from Angola undermined the diplomacy of the UN Security Council Western Contact Group—Britain, France, Canada, West Germany, and the United States—in Namibia, enhanced raids into Angola by the South African Defence Force, and caused deep distrust of the Reagan administration by the MPLA government. Its policy of covert support for the UNITA rebels, which was overwhelmingly endorsed by conservative members of Congress, disrupted the negotiation process. Inherent in Reagan's southern Africa policy was the risk of a regional conflict escalating into an international confrontation. Such confrontation, however, did not occur.

It was to prevent such an eventuality that Reagan's Assistant Secretary of State for African affairs, Chester Crocker, sought ground for negotiation with the MPLA and for dialogue with the Soviet Union, Cuba, and South Africa. Developments after 1985 collectively helped to create a favorable climate for negotiations. A 1986 Comprehensive Anti-Apartheid Sanctions Act, which

THE VICE PRESIDENT
WASHINGTON

January 6, 1989

Dr. Jonas Savimbi
UNITA
P.O. Box 65463
Washington, D.C. 20035-5463

Dear Dr. Savimbi:

Since our exchange of letters in November, the Tripartite Agreement for the departure of Cuban troops from Angola and the independence of Namibia was signed in New York on December 22, 1988. With the implementation of the agreement, the stage will be set for peace in southwestern Africa and for national reconciliation in Angola. I want to join you in welcoming this great diplomatic achievement which holds out so much hope for the Angolan people.

While we take pride in our role as the mediating power, the United States remains mindful of the fact that peace has not yet been achieved within Angola, and that much work remains to be done in pursuit of that goal. UNITA is to be congratulated for its courageous demonstration over more than a decade that solutions to Angola's problems cannot be found through repressive military force.

My Administration will accord the highest priority to the full and prompt implementation of the Tripartite Agreement so that Angolans will be free to settle their own political future without the destructive presence of foreign military forces. I also want to assure you that American diplomacy will continue to encourage African and other interested governments to provide maximum support to a process of negotiation leading to national reconciliation in your country. Until that objective is achieved, my Administration will continue all appropriate and effective assistance to UNITA.

I want to take this opportunity to wish you, your family, and the entire UNITA movement a successful and prosperous New Year. I look forward to seeing you again for exchange of views as the situation evolves in your country and in your region.

Sincerely,

George Bush

Congress overwhelmingly passed to override President Reagan's veto, undermined the administration's policy of constructive engagement with South Africa. In June 1988 South Africa's Defence Force suffered a major military defeat by Cuban-backed MPLA forces at Cuito Cuanavale, Angola.[15] That defeat was a decisive factor in the decision by an overextended South Africa to retrench its military involvement in Angola and to negotiate. The new approach in the Soviet Union under Mikhail Gorbachev helped to relax the tension between the Soviet Union and the United States. Also, by 1988, the Angolan government, faced with the extreme economic and social realities of the war, showed a willingness to negotiate a political settlement. There was a desperate need to restore Angola's war-torn economy to normalcy, to convert its economic potential to reality, and to invest its human and natural resources in alleviating the suffering of masses of the people rather than in a continuing war. By that time, moreover, the MPLA's major military supporters—Cuba and the Soviet Union—had concluded that the Angolan war could not be resolved militarily, that a continued stalemate was a costly drain on their scarce resources, and that a politically acceptable settlement should be sought. For its part, the Reagan administration, believing that a military solution of the Angolan conflict was neither feasible nor desirable and wishing to achieve a foreign policy success before the end of its term, became willing to make a greater effort towards a political settlement. It seems, however, that the turning point in the process was the major defeat suffered by the South African Defence Force at Cuito Cuanavale in June 1988.

Given the favorable climate provided by these developments, negotiations for a southwestern African regional settlement that included the withdrawal of Cuban troops from Angola and the independence of Namibia were held by the governments of Angola, Cuba, and South Africa between May and December 1988. That was the basis of the Reagan administration's policy of linkage, conceptualized by Chester Crocker, the assistant secretary of state for African affairs in 1981. The negotiators were assisted by the governments of the Soviet Union and the United States. Formal agreements, initially signed in Brazzaville, Congo, on 13 December, were finally sealed on 22 December 1988 at the UN headquarters in New York.[16]

The accords defined the steps and timetable for implementation of UN Security Council Resolution 435 regarding the independence of Namibia, the departure of Cuban expeditionary forces from Angola, and the reduction of South African troop strength in Namibia. An initial contingent of 3,000 out of 50,000 Cuban troops departed from Angola ahead of the scheduled date of 1

April 1989. The departure of the entire force was scheduled over a period of 27 months, ending 1 July 1991. The last of the Cuban troops left Angola in May 1991, ahead of the scheduled date.

The agreements did not resolve the internal conflict between the MPLA and UNITA rebels, lead to normalization of relations between the United States and Angola, or end U.S. covert assistance to UNITA. A collective appeal by the frontline states (located between Angola and the Republic of South Africa) to Reagan's successor, George H.W. Bush, to discontinue U.S. assistance to UNITA was rebuffed. After his inauguration in January 1989, President Bush fulfilled his postelection pledge of continued support to Savimbi by renewing the covert military support the Reagan administration initiated at $15 million annually.[17] At its height in 1991 the assistance totaled about $125 million.[18] In the meantime, after mediation efforts by President Mobutu of Zaire and other African leaders at Gbadolite (June 1989) and elsewhere failed to bring about Angolan national reconciliation, military confrontation between the MPLA and U.S.-supported UNITA forces intensified. The renewed U.S. support, under the Bush administration, had obviously strengthened the UNITA leader, Savimbi, to the point where he was no longer very interested in peace negotiations.

Three related developments collectively worked to negate the excuse for the Bush administration's support of UNITA rebels. First of the developments was the collapse of Eurocommunism in 1989. The second was the abandonment of Marxism by the MPLA leadership in 1990, and the third was the much-improved relationship between the United States and the Soviet Union. Following these developments, diplomatic efforts, free of Cold War thinking, resumed in 1991 towards a political settlement. The outcome was an internationally brokered peace treaty signed by the MPLA government and UNITA in the Portuguese town of Bicesse in May 1991. By the treaty MPLA and UNITA agreed to form a national government, a national army, and a multiparty system. Also the MPLA government accepted UNITA as a bona fide electoral opponent. It was, therefore, agreed that Angola's first national elections were to be held in 1992 and monitored by UN representatives.

The elections were held on 29 and 30 September 1992 in an atmosphere of intense distrust and under conditions of dual sovereignty because the armies of the two major rivals had never been demobilized as planned. The elections were monitored by 800 international observers, operating under the umbrella of United Nations Angola Verification Mission (UNAVEM).[19] UN observers certified the elections as free and fair. The results gave the MPLA a parliamentary majority of 129 deputies, while UNITA and other regional parties respectively won seventy and twenty-one seats.

Although MPLA won more seats, its leader, José Eduardo dos Santos, failed to achieve an overall majority, necessitating a run-off for the Angolan presidency. Savimbi would not accept the electoral results. He, along with the Western ambassadors in Luanda and most members of the international community, had expected that he would win the election. Indeed, the UN and Western diplomats had condoned his systematic violation of the Bicesse Accords as well as UNITA's catalogue of violent incidents during the campaign in order to facilitate his electoral victory and to enhance "UN credibility as an agent of the New World Order."[20] But before the run-off could take place, Savimbi, who had failed to demobilize his troops during the cease-fire, took up arms, asserting that the September 1992 elections had been rigged by the MPLA. He felt that he had been cheated by José Eduardo dos Santos in Angola's first general elections, certification of the polling by international observers as free and fair notwithstanding. The only recourse left to him, therefore, was to take power by armed force. A grueling war that gave UNITA control of most of Angola, except the capital city Luanda, ensued. The war devastated the land, especially the infrastructure of such cities as Cuito, Huambo, Uige, and Malange. Two of Savimbi's closest associates were killed along with thousands of other Angolans. Marcelino Moco, an Ovimbundu who had been appointed prime minister of the Angolan National Assembly by the MPLA in a gesture towards national reconciliation, and his entire family were among the casualties.[21] Thousands of refugees fled from the towns, and over a million people faced the prospect of starvation.

Peace talks were reopened in Abidjan, Côte d'Ivoire, on 12 April 1993. The MPLA government accepted a thirty-seven-point peace proposal offered at the conference by the United States, the UN, Russia, and Portugal. UNITA flatly rejected the peace plan. Among other items, the plan had called for a cease-fire, a phased withdrawal of UNITA forces, and simultaneous and gradual insertion of UN personnel to monitor the cease-fire. The peace talks were suspended on 21 May as Savimbi remained intransigent.

The failed diplomatic effort marked the end of America's policy of outright hostility towards the government of Angola. After the rejection of the thirty-seven-point peace plan by Savimbi, President Clinton, who had, in keeping with the policy of his four immediate predecessors, withheld the diplomatic recognition of the government of President dos Santos, did recognize it on 19 May 1993.[22] In addition, he lifted the U.S. embargo on the sale of military hardware to the MPLA and called for UN sanctions against UNITA. These actions notwithstanding, UNITA remained unrelenting.[23]

A third attempt at political settlement was made in November 1994 in Lusaka, Zambia, after Huambo, UNITA's headquarters, had been captured by government forces earlier in the month.[24] The major focus of the attempt was to arrange a cease-fire, sort out practical details of that cease-fire, demobilize the troops and create a single national army, and work out the details of a power-sharing arrangement that would lead to a UN-supervised presidential run-off election in 1996.[25] The government held out promises to UNITA rebels, including the control of four ministries, seven deputy ministerial posts, three provinces, dozens of municipalities and communes, and several ambassador-ships once their guns were laid aside.[26] Just before the peace pact was signed, Angola's National Assembly passed a blanket amnesty covering both warring parties.[27]

On 13 November when agreement on these issues was due to be signed, Savimbi failed to show up for the signing. His excuse was that he feared leaving Angola. The document was signed by proxies on 20 November 1994.[28] Dos Santos shared the view expressed by the U.S. Congress in a letter to President Clinton that the Lusaka Accords represented the "last, best hope for peace in Angola" and invited Savimbi to meet with him "at any time and any place in Angola so we may show our people we are fully engaged together in national reconciliation and reconstruction."[29] Eventually, Dos Santos and Savimbi met in Lusaka and signed the treaty on 6 May 1995. On that occasion Savimbi recognized dos Santos as the president of Angola. He asserted that his struggle was over, that there would be no run-off election, and that he would serve as Angola's vice-president.

Savimbi, more responsible than anybody else for Angola's terrible destruction after twenty-seven years of bitter fighting, honored none of these assertions. The Lusaka protocol, therefore, turned out to be more of a tenuous truce than a peace treaty. Savimbi and his personality cult, UNITA,[30] remained recalcitrant in meeting the terms of the accord. Savimbi's requirement for peace seemed to be some sort of federation which would allow him to administer his stronghold, the agricultural and diamond-rich central highlands, on his own terms. In that way he would be able to promote the interests of the Ovimbundu, Angola's largest nationality group and UNITA's base, as well as counterbalance the role of Angola's other ethnic groups in an Angolan federal government. Indeed, he had formed UNITA in 1966 to ensure that the Ovimbundu would rule Angola after the Portuguese departure from the territory.[31] As long as the peace process denied him this role, Savimbi sought to derail it, believing that his movement was strong enough to avoid defeat by the Angolan forces

United Nations contributions to diplomatic efforts to resolve the Angolan conflict began in December 1988 when the organization created UNAVEM to monitor the phased withdrawal of Cuban troops from Angola. That mission began on 3 January 1989 and was completed on 1 July 1991, thirty-six days ahead of schedule. After the Bicesse Accords (31 May 1991), the UN enlarged and prolonged the mandate of UNAVEM, renamed UNAVEM II, to help verify the cease-fire agreed to in the Bicesse Accords and to monitor elections proposed for September 1992. The enlarged mandate was carried out by a force of 700 military and civilian personnel. As already noted, despite the assurances from UN Special Representative Margaret Anstee and other international observers that the elections were free and fair, Savimbi refused to accept his defeat and resumed the war. Given this situation, UNAVEM II, which had been scheduled to be withdrawn from Angola on 30 November, was reduced to 500 military and eighty civilian staff, and its mandate was extended. The force was later reduced to eighty observers as the war continued.

Negotiations in Addis Ababa (27–30 January 1993) sponsored by the UN and in Abidjan, Côte d'Ivoire (12 April to 27 May 1993) failed to produce a cease-fire. The intransigence of UNITA caused the UN Security Council to impose an embargo on military weapons and petroleum products in areas controlled by the rebel organization. The sanctions were later withdrawn in lieu of the October 1994 UN-sponsored peace talks, chaired by UN Special Representative Alioune Blondin Beye, in Lusaka, Zambia. The talks produced the Lusaka Protocol (20 November) and a cease-fire on 22 November 1994.

Consequently, UNAVEM III, comprising 7,000 troops, was formed. Its mandate was to monitor the cease-fire, supervise the separation of government and UNITA forces, oversee the demobilization of UNITA troops and their integration into the national army, assist in the encampment of troops and clearance of about 10 million land mines, supervise the integration of 5,500 UNITA personnel into the Angolan National Police Force, chair the Joint Commission on the integration of UNITA into the national administration, and deliver humanitarian assistance to about 3.5 million Angolans. UNAVEM III undertook aspects of these tasks, but others and the peace process were delayed by Savimbi's bad faith. After two extensions of its mandate, the mission was withdrawn on 8 July 1996.

After the withdrawal of UNAVEM III, a UN observer mission in Angola (MONUA) was established to assist in the implementation of the provisions of the Lusaka Protocol. It and Alioune Blondin Beye, the UN special representative, too, experienced a series of frustrations in the peace process.[32] Besides, MONUA, three observer countries—Portugal, Russia, and the United States—monitored the implementation of the Lusaka Protocol. Early in June 1998, the three nations were to submit a draft resolution to the UN Security Council, proposing steps to save the peace process and to prevent a renewal of civil war in Angola.[33] On 24 June 1998, the Security Council agreed to allow UNITA until 1 July 1998 to comply with the terms of the Lusaka Protocol. After that date, the Council said it would freeze UNITA's foreign bank accounts and ban its diamond exports unless it relinquished the central highland strongholds and took major steps to demobilize its armed forces. Shortly after the decision, UN Envoy Beye and five members of MONUA died in a plane crash near Abidjan on 26 June 1998 on their mission to advance the peace process in Angola.[34]

It is regrettable that neither Africa as represented by the OAU, a consensus body, nor the outside world sufficiently exerted itself to bring the peace process in Angola to finality. Troops from Zimbabwe, Namibia, and Botswana attempted for more than a year up to the end of 1997 to maintain the cease-fire but could not enforce peace in the troubled African country. Because of pressures from the U.S. government, among other reasons, the UN was unable to invest adequate resources in the peace process to address the legacy of the Cold War and Portuguese colonialism in Angola. Some of its member states failed to fulfill their assessments or pledges to the organization, while others became leery of the fits and starts in the Angolan peace process. Implementation of UN-sponsored measures against UNITA—the closure of its overseas offices, travel restrictions on its leadership, a ban on unauthorized flights into UNITA-held areas, and on the sale of oil and weapons of war—was not strictly carried out by UN member states. After the end of the Cold War, there appeared to be no incentive for the United States, the sole remaining superpower, and its allies to invest in the Angolan peace process since, despite the years of war, their basic interest in the southern African nation, oil, continued to be met. Cuban troops had done a yeoman job during their presence in the country to protect American oil companies against sabotage by rebel forces and the South African government. Altogether, therefore, Angola was the victim of a combination of forces: its own history and internal dynamics, external militaristic intervention during the Cold War, and neglect by the great powers after the end of that war.

Steps towards National Reconciliation

Although the diplomatic initiatives failed to resolve the conflict, they were
definite steps towards national reconciliation. In 1990 the MPLA renounced
Marxism and one-party rule. This paved the way for the 1992 elections, the
results of which were rejected by Savimbi. In 1994 the National Assembly
passed a general amnesty covering all warring parties. Also in 1994, at the
Lusaka peace negotiations, the MPLA offered its goodwill to UNITA, and
subsequently President dos Santos in January 1995 invited Savimbi to meet him
at "any time and any place in Angola." With these steps it was hoped that
Savimbi and his supporters would reciprocate so as to foster national reconciliation and reconstruction.

A number of Savimbi's UNITA supporters did so by deserting him to accept
the government's offers and to participate in a coalition government. Integration
of UNITA troops into the national military began in June 1996. A sizable
demobilization took place as thousands of soldiers turned in their weapons and
were provided with food and other supplies to start a new life. By the end of
1996 nine former UNITA generals relocated to Luanda to assume leadership
positions in the armed forces. In July 1997 the integrated Angolan Armed
Forces (FAA), comprising 90,000 men, 10,000 of whom were former UNITA
soldiers, were officially inaugurated. Earlier, on 11 April 1997, UNITA had
joined the MPLA and ten smaller political parties to form a Government of
Unity and National Reconciliation (GURN). As stipulated by the Lusaka
Protocol, UNITA filled seventy National Assembly seats it had won in the 1992
elections and was also given control of four of twenty-eight ministries and eight
of fifty-five vice-ministries. A position, leader of the largest opposition party,
was created for Savimbi. The perks of the position included a state residence,
a private bodyguard, and regular consultation with President dos Santos.
UNITA representatives in the Angolan Parliament participated vigorously in
debates in July 1997 over a resolution that condemned UNITA for failing to
demobilize in flagrant violation of the Lusaka peace accord. By June 1998
government authority had extended into all but four UNITA-controlled areas.
Thus, by that time, Angola was able to experience its longest period of relative
stability since the departure of Portugal in November 1975.

The desertion of Savimbi's major external supporters—the United States and
South Africa—improved the prospects for peace in Angola. In addition, it was
hoped that the wars in Zaire and Congo-Brazzaville in 1997 would enhance
Angola's prospects for peace. The Angolan Armed Forces intervened in both
wars, which ousted two of Savimbi's regional supporters—the late Mobutu Sese

Seko and Pascal Lissouba from the two countries. The removal of the two effectively shut two backdoors for UNITA's arms and logistical supplies. Savimbi was thus expected to be more inclined to adhere to the Lusaka Protocol and to participate in GURN.

In spite of these positive developments, key obstacles to peace, stability, national reconciliation, and reconstruction in Angola remained. The apparent uncompromising thirst for power and the unrelenting distrust exhibited by MPLA and UNITA leaders for each other comprised one such obstacle. More than two and a half decades of war and disappointment created a monumental mutual distrust in dos Santos and Savimbi. Consequently, the protracted struggle for power and control of national wealth produced in Angola generally, not just in its leaders, a frontier culture which tended to erode traditional African standards of compromise and restraint. Hence, the Lusaka agreement turned out to be more of a truce than an end to the war. Neither dos Santos' government nor Savimbi's UNITA had the "political will" to fully comply with its provisions.

The MPLA government comprised another obstacle. Its leader's power is monumental. It is egregiously corrupt, incompetent, and unpopular. It smothers investigations into corruption in the administration and into divisional and factional fighting within the MPLA. Like UNITA, it is intolerant of opposition. Opposition to the MPLA, before the formation of GURN, was considered a treason. Ever since it took control of Luanda at independence in November 1975, it has been obsessed with the idea of wiping out UNITA. Its ministry of interior operates a dreaded secret police. Its mismanaged socialist policies helped to wreck Angola's economy. Generally, it does not respect the provisions of Angola's 1991 constitution guaranteeing the protection of basic human rights. Not only does it lack the ability to effectively enforce those provisions, it also inhibits independent investigations of human rights abuses. President dos Santos has a tight grip on the media. His government restricts freedom of expression and association. Although it claims that it holds no political opponents in custody, it uses the security forces and the regional governors, appointed by the president as his representatives, routinely to serve its own interests, including the detention and harassment of critics. Although the civilian authorities maintain control of them, the security forces have frequently committed human rights abuses, especially in areas to which the government recently extended its authority and which had been under UNITA control. This is part of the "context" that UNITA termed unfavorable to the extension of state administration to the four areas it controlled.

Another part of that context regarded as unfavorable by UNITA is the judiciary. The Angolan judiciary is not independent of President dos Santos and his MPLA-led government[35] even though the constitution provides for an independent judiciary. President dos Santos has strong appointive powers, including the appointment of Supreme Court justices, with no requirement for confirmation by the National Assembly. Furthermore, the judiciary lacks the means, experience, and training to be truly independent of the president and the ruling coalition government. It does not ensure due process and functions only in parts of the country.

Until his death in February 2002 in a battle with government troops, Savimbi and his future remained the most daunting obstacles to Angola's national reconciliation and reconstruction. He had an unquenchable passion to become president of Angola. That personal ambition overrode any idea of peace and national reconciliation as he demonstrated in his rejection of the results of the 1992 elections. Regarding UNITA's inclusion in GURN as "mere crumbs from the table of power," Savimbi flatly refused to assume the position of leader of the largest opposition party created for him in Luanda, where he insisted that his safety was at risk. In 1997 he proposed that he should be "appointed 'special adviser to the president with executive powers' and that this job description should be written into the Constitution."[36] Dos Santos rejected the idea out of hand. Furthermore, Savimbi consistently showed bad faith to both the UN and President dos Santos as he continued to rearm about 15,000 battle-hardened cadres (through Zambia after the ouster of Mobutu and Lissouba)[37] while negotiating with the organization and the Angolan president. That was how he adeptly manipulated conservative forces and policymakers in Washington during the Carter, Reagan, and Bush administrations with his rhetoric of struggling for the democratization of Angola and fighting against communism in southern Africa to sustain his war-making against the MPLA and his own nation. With no apparent communist and Soviet ideological threat to southern Africa, Savimbi continued the war to remind the government that he had the ability to make Angola ungovernable. All along, Savimbi was able to sustain this behavior in spite of prohibitions by UN Security Council Resolutions 864 (November 1993), 1127 (August 1997), and 1130 (September 1997).[38]

The failure of Angolan national reconciliation during his lifetime is attributed in large part to Savimbi's character. He absolutely refused to convert from military to political leader. He was unable to accept short-term defeat and build a long-term base of support outside his traditional Ovimbundu constituency by exploiting the failures of the MPLA government. However, national reconciliation was also adversely affected by the fact that both sides in the conflict had access to Angola's mineral wealth until late in the 1990s, greater resources and more external allies gave the government a clear military advantage.

Effects and Ramifications of the Conflict

The Angolan conflict had several internal and external effects and ramifications. It affected the course of Soviet-American détente for at least twelve years. Rivalry between the two superpowers escalated the conflict and made Angola a battleground for principles and policies largely irrelevant to its critical needs. Furthermore, the conflict brought about a shift in American policy (from limited involvement, happy to follow the lead of Western European powers, to activism and leadership) towards southern Africa. It also manifested a strange set of alliances. The Soviet Union and Cuba supported the MPLA, while China, the United States, and South Africa supported UNITA. MPLA's Soviet- and Cuban-supported initial victory in the conflict, made possible by the U.S. Congress' exercise of its general legislative powers, foreshadowed the intervention of the two powers in the Ethiopia-Somalia conflict over the Ogaden in 1977. This intervention further undermined the Soviet-American détente.

While not recognizing the MPLA government (until 19 May 1993), the United States maintained trade relations with Angola, became Angola's largest trading partner (largely because Angola's oil was exploited by American companies), and engaged in direct diplomatic negotiations with its representatives. The MPLA used Cuban soldiers (whose presence on Angolan soil American administrations cited to deny the Angolan government diplomatic recognition and to delay the implementation of UN Security Council Resolution 435 [1978] on Namibia) to protect and to guard American oil installations in Angola against UNITA rebels and South African saboteurs. Tensions between the United States and the Soviet Union moderated substantially but without leading to an immediate end of the conflict and the tragedies in Angola.

The war forced the government and the rebel forces into greater dependence on external forces—the MPLA on the Soviet Union and Cuba and the UNITA rebels on the United States and South Africa. Increased Angolan reliance on Cuba and the Soviet Union forced the country into an East-West contest that delayed cooperation with Western-controlled financial institutions, such as the International Monetary Fund and the World Bank, which were essential to the country's economic and social development. Its reliance on Cuban expeditionary forces and Soviet weapons consumed critical revenue Angola needed for its economic and social development.

The war affected every area of Angolan society. Politically, since 1975 when the Portuguese left without formally transferring power to any political group, Angola has had little to celebrate during each independence anniversary beyond its precarious survival. Since then a generation of Angolans born during the war that raged for twenty-seven years has grown up and experienced, more than anything else, the tragedies and ruin of a country at war sustained for so long by external forces and the inordinate political ambitions of selfish leaders. One of Africa's bloodiest, the war cost about two million lives.[39] About 78,000 Angolans—men, women, and children—were maimed, their legs amputated by land mines planted in fields, agricultural lands, and by the roadside. Primary health care services virtually collapsed due to the war and underfunding. Therefore, widespread disease and malnutrition took their toll among the young and the old; one child in four died before the age of five. In many parts of the country, virtually the only medical services available were those provided by international nongovernmental organizations, funded by foreign donors. About one-half of the country's estimated 11 million population became displaced by the war. Angolan refugees in neighboring countries added to the economic and social problems of those states.

As the war dragged on, the MPLA government engaged in acts of political corruption and misrule. Acting with zealotry and callous intolerance, it banned opposition groups, jailed critics, repressed organized religion, and assumed absolute control over the press.[40] For their part, UNITA rebels burned, dismembered, and drowned individuals within and without their movement who were suspected of disloyalty.

In a country where there was no tradition of a strong independent judiciary, the collapsed security situation contributed to the demise of judicial safeguards and due process of the law. Atrocities were thus committed and civilians killed with impunity and no fear of reprisals. Deepening poverty and institutional decay bred conditions for widespread banditry and criminality. This situation was facilitated by three forces: the proliferation of weapons among Angolan nationals, soldiers and civilians alike; the engagement of government security forces in widespread pillage of civilian property during military operations; and the failure of the police and security forces, themselves deeply involved in criminal activity, to investigate crimes.

The war stunted the economic and social development of Angola, apart from the oil industry. Military conscription, by both UNITA and the government, depleted the rural labor force, and many peasant households lost most of their livestock. In this manner the war ravaged Angola's agricultural production,

especially of coffee and food crops, and agroprocessing. Hence, once agricultur-
ally self-sufficient and with the potential to feed much of southern Africa,
Angola now imports food, and in the 1990s it was heavily dependent on
international food aid to the tune of 200,000 tons a year.[41] Coffee production,
a major source of foreign exchange during the years of Portuguese imperial
control, fell from 5.2 million sacks in 1974 to 283,000 sacks in 1983.[42] The
collapse of commercial agriculture and the general decline of economic
activities closed off opportunities for the poorer peasant families who had
insufficient land to meet their food needs to supplement their own production
with income from employment as seasonal or marginal laborers.

UNITA insurgents, using land mines and terrorist tactics, reduced the
security radius in Angola's fertile central highlands. It was unsafe for farmers
to cultivate the land and/or harvest and transport their crops to the markets as
the insurgents effectively shut down road transport, destroyed bridges, and
blocked rail traffic. In effect, war denied Angola a unified national market and
instead promoted "a coastal enclave economy, cut off from the rest of the
country, using oil revenue to import virtually all goods and services."[43] The
major east-west transportation artery, the 800-mile Benguela Railway that
stretches from Angola's Atlantic port of Lobito to Zaire's border with Zambia,
has remained only in partial operation because of UNITA mines and sabotage.
The disruption of the railway deprived the Angolan government of enormous
revenues: It had earned $100 million annually prior to 1975 from Zairean and
Zambian traffic on the line.

The production of diamonds and iron ore also suffered. While the government depended on Western-developed and Western-consumed oil production
to pay for military weapons and keep its economy afloat, UNITA relied on
revenue from smuggling diamonds in order to purchase weapons. It is estimated
that it smuggled $10 million worth of diamonds per week through Zaire in order
to do so.[44]

The government spent more than 50 percent of Angola's oil revenues of
about $2 billion a year on counterinsurgency and defense, including the
maintenance of Cuban troops, whose numbers rose from 15,000 in 1976 to
50,000 in 1988. An estimated $1 billion was spent every year to purchase
military equipment from the Soviet Union.[45] In 1993 the government spent $475
million on the military, $18.5 million on health, and $12 million on education.[46]
Thus, the school system, already suffering from the neglect of colonial years
which left Angola with an illiteracy rate of 95 percent, became more under-
funded and understaffed, thereby crippling the quality and quantity of human

resources needed for Angola's national development. For these reasons and a fall in investment, industrial production also declined sharply.[47]

Even after the death of Savimbi, Angola remains sharply divided. The extension of state administration throughout the country is still incomplete. Thousands of UNITA soldiers remain outside the peace process, and far too many deaths and human rights violations continue on a regular basis.[48] Thousands of the demobilized soldiers on both sides remain a threat to the recovery of the Angolan society. Many, initially recruited as boys, with little, if any, education, are believed to have rejected the idea of scratching out a living at farming and have taken up banditry, a lifestyle closer to what they have grown used to and far more lucrative than farming. Banditry, therefore, has been on the rise, regularly sending ambushed victims on the roads and uncontrolled buffer zones to such Angola's hospitals as those in Huambo and the port city of Lobito.[49] In addition, poorly paid and supervised government soldiers contribute to the increasing wave of criminality. Gun battles between Angolan police and the army occur regularly.[50]

Political and economic stability continues to be hampered by the devastation of the prolonged conflict. The government has neither jobs nor formal schooling for its people, including the demobilized soldiers, despite Angola's vast natural resources—oil, diamond, coffee, cotton, rich farmland—which are enough to make it one of the wealthiest countries in Africa. In 1995, Angola had a staggering $11.3 billion debt and in 1996 an inflation that was estimated at over 1,600 percent.[51] For years, the lack of assurances about the credibility of the peace process obstructed the government's search for funding for its development program and plans for demining, rebuilding bridges and roads, and reopening clinics and schools. In view of these and the probable aftershocks of its massive trauma, the path to peace, stability, reconstruction, and national consolidation in Angola remains an arduous one.

Specifics of U.S. Intervention

U.S. intervention in the Angola conflict was a product of America's immediate post-World War II policy towards non-self-governing territories around the world. That policy sought to contain the spread of communism and Soviet socialist ideology, to preserve America's sources of vital raw materials, and to protect America's friends and allies. To promote these goals in regions such as Africa, where it had few direct responsibilities, the United States supported Western European colonial powers in order to strengthen their control over their colonial territories. In spite of the Franklin D. Roosevelt-sponsored Atlantic

Charter (August 1941), those powers were assured that the United States had no intention of promoting a premature grant of independence to their colonies. Initiated by the Harry S. Truman administration, the policy was influenced by two geopolitical considerations: Portugal was a NATO ally from which the United States leased its strategic base at Azores and which therefore the United States could ill afford to alienate. The policy was continued by Truman's immediate successor, Dwight Eisenhower. Consequently, during his administration the United States played no constructive role in mediating or resolving the anticolonial struggle in Portuguese colonies, including Angola. Instead, it provided Portugal, as a NATO ally, the military aid and counterinsurgency training it needed to suppress nationalist movements. In addition, it provided diplomatic support within and outside the United Nations. For example, in December 1960, the administration ordered the U.S. ambassador to the UN to abstain from voting on General Assembly Resolution 1514, which called for self-determination in colonial territories.

John F. Kennedy, who succeeded Eisenhower, faced, in addition to the realities that had confronted his predecessors, an escalating crisis in the Democratic Republic of the Congo (DRC) that was perceived solely in terms of the ongoing East-West ideological conflict. Given this, the decolonization of Angola became part of his ordeal in Africa as he sought to balance American geopolitical and security interests with a U.S. commitment to self-determination and independence for all people. His administration reasoned that change in Africa was inexorable and that any attempt to block it would only benefit the communists.[52] Therefore, because Portugal would probably be unable to hold onto Angola forever, the United States should support UN measures to promote self-determination in Portuguese colonies and to establish contact with a possible successor regime. This was the rationale for U.S. linkage with, and modest assistance to, the Holden Roberto-led FNLA. The same rationale motivated the Kennedy administration's symbolic affirmative vote on a UN Security Council resolution introduced by Liberia to promote self-determination in Portuguese colonies. The affirmative vote received mixed domestic and international reactions. Conservatives and Republican senators criticized it as the product of "misguided idealism" and the wrong way to treat an ally. Robert D. Murphy, former undersecretary of state in the Eisenhower administration, condemned the vote as a "matter of deep concern" that the United States had joined the Soviet Union to vote against its own ally.[53] Liberals and civil rights advocates praised the vote. "At long last," asserted a *New York Times* editorial, "the United States will determine its own political priorities in respect to the colonial (and ex-colonial) areas, and will not necessarily be bound by the policies of other countries, even [its] closest allies."[54]

Overseas, the inflexible and obsolescent Portuguese dictator Antonio de Oliveira Salazar vehemently denounced the vote as a betrayal and maintained that Angola was a domestic issue that warranted no international scrutiny and interference. British and French leaders joined him to admonish President Kennedy to refrain from provoking Portugal and encouraging violent radicalism throughout Africa.

The Kennedy administration was not deterred. It capitalized on the disenchantment within the Portuguese military with Salazar's domestic and colonial policy to encourage high-ranking officers to foment an overthrow of Salazar's regime and to change colonial policies in return for economic assistance. Laxity on the part of the officers foiled the plot. Kennedy, on the other hand, supplied arms to FNLA, initiated an educational program at Lincoln University in Pennsylvania in 1962 for exiled Angolans, and supported UN resolutions calling for decolonization, among other goals, in Angola and other Portuguese colonies. When these produced no positive results, Dean Rusk, the administration's Secretary of State, set up a Task Force on Portuguese Territories in Africa in June 1962 to recommend how the administration could deal with Portugal. Chaired by the Assistant Secretary of State for African affairs, G. Mennen Williams, the task force recommended that the administration unequivocally oppose Portugal's policy and recognize, at the appropriate time, a provisional Angolan government. In addition, the Task Force recommended that the administration should

1. send an envoy to Portugal to inform Salazar that the United States expected far-reaching colonial reforms;
2. convince France and Britain to coordinate pressure on Portugal;
3. explore whether the Vatican, Spain, and Brazil would be willing to intercede;
4. formulate an agenda for U.S. activities at the UN;
5. respond favorably to any reasonable request for economic assistance to Portugal if the regime liberalized its colonial policy; and
6. act discreetly in these matters in order to minimize the possibility of losing the base at the Azores.[55]

Subsequently, the recommendations were promulgated in a National Security Action Memorandum 60—the highest form of presidential authorization in foreign policy—in spite of the fears of the Pentagon that the policy could undermine U.S. capability to respond to crises in Europe, the Middle East, and Africa.[56] After approval by Kennedy, the Department of State began to implement the suggestions. In response to revelations about U.S.-NATO weapons being used by the Salazar regime in Angola, Kennedy asked Dean Rusk to halt U.S. military assistance to the Portuguese-NATO division.

U.S. Policy on Angola and the Azores Bases

The Kennedy administration was concerned about U.S. security interests in a united NATO and U.S. access to the Azores bases leased from Portugal. The bases, whose lease was to expire in December 1962, were militarily significant for refueling and communications and antisubmarine surveillance. They had been used in a succession of crises: in 1958 to shuttle U.S. marines to Lebanon, to move American troops and equipment to Berlin in the fall of 1961, and to transport thousands of UN troops to the Congo in 1960 and 1961. The Joint Chiefs of Staff considered them indispensable in an emergency build-up of Western forces in Europe or the Middle East. Kennedy's goal was to preserve these interests while at the same time pursuing the Angola policy and thus enhancing American standing in Africa and the UN. Both interests were to be served at the same time.[57] The thorny problem was that Salazar not only flatly refused to compromise on Angola but also adamantly linked the American lease on the mid-Atlantic Azores bases to U.S. policy on Angola. That was his most significant trump card.

The advice President Kennedy received on how to resolve the policy issue was diametrically conflicting. The Pentagon, the former Secretary of State, Dean Acheson, C. Burke Elbreck, U.S. ambassador to Portugal, and congressional critics fed Portuguese propaganda by a Portuguese-retained New York public relations firm—Salvage and Lee—insisted that the administration had no choice but to yield to Salazar in order to retain the lease on the Azores. Acheson, the leading advocate of this position and the most vocal critic of Kennedy's Angola policy, openly doubted that Africans had the capacity to rule themselves. Opposing this view, Adlai Stevenson, U.S. ambassador to the UN, G. Mennen Williams, and other advocates of a constructive Angola policy argued that the Kennedy administration should firmly resist Portuguese efforts to link the Azores to U.S. policy on Angola. It should, rather, "insist that the Azores base is vital not only to the defense of the United States but to all NATO [countries], including Portugal [and] should be treated as a NATO matter."[58] Chester Bowles, Undersecretary of State, preferred turning the Azores base over to NATO. Portugal, in his view, could leave the Alliance if it found the idea reprehensible. The Deputy Assistant Secretary of State for African affairs, Wayne Fredericks, went further and suggested that the administration did not need to bother. In case of war, the United States, he opined, could seize the Azores and use them as it wished.[59]

Kennedy was not convinced by the military arguments. Secretary of Defense Robert S. McNamara held that the military necessity of access to the Azores must remain preeminent and that further public pressure on the Portuguese regarding the use of American-supplied equipment in Angola should be avoided, but Kennedy ordered the revocation of several commercial licenses granted by the Department of Defense to sell arms to Portugal. Additional warnings sent to Salazar to effect immediate political changes in Angola received no positive response. Kennedy seriously contemplated the probable political consequences—at home and overseas—of losing the Azores. It was at that stage that Secretary of State Rusk, who had looked askance at the administration's Angola policy, proposed the "postponement of all discussions and action on Angola pending a settlement of the Azores question."[60] Rusk proceeded to Lisbon for a twenty-two hour visit after visiting the capitals of the leading Western European nations. He met Salazar for two hours and presented the Portuguese leader his proposal. First, Portugal should accept the UN appointment of an internationally recognized figure as a rapporteur to investigate, with full Portuguese cooperation, conditions in Angola. This, he assured him, was a means of splitting the Afro-Asian bloc. Second, he told Salazar that the Azores would be negotiated after a complete review of bilateral relations. The deal was struck.

Thus, the Kennedy administration capitulated to Portugal on the colonial question in Angola in September 1962 when it reassured Salazar that its efforts had been designed not to force Portugal out of Africa but to encourage measures that would enable it to complete the work it had begun in the continent. Foreign policy tends to require some trade-offs. In this case the Kennedy administration subordinated its interest in legitimate national self-determination and decolonization in Angola to U.S. national security interests in the Azores and NATO alliance. Following this trade-off and reassurance of the Portuguese, the administration ceased all contact with Roberto and other African nationalists in Portuguese-occupied Africa. In the UN it voted against two Security Council resolutions that called for self-determination and independence for Angola and economic sanctions and arms embargo against Portugal.[61] Portugal continued to use U.S.-supplied weapons in its African wars, and Salazar refused to renew the agreement on the Azores, extending the terms only for one year.

Following the assassination of President Kennedy in November 1963, President Lyndon B. Johnson inherited the administration's policy of capitulation to Portugal on the Angolan colonial question. To him the NATO alliance and the Azores were so important to U.S. national security interests that he concluded they could not be compromised by continued pressure on Portugal to decolonize Angola. Therefore, he encouraged a moderate and evolutionary settlement to the colonial question in the whole of Portuguese-controlled Africa. Furthermore, his escalation of U.S. involvement in Vietnam after 1964 and his subsequent domestic difficulties absorbed his administration's energies almost exclusively. Portugal, which became one of the administration's staunchest supporters in that war, was provided training for its military personnel as well as other military and economic assistance amounting to $28.4 million and $54.9 million, respectively, between 1963 and 1968.[62] Angola, on the other hand, was put on the back burner during the administration's tenure, which ended in January 1969.

The Angola Policy: From Nixon to Clinton

President Johnson's successor, Richard M. Nixon, put Angola even further back on the back burner after his review of U.S. policy towards white minority-controlled southern Africa. His open support for Portugal, dating from his years as vice-president in the Eisenhower administration, was reinforced by the recommendations of Option II of an interagency study he and Henry Kissinger, his adviser on national security, had commissioned in 1969. As noted above and in Chapter 4, Option II of the study asserted that the white minority regimes were in southern Africa to stay, that they alone were capable of bringing about positive change to the region; that the nationalist forces seeking to overthrow them violently were incapable of doing so but would only create opportunity for the Soviets to fish in the region's troubled waters. Therefore, the administration should materially and diplomatically support the minority regimes and so reduce a major irritant in U.S. relations with Portugal.

In view of his perception of the centrality of the Azores base to U.S. relations with Portugal and to NATO, President Nixon began to implement this recommendation in 1970. By December 1971 his administration concluded an executive agreement with Portugal, renewing the lease on the Azores until February 1974. Consequently, Portugal was granted U.S. economic and military assistance, including the training of its military personnel, sale of aircraft and other dual-purpose equipment, defoliants, and strategic intelligence. In addition, the administration encouraged U.S. private capital investment in Angola. As a whole the official and private assistance enormously facilitated Portugal's war and counterinsurgency operations in Angola. The administration assisted Portugal even further diplomatically by vetoing or abstaining from every UN Security Council and General Assembly resolution concerning Portugal's colonial wars. It assumed that Portugal was effectively containing the nationalists in Angola and its other colonies in Africa. However, to the administration's surprise, Marcello Caeteno's Portuguese government was overthrown by war-weary officers of the Portuguese Armed Forces in April 1974. That event ultimately brought about the collapse of the Portuguese colonial empire in Africa.

Other specifics of U.S. role in the war during the administrations of Gerald Ford, Jimmy Carter, Ronald Reagan, and George H.W. Bush have been discussed above. Here, a recapitulation of the most salient aspects of the role of the administrations is in order. Following the collapse of Portuguese colonial empire in Africa, the Ford administration began a major covert operation in Angola that was designed to promote America's ideological and geopolitical interests and to prevent the African country from falling under imagined Soviet domination. First, using the CIA, it undermined a 15 January 1975 agreement at Alvor, Portugal, for a transitional government and independence process which Portugal had worked out with the three Angolan nationalist movements. Unwilling to allow a negotiated settlement among the Angolan factions at the early stages of the conflict, the administration did not stop there. Rather, it proceeded to derail an agreement leaders of the three movements had signed in June 1975 at Nakura, Kenya, under the auspices of the OAU and the chairmanship of Kenyan President Jomo Kenyatta. Its strategic intelligence arm, the CIA, spent more than $1 million recruiting mercenaries to fight for the FNLA/UNITA alliance which it had forged. Furthermore, the CIA trained FNLA/UNITA combat units and carried out a disinformation campaign against the MPLA and its Cuban and Soviet supporters.[63] U.S. military personnel carried out reconnaissance flights and supply missions for the FNLA/UNITA alliance and collaborated with the government of South Africa to ferry American military aid from Zaire into Angola for the alliance.

In addition to these measures, Henry Kissinger, President Ford's secretary of state, urged Gulf Oil Corporation to discontinue its royalty payments to the MPLA. Kissinger did so in spite of the fact that the MPLA had mandated the oil company to continue its exclusive operation in Cabinda and had guaranteed the safety of the company's employees. Gulf resisted Kissinger's pressures but was compelled to put the payments into an escrow bank account when Kissinger threatened to investigate an alleged international bribery by the Corporation. Kissinger capped his intervention measures by dismissing from office Assistant Secretary of State for African affairs, Donald Easum, for opposing U.S. covert intervention in the Angolan war of political succession. He replaced him with Nathaniel Davis. This action caused domestic uproar among Africanist scholars and much consternation in Africa for Davis had served as ambassador to Chile in 1973 when Kissinger arranged the military overthrow and assassination of President Salvador Allende. Davis resigned on 31 August 1975 in protest against covert military assistance totaling $24.7 million to FNLA and UNITA.[64] By these measures, the Ford administration deliberately plunged Angola into war as it armed FNLA and UNITA, assisted by the apartheid regime in South Africa and Mobutu of Zaire, to fight the MPLA. In turn, the MPLA sought and obtained military assistance from Cuba and the Soviet Union.

As the war escalated, Portugal annulled the Alvor Accords, dissolved the transition government, and called off the elections scheduled for October 1975. The U.S.-supported FNLA/UNITA and South Africa/Zaire alliance waged war in order to seize Luanda, the capital, before 11 November 1975, the date of independence. With the assistance of Cuban expeditionary forces and Soviet logistical and military support, MPLA held the capital. On 11 November Portuguese officials proclaimed the independence of Angola without handing over power to any of the nationalist movements. Already controlling the capital, MPLA assumed that power. It held its ground with the aid of more Cuban troops. Its victory, though precarious, was assured by the passage of Clark/Tunney Amendments to the Defense Appropriation and Security Assistance Acts of 1976, prohibiting "assistance of any kind" (promoting or augmenting military or paramilitary operations) to any of the factions in the Angolan conflict.[65] In view of the prohibition, South Africa also terminated its intervention.

The Ford administration vehemently protested against the prohibition, arguing that it deprived the president of flexibility in formulating a foreign policy that was in America's national security interest.[66] It refused to extend diplomatic recognition to Angola so long as Cuban troops remained there and abstained from voting when the UN admitted the new nation into its membership on 1 December 1976.

During the 1976 presidential election campaigns, Jimmy Carter, who eventually succeeded President Ford, said that he intended to normalize U.S.

relations with Angola.[67] As president-elect, he reiterated that intention. During his confirmation hearings before the Senate Foreign Relations Committee, his UN Ambassador-Designate, Andrew Young, expressed a similar intention when he asserted that Cuban military forces in Angola were a force for stability and order in the African country. Cyrus Vance, Carter's secretary of state, favored delinking U.S. relations with Angola from the ideological struggle with the Soviet Union and its allies. He advocated an affirmative and constructive approach to Africa that avoided East-West confrontations and responded to problems in their local realities.[68] Although, according to this view, the Carter administration conducted negotiations with the Angolan government, it maintained the Ford administration policy of nonrecognition of the Angolan government before the withdrawal of Cuban troops. This outcome was a consequence of the influence of Carter's national security adviser, Zbigniew Brzezinski, a globalist who believed in responding to crises in Third World countries on the basis of the East-West ideological struggle. He was, therefore, totally opposed to any normalization of relations with Angola so long as Cuban forces remained in the country.[69]

This position, which proved decisive for President Carter's denial of formal recognition to the Angolan government, was hardened when in March 1977 the Congo National Liberation Front (FNLC), based in Angola, invaded Zaire's Shaba province. Although that invasion and a subsequent one in May 1978 were repulsed by a coalition of French, Belgian, and Moroccan forces, the Carter administration blamed it on Cuba and the Soviet Union. Furthermore, when the Soviet Union and Cuba intervened in the Ogaden War (1977–1978) between Ethiopia and Somalia, the administration contemplated providing military assistance to UNITA and advocated a repeal of the Clark Amendment, which it complained had constrained its ability to compete with the Soviet Union in Africa.[70] Globalists in the administration and neoconservative forces in the nation, such as the American Heritage Foundation, Freedom House, Social Democrats (U.S.A), and the Committee on the Present Danger, urged it to renew such assistance to UNITA.

Cyrus Vance and Andrew Young in the administration and critics of the administration's policy persisted in their advocacy of an affirmative and constructive Angola policy including normalization of relations between Angola and Zaire, a Namibia settlement under UN auspices, and diplomatic recognition of Angola prior to the withdrawal of Cuban troops. Toward these ends, the administration began direct and formal communications with the MPLA government that culminated in normalization of relations between Angola and

Zaire and negotiations involving the UN Contact Group of Five nations, Angola, and the Republic of South Africa on the independence of Namibia. The Group was led by U.S. Ambassador to the UN, Donald McHenry, and British Foreign Secretary, David Owen. The negotiations produced an agreement that became the basis of UN Security Council Resolution 435 (1978) for the independence of Namibia. These positive outcomes did not result in normalization of U.S.-Angolan relations, nor did they prevent conservatives like Jesse Helms in Congress from mounting efforts in 1980 to repeal the Clark Amendment. The attempts reflected frustration at developments in such Third World countries as Nicaragua, Afghanistan, Iran, and the Horn of Africa during 1977–1980 which the Carter administration was unable to contain.

Upon succeeding President Carter in January 1981, Ronald Reagan desired to overthow what he believed were revolutionary regimes in the Third World and to reverse perceived Soviet geopolitical gains made possible by those regimes.[71] To do so he enunciated a policy—the Reagan doctrine—to aid rebels, labeled "freedom fighters," seeking to overthrow such regimes assisted by Soviet and Cuban governments. Leading members of his administration, including CIA Director William Casey, National Security Adviser Richard Allen, Secretary of State Alexander Haig, and Defense Secretary Casper Weinberger, had direct contact with UNITA leadership, promising it U.S. material support, regardless of the Clark Amendment.[72]

Following this, the administration embarked upon a fourfold strategy to deal with the Angolan situation. First, it renewed U.S.-South African military contacts and adopted a policy of constructive engagement with the government of the Republic of South Africa as developed by the Assistant Secretary of State for Africa, Chester A. Crocker. This policy virtually gave South Africa a free hand to continue its destabilization of Angola and its neighboring states while at the same time it defended such acts in international forums. South Africa thus escalated its support for UNITA against the Angolan government. Second, the administration explicitly encouraged South Africa, Saudi Arabia, Morocco, Israel, and Zaire to lend material assistance to UNITA.[73] Consequently, the administration shipped arms through Honduras, Belgium, and Switzerland to South Africa. These arms were then sent to UNITA, while Saudi Arabia, starting in 1981, supplied Morocco with $50–$70 million annually for training UNITA military personnel. For its part, Israel trained UNITA forces in Namibia and Zaire in return for U.S. high-tech weapons. Third, the administration adopted a policy of linkage, linking both the normalization of U.S.-Angolan relations and the implementation of UN Security Council Resolution 435 regarding the independence of Namibia with the withdrawal of Cuban troops from Angola. Angola rejected such linkage. It insisted that South African military forces which necessitated the presence of the Cubans must first withdraw from its territory.

The Reagan administration embarked on the fourth strategy in 1985 because of growing Cuban military presence in Angola in response to its own covert activities against the Angolan government. In that year, President Reagan persuaded Congress to repeal the Clark Amendment. To do so, he worked in concert with conservative forces and agents lobbying for UNITA and powerful voices in the Pentagon urging U.S. resolve to stand up to the Soviets in a regional conflict. Thenceforth, to avoid scrutiny by Congress, President Reagan provided UNITA only covert military support, which included antiaircraft missiles and weapons, 106 mm recoilless rifles, ammunition, and fuel. The assistance effectively abetted the military cooperation between the rebel movement and South African Defense Force inside Angola. The voices of human rights activists, mainstream media, and the Congressional Black Caucus against the covert support were completely ignored. Therefore, the covert assistance continued beyond the Reagan administration into that of George H.W. Bush, costing the U.S. Treasury more than $110 million from 1986 to 1989.

While part of the rationale for the military assistance to UNITA was to make Soviet support for Angola more costly, the goal was to bring about the collapse of the Angolan political economy and the ascendancy of the Jonas Savimbi-led UNITA. Needless to say, neither goal was achieved, but the policy compromised U.S. credibility as a mediator in African conflict resolution.

Meanwhile, the administration had initiated direct bilateral negotiations with the Angolan government by January 1982 on its linkage policy and a specific timetable for the withdrawal of Cuban troops. The Angolan government maintained its position on the policy. The Angolan war, thanks to U.S. military support and South Africa's destabilization measures, continued, devastating the Angolan population, economy, infrastructure, and ecology, and forcing the government into greater dependence on Cuba and the Soviet Union. Ironically, while South Africa and right-wing groups such as the American Heritage Foundation and the United States-Namibian Trade and Cultural Council were sabotaging the operations of U.S. firms and investments in Angola, the Reagan administration encouraged such operations and investments. Crocker asserted that such operations served as a moderating influence on the Angolan government and worked to discourage Soviet and Cuban presence in Angola. At the same time the United States became Angola's largest trading partner.

In February 1984 Crocker mediated an agreement between Angola and South Africa at Lusaka, Zambia. Because of the high cost of its military incursions into Angola, the South African government concluded that the conflict in Angola and Namibia could be resolved politically rather than by military force. The consequent Lusaka Accords called for the disengagement of South African and Angolan forces in southern Angola and the establishment of a joint South African-Angolan team to supervise the withdrawal of South Africa's troops. South Africa failed to abide by the terms of the agreement. The agreement collapsed by June 1984 and the conflict simmered. On 7 October 1985 the United States joined other members of the UN Security Council to condemn South Africa for its military incursions into Angolan territory. It did so again in November 1987 when the Security Council demanded that South Africa cease its continued and intensified acts of aggression against Angola.

Definitive diplomatic negotiations took place after South Africa, having suffered a military defeat at Cuito Cuanavale, Angola, in June 1988, decided to seek a political solution. The new ideas of Mikhail Gorbachev regarding restructuring Soviet political economy and reducing Soviet military involvement in the Third World contributed to the general atmosphere and outcome of the negotiations. Formal agreements on the timetable for the withdrawal of Cuban troops from Angola and the independence of Namibia under UN Security Council Resolution 435 were signed at the UN headquarters in New York on 22 December 1988.

The agreements did not end U.S. covert assistance to UNITA. In spite of demands by liberal members of Congress to end such assistance and to normalize relations with the Angolan government, the covert assistance continued. President George H.W. Bush had determined that he would not allow an Angolan government victory on the battlefield. Therefore, after his inauguration on 20 January 1989, he honored his postelection pledge to continue to provide UNITA all "appropriate" and effective assistance until a political settlement, acceptable to the United States, between it and the Angolan government was achieved. Within the first year of his administration, he provided UNITA with $50 million in military assistance.

However, despite its military support to UNITA, the Bush administration sustained its communication with the Angolan government in order to persuade it to negotiate a reconciliation with Savimbi.[74] The administration also indicated its willingness to establish a low-level diplomatic representation in Luanda and to end its opposition to Angola's application for membership in the International Monetary Fund and the World Bank. Negotiations for national reconciliation were held in June 1989 at Gbadolite, Zaire. Arranged by President Kenneth Kaunda of Zambia and hosted by Mobutu in the presence of representatives of eighteen African countries, the negotiations produced a peace plan calling for an end to the war, a commitment to national reconciliation, a temporary exile for Savimbi, integration of UNITA into existing government structures, and the establishment of a mechanism to implement the plan. Shortly after the Gbadolite summit, Savimbi repudiated the terms of the plan. Efforts to revive the plan failed due to Savimbi's insistence on his own plan for a transitional government and free and fair elections, which the Bush administration supported. By the end of the year heavy fighting resumed. The Gbadolite efforts collapsed completely by mid-January 1990.

After the collapse of the Gbadolite peace plan and the renewed fighting, Portugal, the former colonial power, worked to bring the Angolan government and UNITA together to find a solution to the conflict. In the process Portugal demonstrated greater neutrality than the U.S. administrations had done. Its series of efforts in the renewed negotiation process were supported and assisted by the Bush administration even though the administration simultaneously requested from Congress additional covert funding for UNITA. To counteract both this and the relentless U.S.-UNITA destabilization measures, the Angolan government introduced a number of reforms. It liberalized the Angolan economy, abandoned Marxism-Leninism, and declared its intention to institute a multiparty system. These reforms and the rapidly changing U.S.-Soviet relations enhanced the negotiation process to the extent that after both the United States and the Soviet Union had held discussions with each of the warring Angolan leaders, general principles for a peace settlement were hammered out in December 1990. The five parties involved in the negotiation process—the Angolan government, UNITA, Portugal, the United States, and the Soviet Union—accepted those principles. The Angolan government and UNITA, having agreed to a cease-fire set for 15 May and to hold general elections between September and November 1992, signed the resultant Bicesse Accords on 31 May 1991.

The Bush administration expected that Savimbi would win the national elections. Thus, it continued to support UNITA by providing it with more than $30 million in covert funding through the CIA.[75] It also maintained contact with the Angolan government, opened a liaison office in Luanda on 10 June 1991, and allowed the Angolan government to establish an Observer Mission at the headquarters of the Organization of American States in Washington, DC.

As discussed above, the national elections were held over two days (29–30 September 1992). Savimbi rejected the results, ignoring overtures by both the United States and the UN to accept the international community's determination regarding those results. He chose to renew the war, mounting attacks on Luanda and on major Angolan provinces and cities. The Bush administration blamed the postelection violence on the government and its "winner-takes-all" attitude and called for a settlement that included power sharing. Implicitly, by refusing to extend diplomatic recognition to the freely elected Angolan government, it encouraged Savimbi to reject the run-off election and to persist in his defiance and war mongering, using U.S. weapons he had stockpiled prior to the elections.

Savimbi intensified his military operations in January 1993, threatening U.S. companies and economic interests in Cabinda. He thwarted efforts at peace negotiations at Addis Ababa, Ethiopia, throughout January and February. By April he accepted to resume negotiations at Abidjan, Côte d'Ivoire, because of pressures from the UN, the succeeding Clinton administration, and Congress. However, those negotiations collapsed when Savimbi rejected the terms of the proposed peace plan. He insisted that the Angolan government should accept the new military reality in the country, power sharing, and decentralization. Upon the collapse of the peace talks, President Clinton extended diplomatic recognition to Angola on 19 May 1993. He expressed his hope that UNITA would accept a negotiated settlement and would become part of the Angolan government. Savimbi dashed those hopes. Doing so ended his alliance with U.S. administrations as well as America's eighteen years of total hostility towards the government of Angola.

Conclusion

The United States was not neutral in the Angola war of political succession. It did not play the role of an honest broker from the colonial beginnings of the conflict and throughout its duration. The consequences of U.S. intervention are incalculable in terms of bloodshed, human anguish and suffering, and squandered material resources. The intervention exacerbated and prolonged the conflict. It contributed enormously to the death toll, human suffering, damage to the economy and infrastructure, the education and health systems, agriculture and food production brought about by the war. It stalled all aspects of economic and human development in the southern African nation and for years made the Angolan government more dependent on Cuba and the Soviet Union.

Given the outcome of the war, U.S. intervention was a colossal and tragic miscalculation on all accounts. American resources were squandered over seventeen years. For example, through the CIA and its secret contingency funds, $31.7 million was spent procuring arms for FNLA/UNITA during the first year of the war. This amount does not include several million dollars for the salaries and operational expenses of the hundreds of CIA employees and the CIA facilities involved in the intervention program charged to the agency's 1976 FY personnel and support budget. In addition, $15–$60 million a year was spent supporting Savimbi from 1986 to 1990. The U.S. client Savimbi proved by his actions that he was neither the democrat he professed to be nor the freedom fighter U.S. administrators declared he was. He murdered his colleagues who disagreed with his views. He returned to war rather than accept the results of an election he had lost and which had been certified by the UN and international observers as free and fair. He was killed in February 2002, fighting against Angolan government forces without achieving his political goals that had been nurtured and encouraged by U.S. administrations.

The intervention served no positive U.S. national security interest. The United States had little or nothing to gain. At the time, beyond the Robusta coffee it sold to American markets and the relatively small quantity of petroleum Gulf Oil Corporation pumped from Cabinda, Angola was of little, if any, importance to U.S. national security and economy. Major U.S. private interests, such as Gulf Oil Corporation, Boeing, and Mobil were not threatened by the MPLA but were indeed negotiating business deals with it. The intervention was a manifestation of Kissinger's fascination with geostrategic theorizing as well as his preoccupation with any perceived attempt by the Soviet Union to expand its global reach. He rejected the advice of his top assistants to seek diplomatic solutions in Angola and instead pushed the CIA into covert operation in the African nation. Kissinger saw the Angolan conflict "solely in terms of global politics. He was unalterably determined to ensure that the Soviets would not be permitted to make a move in any remote part of the world without being confronted militarily by the United States.

The intervention had elements of incongruity. U.S. administrations bonded with the government of the Republic of South Africa—condemned by the UN as illegally occupying Namibia, detested at home and abroad because of its policy of apartheid, trampling on the fundamental rights of the vast majority of its population—in order to intervene in Angola. This was damaging to America's credibility in Africa. Equally damaging and incongruous was the fact that after it had blocked executive branch's covert operations in Angola,

Congress reversed itself, and its members allowed themselves to be co-opted by Presidents Reagan and Bush the elder in their covert and destructive activities in Angola. Deference to the executive branch inhibited Congress from performing its constitutional role as coequal manager of American foreign policy. These elements of the policy's incongruity were fostered by the paucity of powerful constituencies in the United States for African countries. Because TransAfrica and the Christian church-sponsored Washington Office on Africa devoted more effort to ending apartheid in South Africa, they exerted little or no pressure to prevent the Reagan-Bush administrations' covert activities to assist UNITA. On the other hand, conservatives, including the Cuban American National Foundation, eager to bleed and humiliate Cuban military forces in Angola, lobbied Congress to support UNITA.[76]

If the geostrategic and ideological goal of the intervention was to deny Angola to the Soviet bloc, the intervention should have terminated after the end of the Cold War, the disintegration of the Soviet Union, the withdrawal of Cuban troops, and the transformation of Angola from a Marxist-Leninist state to a capitalist one. That did not occur. Instead, U.S. material, military, diplomatic, and financial support for Savimbi continued after these developments. In the final analysis. the intervention did not in any demonstrable way promote any vital national security interest of the United States.

Notes

1. Tony Hodges, *Angola from Afro-Stalinism to Petro-Diamond Capitalism* (Bloomington: Indiana University Press, 2001); A. W. Pereira, "The Neglected Tragedy: The Return to War in Angola, 1992–3," *The Journal of Modern African Studies*, Vol 32, No. 1 (1994), pp. 1–28; John A. Marcum, "Angola: War Again," *Current* History, Vol. 92, No. 574 (May 1993), p. 218; John A. Marcum, *The Angola Revolution* (Cambridge, MA: MIT, 1978); Christine M. Knudson with I. William Zartman, "The Large Small War in Angola," *The American Academy of Political and Social Science,* 541 (September 1995), pp. 130–143; Raymond Copson, *Africa's Wars and Prospects for Peace* (Armonk, NY: M.E. Sharpe, 1994); Anthony G. Pazzanita, "The Conflict Resolution Process in Angola," *The Journal of Modern African Studies*, Vol. 29, No. 1 (March 1991), pp. 83–114; I. William Zartman, *Ripe for Resolution: Conflict and Intervention in Africa* (NY: Oxford University, 1989); James S. Coleman and Richard Sklar (eds.), *African Crisis Areas and U.S. Foreign Policy* (Berkeley: University of California Press, 1985); Arthur Gavshon, *Crisis in Africa: Battleground for East and West* (New York: Harmondsworth, 1981); Tony Hodges, *After Angola: The War over Southern Africa* (New York: Penguin, 1976); R. LeMarchand (ed.), *American Policy in Southern Africa: The Stakes and the Stance* (Washington, DC: University Press of America, 1978).

2. Arthur J. Klinghoffer, *The Angolan War: A Study of Soviet Policy in the Third World* (Boulder, CO: Westview, 1980), p. 2.

3. Quoted in Gerald J. Bender, *Angola Under the Portuguese: The Myth and the Reality* (Berkeley: University of California Press, 1978), p. xix; see also p. 147.

4. For details on the ethnic division within Angolan society, see Zak Laidi, *The Superpowers and Africa* (Chicago: University of Chicago, 1990), pp. 59–65; Knudsen and Zartman, "The Large Small War in Angola," pp. 132–133.

5. John Marcum, "Angola: Perilous Transition to Independence," in G.M. Carter and P. O'Meara (eds.), *Southern Africa: The Continuing Crisis* (Bloomington: Indiana University Press, 1982), p. 185.

6. William Minter (ed.), *Operation Timber: Pages from the Savimbi Dossier* (Trenton, NJ: Africa World, 1988), p. 7; James Ciment, *Angola and Mozambique: Postcolonial Wars in Southern Africa* (New York: Facts on File, 1997), pp. 94–116.

7. See Mohamed A. El-Khawas and Barry Cohen (eds.), *National Security Memorandum 39: The Kissinger Study of Southern Africa* (Westport, CT: Lawrence Hill, 1976); John A. Marcum, "Lessons of Angola," *Foreign Affairs*, Vol. 54, No. 3 (April 1976), pp. 407–425.

8. Quoted in Klinghoffer, *The Angolan War*, p. 32.

9. Ted Galen Carpenter, "The New World Disorder," *Foreign Policy*, No. 84 (Fall 1991), p. 34; Chester A. Crocker, "The United States and Angola," *Current Policy,* No. 796 Washington, D.C.: U.S. Department of State, Bureau of Public Affairs, 18 Feb. 1986).

10. *The Washington Post* (12 January,. 1989), p. 1; Pauline Baker, "The American Challenge in Southern Africa," *Current History*, Vol. 888, No. 538 (May 1989), p. 211; Marcum, "Lessons of Angola," p. 169; Richard Hull, "United States Policy in Southern Africa," *Current History*, Vol. 89, No. 547 (May 1990), pp. 193–196, 228–231.

11. See Charles W. Freeman, Jr. "The Angola/Namibia Accords," *Foreign Affairs*, Vol. 68, No. 3 (Summer 1989), pp. 125–141; Chester A. Crocker, "Southern Africa: Eight Years Later," *Foreign Affairs*, Vol. 68, No. 4 (Fall 1989), pp. 144–164.

12. Phyllis M. Martin, "Peace in Angola," *Current History*, Vol. 88, No. 538 (May 1989), pp. 229–232, 246–248.

13. John A. Marcum, "Africa: A Continent Adrift," *Foreign Affairs*, Vol. 68, No. 1 (1988/89), pp. 163/164.

14. Chester A. Crocker, "South Africa: Strategy for Change," *Foreign Affairs*, (Winter 1980/81), pp. 323-351; Hebert Howe, "United States Policy in Southern Africa," *Current History*, Vol. 85, No. 511 (May 1986), pp. 206–208, 232–234; Lisa Alfred, "U.S. Foreign Policy and the Angolan Peace," *Africa Today* (1st and 2nd Quarters 1992), pp.73–88.

15. For details, see Horace Campbell, "The Military Defeat of South Africans in Angola," *Monthly Review*, Vol. 40, No. 11 (April 1989), pp. 1–15; Marcum, "Lessons of Angola," pp. 164–166.

16. "Dossier: Southern African Accords," *AWEPPA NEWS BULLETIN*, Association of West European Parliaments for Action Against Apartheid (January/February 1989), pp. 5–8; "Tripartite Agreement on Southwestern Africa: Blueprint for Peace for Namibian Independence," *Southwestern Africa: Regional Brief* (Washington, DC: U.S. Department of State, December 1988).

17. Marcum, p. 168.

18. J.A. Marcum, "Angola: War Again," *Current History*, Vol. 92, No. 574 (May 1993), p. 218.

19. Marcum, "Angola: War Again," pp. 220–223.

20. Victoria Brittain, "Angola: Against the Odds," *New Statesman and Society* (16 October 1995), pp. 20–21.

21. Anthony W. Pereira, "Peace in the Third World," *Dissent*, Vol. 40, No. 3 (Summer 1993), p. 293.

22. "Ending Long Hostility, U.S. Plans Ties with Angola's Government," *The New York Times* (19 May 1993); "Washington Recognizes Angola Government," *The New York Times*, International Section (20 May 1993).

23. See "Why Angola's Rebels Will Fight On and On," *Economist* (22 November 1993), pp. 42–43.

24. *The Economist* (10 December 1994), p. 44.

25. Karen Gellen, "UN Brokers Peaceful Transition in Angola, Mozambique," *Africa Recovery* (UN), Vol. 8, No. 3 (December 1994), p. 15.

26. *The Economist* (10 December 1994), p. 44.

27. Gelen, in "UN Brokers Peaceful Transition," p. 15.

28. Editorial, "Angola on the Brink of Peace," *The New York Times* (26 November 1994).

29. José Eduardo dos Santos, "Angola Needs the World's Help in Making Peace Triumph," *The Christian Science Monitor* (19 January 1995), p. 19.

30. James Ciment, *Angola and Mozambique: Postcolonial Wars in Southern Africa* (New York: Facts on File, Inc., 1997), p. 12.

31. Ciment, *Angola and Mozambique*, pp. 41, 98–99.

32. "UN Says Angolan Rebels Still Armed," *The Washington Post* (2 June 1998), on the World Wide Web (8 June 1998).

33. Robert H. Reid, "Angola Peace Process in Trouble," *The Washington Post* (6 June 1998), on the World Wide Web (8 June 1998).

34. "UN Chief Calls for Angolan Peace," *New York Times* (29 June 1998) on the World Wide Web (30 June 1998); Tim Sullivan, "UN Envoy to Angola Confirmed Dead," *Washington Post*, on the World Wide Web (29 June 1998); Tim Sullivan, "Plane Carrying U.N. Envoy Found," *The Washington Post* on the World Wide Web (27 June 1998).

35. U.S. Department of State, *Angola: Country Report on Human Rights Practices for 1997*, (30 January 1998) on the World Wide Web (6 June 1998).

36. "Angola: It's Not Yet Over," *Africa Confidential*, Vol. 38, No. 4 (14 February 1997), pp. 2–4.

37. *Africa Confidential*, Vol. 48, No. 1 (January 1998), p. 4.

38. The White House, "Clinton Notifies Congress of Sanctions Against UNITA," *Africa News On Line* (15 December 1997).

39. Editorial, "Angola on the Brink of Peace," *The New York Times* (26 November 1994); Peter Hain, "Angola: Africa's 'Pol Pot'" *New Statesman and Society* (6 October 1995), p. 14.

40. Hodges, *Angola from Afro-Stalinism to Petro-Diamond Capitalism,* pp. 83–88.

41. Hodges, *Angola from Afro-Stalinism to Petro-Diamond Capitalism,* pp. 84 and 170.

42. John A. Marcum, "Angola: Twenty-five Years of War," *Current History*, Vol. 85, No. 511 (May 1986), p. 199.

43. Hodges, *Angola from Afro-Stalinism to Petro-Diamond Capitalism*, p. 92.

44. *The New York Times* (5/6 May 1993), p. A 6.

45. Crocker, "Southern Africa," p. 146; Marcum, "Angola: Twenty-five Years of War," p. 193.

46. *The New York Times* (5/6 May 1993), p. A 6.

47. *African Economic Digest* (7 November 1988).

48. U.S. Department of State, "Albright Meets dos Santos, Regrets Savimbi's Absence," *Africa News On Line* (12 December 1997).

49. Suzanne Daley, "Ex-Rebels Adrift in an Angola Without a War," *The New York Times* (17 June 1997).

50. Hain, "Angola: Africa's 'Pol Pot'," p. 14.

51. Daley, "Ex-Rebels Adrift in an Angola Without a War."

52. John F. Kennedy, "A Democrat Looks at Foreign Policy," *Foreign Affairs*, Vol. 36, No. 1 (October 1957), pp. 52–53.

53. Richard D. Mahoney, *JFK: Ordeal in Africa* (New York: Oxford University, 1983), p. 190.

54. "The Vote on Angola," *The New York Times* (18 March 1961), cited in George Wright, *Angola: The Destruction of a Nation: United States' Policy Toward Angola Since 1945* (London: Pluto, 1997), p. 34.

55. Wright, *Angola: The Destruction of a Nation*, p. 38.

56. Mahoney, *JFK*, pp. 201–202; Wright, *Angola: The Destruction of a Nation*, p. 38.

57. Mahoney, *JFK*, p. 203.

58. Mahoney, *JFK*, p. 211.

59. Mahoney, *JFK*, p. 214.

60. Mahoney, *JFK*, p. 217.

61. *Yearbook of the United Nations, 1962* (New York: Columbia University, 1964), pp. 92–93.

62. Wright, *Angola: The Destruction of a Nation*, p. 50.

63. John Stockwell, *In Search of Enemies: A CIA Story* (New York: Norton, 1978), pp. 191–201.

64. Nathaniel Davis, "The Angolan Decision of 1975: A Personal Memoir," *Foreign Affairs*, Vol. 55, No. 1 (1978), pp. 109–124.

65. House of Representatives, Committee on Foreign Relations, "Restrictions on Assistance to Angola," Report No. 94–584, Calendar No. 562, 18 December 1975, pp. 1, 5–6; Gerald Bender, "Kissinger in Angola: Anatomy of Failure," in R. LeMarchand (ed.), *American Policy in Southern Africa*, pp. 102–103.

66. Henry Kissinger, "Implication of Angola for Future United States Foreign Policy," *U.S. Department of State Bulletin*, Vol. lxxiv, No. 1912 (16 February 1976), pp. 175–176.

67. "Governor Jimmy Carter on Africa," *Africa Report* (July–August 1976), p. 11.

68. Cyrus Vance, "Elements of United States Foreign Policy Towards the Soviet Union," *U.S. Department of State Bulletin*, Vol. 78, No. 2017 (August 1978), p. 16.

69. Zbigniew Brzezinski, *Power and Principle: Memoirs of the National Security Advisor,* *1977–1981* (New York: Farrar, Straus & Giraux, 1983), pp. 56 and 184.

70. Walter Pincus and Robert Kaiser, "Clark Fears Revived Role in Angola," *The Washington Post* (24 May 1978), pp. A1, A16; E. Walsh, "Carter Criticizes Hill Restraint on U.S. Role Abroad;" *The Washington Post* (17 May 1978); Hearings, *U.S.-Angola Relations,* House of Representatives, Foreign Relations Subcommittee on Africa, 25 May 1978 (Washington, DC: U.S. Government Printing Office, 1978), pp. 9, 14–15, 19.

71. Stephen R. Weissman, *A Culture of Deference: Congress's Failure of Leadership in Foreign Policy* (New York: Basic Books, 1995), pp. 117–118.

72. Wright, *Angola: The Destruction of a Nation,* p. 109.

73. Weissman, *A Culture of Deference,* pp. 119–120; Wright, *Angola: The Destruction of a Nation,* p. 110.

74. W. Clark, Jr., "National Reconciliation Efforts for Angola," *Current Policy,* No. 1217, U.S. Department of State (October 1989), p. 1.

75. Hearing, *Potential for U.S. Private Activity in Angola,* House of Representatives Foreign Affairs Subcommittee on Africa, 3 March 1992 (Washington, DC: U.S. Government Printing Office, 1992), pp. 73–74.

76. Stockwell, *In Search of Enemies,* p. 43; See also William Colby, *Honorable Men* (New York: Simon & Schuster, 1978), pp. 339–340.

CHAPTER 8
The United States and the Genocide in Rwanda, 1994

Demonstrably, internal conflicts within individual African states have tended to set off chain reactions and spill-over effects in their specific regions. Indeed, this was the experience of the whole African continent throughout the last two decades of the twentieth century. As a result every region experienced political and economic instability and became a victim of several other consequences and effects of those internal conflicts that began in specific states.

Throughout the 1980s, the apartheid government of South Africa attacked neighboring states—Angola, Mozambique, Botswana, and Zimbabwe—in order to eliminate the bases and supply lines of its internal enemies—the African National Congress (ANC), and the Southwest African Peoples Organization (SWAPO). It actively supported and abetted two rebel groups—the Mozambique National Resistance Movement (RENAMO) and the National Union for the Total Independence of Angola (UNITA)—against their own governments as a way of punishing and undermining the governments of the two respective states.

At a phase of Angola's protracted war of political succession (1975–2002), Mobutu Sese Seko of Zaire allowed his country to become a staging area for UNITA rebels against the neighboring Angolan government. Mobutu was continuing his support for the United States against the Soviet Union during the Cold War. Up to 1993 when the Clinton administration offered diplomatic recognition to the government of Angola, he served as Washington's conduit for covert support for UNITA. That role as a conduit continued (but not for the United States) after the normalization of relations between the United States and Angola. Mobutu and the rulers of Togo and Burkina Faso allowed their territories to be used as conduits of weapons UNITA acquired from Bulgaria in return for which they received large gifts of diamonds. According to the report of a UN Security Council expert panel which investigated violations of UN sanctions against UNITA:

UNITA used Zaire as a base for the stockpiling of weapons [as well as] Zairean end-user certificates as the means by which arms brokers working for [it] were able to obtain the weapons Savimbi wanted. Mobutu provided Savimbi with the Zairean end-user certificates, and in return Savimbi gave Mobutu diamonds and cash.[1]

After Mobutu's ouster from Zaire, UNITA received a safe haven in Rwanda for its operations. In return for the favor, it became a de facto ally of its benefactor in the war in the Democratic Republic of the Congo (DRC, formerly Zaire) against President Laurent Kabila.

The Angola war subsequently spread sporadically into neighboring Namibia. In 1999 the Namibian government authorized Angola to operate on its territory against Savimbi and his UNITA associates. For its part, UNITA diverted some of its ammunition to separatists in Namibia's Caprivi Strip in retaliation to Namibia's alliance with the Angolan government. The result was a series of military confrontations during which Namibian authorities cracked down on the rebels and were themselves accused of human rights violations. The government of Angola itself intervened in the civil wars of its two neighboring countries of Congo-Brazzaville and Zaire in 1997 to advance its own geopolitical and strategic interests. In both cases, it helped to install friendly governments and end the two Congos' previous role as rear bases for UNITA and the Front for the Liberation of the Enclave of Cabinda (FLEC). The severe damage inflicted on Angolan economic infrastructure by UNITA and South Africa adversely affected the economies of Zambia and Zaire as they relied on the much costlier and longer route through South Africa rather than the Benguela railway for their exports and imports.

The civil war in Sierra Leone started as an offshoot of a civil war in Liberia. It necessitated, as did the Liberian civil war before it, the intervention of the Economic Community of West Africa's Monitoring Group (ECOMOG). It spread several years later into neighboring Guinea-Conakry. The 1994 Rwanda conflict spread into the DRC while six neighboring countries, for one reason or another, intervened in the civil war in the DRC shortly after the ouster of Mobutu in 1997. The protracted war in Sudan influenced and was influenced by the Eritrean liberation struggle and the Tigrean-led insurgency against the government of Ethiopia. Ugandan support for the Sudanese People's Liberation Army (SPLA) led the Sudanese government to train and support rebels in northern Uganda against their government. Uganda also hosted, trained, and used Rwandan Patriotic Front (RPF) rebels in its own internal war and later armed them to invade Rwanda. These calculated discrete actions escalated the respective conflicts and their consequences.

Beyond Africa, the series of internal conflicts within the continent played into the hands of Afro-pessimists and detractors who had lost faith in Africa's present and its future. Afro-pessimists perceived Africa as a continent on the edge of an abyss of despair, chaos, and futility, as little more than a gigantic basket case. A manifestation of the pessimism was the fatigue of aid donors, which reached its nadir in 1994 when the U.S. government torpedoed UN intervention to prevent genocide in Rwanda. The aftermath of that behavior was the adoption in 1996 of the African Crisis Response Initiative (ACRI) to train and equip African militaries who would intervene in African crises and so spare the United States and other nations from such hazards. The policy was preceded by the Clinton administration's Presidential Decision Directive-25 (PDD-25). Faced, among other things, with a barrage of criticism by Congress and the American people following the death of eighteen American soldiers leading a UN mission in Somalia, President Clinton issued the directive, which stipulated the conditions under which the U.S. military would participate in multilateral peacekeeping and enforcement operations under the auspices of the United Nations.

This chapter looks at the origins of the Rwandan conflict and examines the U.S. role in the failure of the international community to stop the genocide in 1994. What were the circumstances of that role? What could the U.S. government—the Clinton administration—have done to save lives and so avert the genocide?

Origins of the Rwanda Conflict

The conflict which culminated in the massacre of about 800,000 Tutsi and moderate Hutu in 1994 had precolonial and colonial origins among its other sources.[2] The exclusion of specific ethnic communities from effective political participation, together with the cumulation of events in the country's past, is the major root of the conflict. The politics of exclusion became the building block for other events in which all the actors and factors in the country's history interrelated and interacted. Exclusion led to political insurrection. In its turn, insurrection led to repression and repression to refugee flows into other states.[3] The refugee situation in other states such as Uganda produced further political exclusion and alienation and, ultimately, revanchist invasion.

The history of the Hutu of Rwanda under a Tutsi monarchy, a root cause of the conflict, was aggravated and ultimately rendered all the more painful by the constraints and discrimination brought about by European imperial overrule. Germany, which had ruled Rwanda as part of German East Africa, and Belgium,

Map 8.1 Rwanda

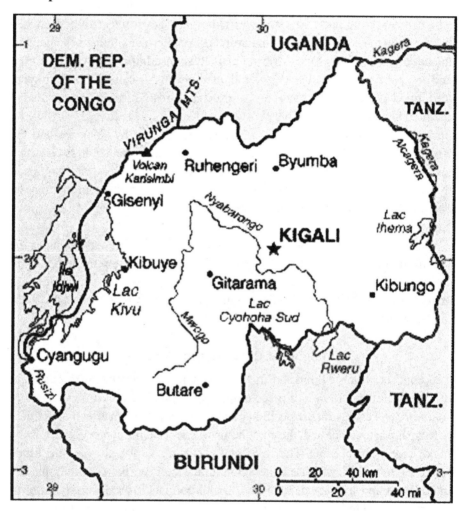

Adapted from CIA - *The World Factbook 2002*.

which obtained the territory as a League of Nations mandate after Germany lost all its African colonies after World War I, racialized Tutsi and Hutu identities. Both imperial rulers favored the Tutsi, Rwanda's minority ethnic group, over the Hutu majority in education and employment. A pastoral people, the Tutsi, who had arrived in the area in the fifteenth century, formed the dominant caste under a feudal system based on cattle herding in precolonial times. Their monarchs had initiated a process of polarizing and politicizing ethnic groups years before the imposition of European imperial control over the territory. They also maintained a flexible and reciprocal patron/client relationship with the Hutu.

The process was intensified by colonial administrative practices. The German and Belgian policy of "indirect rule," using Tutsi monarchs as agents of local government, favored and strengthened Tutsi hegemony. The policy intensified precolonial differentiation between the Tutsi minority and the Hutu majority by inscribing ethnic identification on identity cards, relegating the vast majority of the Hutu to particularly onerous forms of forced cultivation and labor, and actively favoring the Tutsi in access to colonial administrative posts, education, and jobs in the modern sector. Above all, it solidified the precolonial flexible patron/client relationship between the Tutsi and the Hutu, did away with the system's mutual obligations, and accentuated ethnic cleavage based on the racist theory that the Tutsi were cousins of Europeans and so superior to the Hutu. Thus, by the end of Belgian colonial rule in 1962, the Tutsi (though not all of them) were wealthier and more powerful than the majority Hutu.

In November 1959, citing a history of oppression and exploitation under a Tutsi-dominated monarchy, the Hutu revolted. The revolution, together with belated attempts by Belgian colonial administrators to redress past injustices, brought about the end of Tutsi domination and the eventual accession of the Hutu to political power after independence in 1962. The Tutsi monarchy was abolished and with it the political and administrative Tutsi structures on which, for about five decades, the Belgians had based their colonial policy of indirect rule. Also, an estimated 20,000 Tutsi were killed, and thousands of others took refuge in neighboring countries—Uganda, Zaire, and Tanzania. That the 1959 revolt produced such radical changes when the Belgians were still fully in control of the territory suggests that it was teleguided: It is plausible that the revolt "was largely inspired, engineered, and assisted by Belgian administrators, in Brussels and in Kigali, acting in close collaboration with the Catholic Church."[4] The replacement of one group of rulers by another introduced a new dimension of political and social instability as well as the potential for future ethnic violence. From the date of their political ascendency in 1962 to 1994, the Hutu carried out systematic political violence against the Tutsi in order to maintain their power. Thousands of Tutsi who survived the violence fled into Uganda, Zaire, and Tanzania. Except in Tanzania, the refugees were denied citizenship through naturalization. Thus, very significantly for Rwanda, the revolution of 1959 and the political changes it brought about marked the beginning of a cycle of turbulent clashes for power, in which the capture of the state from political opponents became a violent zero-sum game in which the winner took all and the toll of casualties successively increased. This

> is the key to understanding both the 1959 Rwandan revolution, which led to the overthrow of the Tutsi monarch and the capture of [political] power by Hutu politicians, and the invasion 30 years later by the sons of Tutsi refugees under the banner of Rwanda Patriot Front.[5]

In 1982 Milton Obote of Uganda expelled Rwandan refugees from his country. Many of them fled to northern Rwanda into crowded refugee camps where they lived for three years. The Hutu-controlled Rwanda government refused to acknowledge the right of these people to live in the country. Most were sent back to Uganda. There, in 1988 these children of the Tutsi exiles formed the RPF. From their land of exile, they began to carry out armed incursions into Rwanda, adding to the seeds of the country's ethnically defined refugee problem. Members of the armed wing of the RPF joined Yoweri Museveni's National Resistance Movement against Milton Obote. When Museveni overthrew Obote, many Rwandans who had assisted him received influential positions in his government and within his National Resistance Army, arousing immediately the hatred of Ugandans because they were foreigners. Thus, from being an asset, the Rwanda community in Uganda became a liability to Museveni. Among other groups, noncommissioned officers within the National Resistance Movement who saw the predominance of Tutsi officers in the higher ranks as a hindrance to their own promotions wanted them expelled.

Museveni adopted a two-pronged approach to deal with this Tutsi problem. The Uganda government, under his regime, denied the Tutsi citizenship rights by establishing an ancestry requirement for Ugandan citizenship. Museveni chose to send them back to Rwanda with a plan to return the favor they had accorded him in overthrowing Milton Obote. By these measures "Uganda exported its own political crisis to Rwanda in the form of Rwanda Patriotic Front, which [subsequently] began a series of invasion into Rwanda in 1990."[6]

In Rwanda, although relations between the Tutsi and the Hutu had improved during the period 1973-1990, and the Rwandan polity was apparently healthier than others in the region, the Tutsi still perceived themselves as victims of exclusionary policies in and outside of their country as ethnicity served as a strong political tool for acquiring power and the perquisites of office. Therefore, in October 1990, the military wing of the RPF attacked the Hutu President Juvenal Habyarimana from its base in Uganda. Evidently, just as the 1959 Hutu revolution drew its dynamic from the oppressiveness of Tutsi hegemony, so the RPF's 1990 invasion sought to end the pattern of exclusiveness and ethnic domination institutionalized by that revolution. After that invasion the Habyarimana regime abandoned its efforts at internal reforms such as the institution of multiparty politics and a free press and made the Tutsi the target of its hostility.

Demographic pressures contributed to the conflict. With an estimated population of 7.6 million (1997) and a density of 590 people per square mile, Rwanda is overpopulated. About 90 percent of its population depends on agriculture for its livelihood. Before 1990 the Habyarimana government had explored the possibility of settlement schemes elsewhere—Zaire, Tanzania, Gabon—as he believed that the available land could not provide for the livelihood of the Rwandan population. Claiming insufficiency of land for the population in the country, the regime refused to allow the repatriation of the refugees, largely children of the Tutsi who had fled the country during the previous violent clashes. Many of the refugees, Tutsi as well as Hutu, were treated as second-class citizens in their land of exile.

Meanwhile, by 1990 the Rwanda government sought to reexamine the refugee problem, The attempt was undermined by the RPF attack on Habyarimana in October 1990 referred to above. From that time his government began to see the Tutsi as internal enemies and supporters of the RPF and so permitted a policy of internal repression against them. His government also began to purchase and distribute weapons for internal warfare.

The land and exile problem was aggravated by economic decline. Like other African countries, Rwanda experienced severe economic hardships and difficulties during the 1980s. Unfavorable terms of trade in international economic relations and falling commodity prices, especially coffee, the major Rwandan foreign exchange earner, took their toll on the livelihood of Rwandans. Transport costs rose in response to an international surge in oil prices, increasing the price of consumer goods. The gap between the rich and the poor widened markedly, contributing to the level of public uneasiness and social tension. After resisting for several years, the government was forced by the deteriorating economic situation to accept an economic adjustment program worked out by International Monetary Fund and the World Bank in 1990 and approved in 1991. Implementation of the provisions of the program did not markedly improve the economic situation or bridge the gap between the rich and the poor. Rather, it contributed to increased impoverishment of the rural Hutu population as well as to resentment among civil servants and other non-agricultural wage and salary earners. In doing so, it elevated uneasiness and social tension and made large numbers of people susceptible to hate propaganda and active and tacit participation in the genocide in April 1994.

In the meantime, Hutu opposition parties and the RPF had gained ground against the Hutu government forces. In 1993, the government of Tanzania brokered a power-sharing agreement—the Arusha Accords. Under the terms of the Accords, the Rwanda government agreed to share power with the Hutu opposition parties and the Tutsi minority in a provisional government that was to be established by 31 December 1993. Contingents of UN peacekeepers (UNAMIR) were to be deployed to Rwanda to patrol a cease-fire, to assist in demilitarization and demobilization, and to help provide a secure environment so that the exiled Tutsi could return home. RPF was to be integrated into the armed forces and multiparty elections held in 1995. These terms were rejected by Hutu extremists who set out to terrorize the Tutsi and Hutu politicians who supported the peace process.

The immediate cause of the genocide[7] of 1994 was the death of both Habyarimana and the Hutu President of Burundi, Cyprien Ntariyamira, in a plane crash on 6 April 1994 as they were returning from a peace conference in Dar es Salaam, Tanzania. Hardliners in the military/presidential guard are suspected[8] to have shut down the plane as it approached the runway. Perhaps, this was done to make it seem as if the act was the work of the Tutsi, whose ethnic relatives in the Burundi Army had assassinated the first democratically elected Hutu president of the country five months earlier in October 1993. In Kigali, almost immediately after the death of Habyarimana, the presidential guard began a systematic execution of prominent Tutsi and moderate Hutu sympathetic to reconciliation under the Arusha Accords. Parallel killings were carried out by the army and extremist Hutu militia to destroy the leadership of the Tutsi community. In the ensuing tragedy an estimated 750,000 to 800,000 Tutsi and moderate Hutu were murdered within a period of 100 days. The genocide ended in July 1994 when the Tutsi rebels defeated the Hutu rulers. Afraid of Tutsi retribution, about two million Hutu fled to neighboring Burundi, Tanzania, Uganda, and Zaire. About one million others became internally displaced. Members of the former Hutu regime continued to destabilize northwest Rwanda through a low-intensity insurgency.

The war devastated Rwanda's economy, including its educated and skilled labor force. Hundreds of thousands of peasant farmers in northern Rwanda were displaced, with a drastic impact on both coffee and food production. As of this writing, at least 120,000 Hutu suspects of genocide rot in prison in appalling conditions. Rwanda's major institutions of local and central government were destroyed. Its main overland access to the outside world—the road to the Kenyan port of Mombasa—was cut off. The country's fledgling tourist industry, which had become the third largest foreign exchange earner, was destroyed. To maintain internal security, the government increased the strength of its armed forces dramatically, reducing thereby the allocation of national resources to other purposes.

The long-term effects of the horrific bloodshed and brutality continue to be felt throughout central Africa, especially in the DRC, where thousands of Hutu refugees and Congolese citizens died from the ensuing war, epidemics, and deprivation of food and medical supplies. Worse still, inside Rwanda itself, the roots of the conflict remain very much alive. Observers accuse the Tutsi army of politics of exclusion and human rights abuses. The minority Tutsi "fear democracy as an excuse for the majority to reignite the genocide, while the Hutu majority views justice as an excuse for never-ending Tutsi rule, reestablished by invading exiles in mid-1994."[9] Therefore, the fundamental reality in post-genocide Rwanda, under the regime of Paul Kagame, is that one ethnocracy replaced another. The victor's justice took precedence: "Only in one respect is the new Rwanda different: at no other time in the country's history have so many been excluded so ruthlessly—and with so little concern by the international community—from exercising their rights and privileges as citizens."[10]

In spite of the stipulation in the 1948 International Convention on the Prevention and Punishment of the Crime of Genocide that persons committing genocide should be punished "whether they are constitutionally responsible rulers, or public officials or private individuals," none of those responsible for mass killings in Rwanda prior to 1994 had been brought to justice. Perhaps, it is that failure to act on the part of the Organization of African Unity (OAU) and the international community in general that encouraged the culture of impunity as well as the spiral of violence in Rwanda. Spread too thinly at the time and dealing simultaneously with crises in Bosnia, Somalia, and Haiti, the United Nations and the major world powers remained tragically inactive while the massacres went on for ninety days. This was so despite the fact that there had been numerous prior warnings of the violence that erupted on 6 April.[11] Two weeks after the massacre began, the United Nations withdrew the bulk of its 2,500 forces from the country, while the Security Council, bowing to the persistent objection of the United States, failed to reinforce those (about 270) that remained.[12] The United States government under Bill Clinton refused to acknowledge that genocide was taking place. However, belatedly recognizing that serious violations of humanitarian law had been violated in Rwanda and acting under Chapter VII of the UN Charter, the Security Council created the International Criminal Tribunal for Rwanda (ICTR) by Resolution 955 (8 November 1994) after the massacres had ended. Located in Arusha, Tanzania, in accordance with Security Council Resolution 977 (22 February 1995), the tribunal was charged to prosecute individuals responsible for genocide and other serious violations of international humanitarian law committed in Rwanda between 1 January and 31 December 1994. It was also to prosecute Rwandan citizens responsible for genocide and other such violations of international law committed in the territory of neighboring states during the same period. It was expected that the creation and work of the tribunal would contribute to the process of national reconciliation in Rwanda and the maintenance of peace and stability in the Great Lakes region.

Jean Kambanda, a former prime minister of Rwanda, was convicted of genocide in 1998 and sentenced to life imprisonment. He was the first person to be found guilty of genocide by an international court. By 30 June 2002, the Tribunal had indicted eighty persons.[13] In August 2002, General Augustin Bizimungu, chief of staff of the former Rwandan Army was arrested in Angola where he was identified among a number of demilitarized UNITA rebels. In February 2003, Pastor Elizaphan Ntakirutimana and his son, Gerald Ntakiruti-mana, a physician, were convicted for their part in the genocide.[14] By 15 March 2003 ten other individuals—all ringleaders—had been convicted of participating in the 1994 genocide. According to the eighth annual report of the Tribunal covering the period 1 July 2002–30 June 2003, twelve additional accused persons, including Eliezer Niyitegeka, a former interior minister, and Laurent Semanza, a former mayor of Bicumbi, were convicted during the period and judgments in the trials of eight others were expected in the last months of 2003.[15] Three Rwandan news media executives—Hassan Ngeze, Ferdinand Nihimana, and Jean-Bosco Barayagwiza—were convicted of genocide on 3

December 2003 by a three-judge panel for using a radio station and a twice-monthly newspaper to influence ethnic hatred that eventually led to massacres at churches, schools, and roadblocks.[16] The process has been slow, but the tribunal has committed itself to tracking the accused and ensuring their prosecution. In addition to the work of the Tribunal, state prosecutors in Belgium announced in June 2000 that they would try four Rwandan refugees, including two nuns, on charges of war crimes and murder for their alleged involvement in the 1994 Rwandan massacres.[17]

Regional Dimensions of the Conflict

The Rwanda conflict, which traces to the 1959 Hutu revolt against a history of oppression and exploitation under a Tutsi-dominated monarch, evinced few premonitions of a future tragedy for Africa's interlacustrine states in Central Africa. It did not take long for it to draw the whole of Central Africa into a morass of seemingly endless interlinked conflicts, thus opening a Pandora's box of problems for the region. As René LeMarchand has aptly described subsequent developments in the region, the revolt in retrospect

> emerges as the defining moment when an anti-Tutsi, anti-monarchical upheaval sowed the seeds of wider confrontations. Between 1962, when Rwanda became an independent republic under Hutu rule, and the 1994 genocide, the entire region became engulfed in a bitter Hutu-Tutsi struggle, accompanied by periods of massive bloodshed. Each event of political significance in the region during those 32 years was related to the Rwandan revolution: the fall of two monarchies (Rwanda in 1962, Burundi in 1966); the assassination of two leading Hutu personalities in Burundi (Prime Minister Pierre Ngendadumwe in 1965 and President Melchior Ndadaye in 1993); several military takeovers (the 1973 coup in Rwanda and the 1965, 1976, 1987, and 1996 coups in Burundi); the 1972 Burundi genocide of Hutus; the rural uprising in North Kivu [Province of Zaire] in 1993; the 1990 invasion of Rwanda by the RPF, and the 1994 genocide of Tutsis and moderate Hutus; and the transformation of North and South Kivu into a privileged sanctuary for Hutu-sponsored border raids into Rwanda—and the historical threads that link the exodus of the Tutsi populations from Rwanda in the early 1960s to the re-entry of "refugee warriors" some 30 years later are reasonably clear. Less well known is the impact of the Rwandan revolution on Burundi and eastern Congo. In both cases Rwanda refugees played a major role in promoting regional instability.[18]

The most pervasive regional dimension of the conflict is its spillover, in one form or another, into every state of the Great Lakes region, notably Burundi, Eastern Zaire, and also Uganda and Tanzania. With the massive flight of the Hutu and Tutsi Rwandans, violence immediately spread to these countries with devastating consequences. Contributing to the spillovers was the end of the Cold War which enhanced the salience of ethnicity at the expense of ideology and the old Eurocentric concept of state sovereignty. Ethnic conflicts therefore proliferated and spilled across state borders. One effect of all this was the undermining of the concept of state sovereignty.

Four major dimensions of the interlinkage can be identified: a refugee problem, ethnic insecurity and exclusion in Burundi, the collapse of Zaire, and abrogation of commitment to the OAU's principle of nonintervention in the affairs of sister states.

The Refugee Problem

A core regional dimension of the apparently unending conflict in Rwanda is the refugee problem that bedeviled the entire Great Lakes region of Central Africa. From the 1959 Hutu revolt against oppression and exploitation under a Tutsi monarchy, through its overthrow in 1962 to the 1994 genocide, the conflict generated a massive exodus of Rwandan citizens into neighboring states. About three million of the country's seven million survivors fled in 1994. The exodus, 1959 to 1994, aggravated and created problems in every one of the countries, including Rwanda. In their lands of exile, especially Uganda and Zaire, the refugees formed political organizations which launched border raids into Rwanda. Such raids had two major outcomes: increased repression of the Tutsi inside Rwanda and continued swelling of the ranks of Tutsi exiles into neighboring countries where their life became increasingly less certain. For a variety of reasons, including economic and social conditions and xenophobia, enlarged Tutsi communities outside Rwanda exacerbated old tensions between ethnic Tutsis and indigenous citizens of their host countries.

Although in 1980 Tanzania granted citizenship to about 35,000 Rwandan refugees in its territory, few opportunities existed in the republic to assimilate them and later arrivals into its administrative and political structures or commercial hierarchies. In Burundi discrimination in employment against noncitizens reinforced the dire condition of the refugees.

The experience of Rwandan exiles in Uganda best illustrates the dimensions of the problem. In 1982, Milton Obote and his government relentlessly attacked the Tutsi community, which had supported Idi Amin, who overthrew his regime in 1972. It was also supporting Yoweri Museveni's National Resistance Army, which had risen against Obote after his party had been accused of rigging national elections in 1981. Obote expelled Rwanda refugees from Uganda. Remnants of the Rwanda Tutsi community joined Museveni to oust the Obote regime in 1986. Most prominent of those Rwandans was Paul Kagame, who had lived his entire adult life in Uganda. He became Rwanda's president in July 1994.

The impact of the Museveni victory on Uganda and its Tutsi community was significant. On the one hand, the defeat of the Obote regime by a small group of determined fighters contributed to the formation the Rwandan Patriotic Front in 1988. From Uganda RPF carried out border raids into Rwanda. On the other hand, as stated above, the contribution of the Tutsi to Museveni's victory earned them top positions in his government and within the National Resistance Army. Museveni dealt with the jealousy of and hostility toward the Tutsi by denying them Ugandan citizenship and by arming and supplying them to invade Rwanda. The invasion began in October 1990 and culminated in the 1994 genocide.

For Rwanda the return of the refugees confronted the government with a twofold problem. First was the problem of resettling the returnees—both the Tutsi and the Hutu who had fled from the country in 1994 and were suspected by the government to have participated in the genocide of that year. Obviously, the new regime realized that members of the former Rwandan government were using the Hutu returnees to reconstruct their power base. This situation set the stage for a protracted refugee crisis. The second problem was the government's need to consolidate its position among its core Tutsi supporters, many of whom had grown up in exile, while at the same time gaining the confidence of its domestic population—the Hutu—many of whom had recently fled the country.

The government has been unable to address this problem satisfactorily. It does not enjoy the confidence of the Hutu majority. Its rank-and-file supporters would be alienated by any measures taken to win such trust. After the assassination of the top leaders of many of the former opposition movements, few leaders with a strong national following are available to co-opt in order to broaden its base.[19] Finally, the question of individual versus collective guilt in the genocide may never be definitively resolved regardless of the findings of the International Criminal Tribunal for Rwanda. The Hutu majority will carry the burden for the genocide for a long time.

Ethnic Insecurity and Exclusion in Burundi

In Rwanda and Burundi, political developments in one country have produced repercussions in the other because of the ethnic composition and the politics of ethnic insecurity and exclusion in both countries. The Hutu are the majority in each country. The Tutsi minority had the political authority in Rwanda until

1962, regained control in July 1994, and have always been in control in Burundi.

The flight of tens of thousands of Rwanda Tutsi into Burundi as a consequence of the 1959 Hutu revolt and the 1962 overthrow of the Tutsi monarchy became a major vector of conflict in the country. The tales of horror and destruction from the refugees alerted the Burundi Tutsi to a potential Hutu danger. An abortive Hutu-instigated attempt to overthrow the Tutsi government in 1965 heightened that danger. Thus, the failed coup led to the execution of more than a thousand highly-placed Hutu in the central province of Muramvya. Furthermore, with their hegemonic position in the government and the army, the Tutsi massacred virtually all educated Hutu elites in 1972, ensuring thereby a solidly entrenched Tutsi ethnocracy. In 1993 they assassinated Burundi's first popularly elected Hutu President, Melchior Ndadaye, as the quickest way to eliminate the perceived Hutu threat to their hegemony.

The assassination of President Ndadaye inflamed the passions of ethnic Hutu in Rwanda against the Rwanda Tutsi. It escalated hostility and a propaganda campaign in the country against the Tutsi provoked by the invasion of Rwanda by the Tutsi Rwandan Patriotic Front in October 1990.

Collapse of Zaire

The 1959 Rwanda revolution spread to eastern Zaire. There, in 1964, Tutsi refugees joined a short-lived Mulelist insurgency against the government of the DRC. By the alliance, the Tutsi refugees sought to obtain external support in order to recapture power in Rwanda. They fought pitched battles alongside the People's Liberation Army against the Congolese National Army in South Kivu and Northern Katanga provinces. In addition, they launched a series of armed raids into Rwanda. The rebellion was crushed in 1965 through the covert operations of the CIA. The Tutsi and the Congo rebels were both perceived by the U.S. government as the spearhead of communist penetration into the heart of Africa. Hence their elimination by the CIA during the Cold War.

After the breakdown of order in Burundi that began in 1993, following the assassination of President Ndadaye, thousands of Burundi Hutu sought safety in eastern Zaire. Similarly, the 1994 genocide in Rwanda forced more than one million Hutu to flee into the same region to escape the avenging arm of the Tutsi RPF. Included in the exodus were remnants of the all-Hutu Rwandan Armed Forces (FAR) and thousands of others who had been active participants in the genocide. On the one hand, these refugees added to the hardships of the local population and created an uncertainty that helped to rekindle dormant feuds. Soon, local politicians began to take advantage of the new situation to settle old scores with the local Tutsi community.[20] On the other hand, from their refugee camps in eastern Zaire, the remnants of FAR and the Hutu militias, known as *Interhamwe*, launched innumerable cross-border raids into Rwanda. In this they received substantial assistance from their host and ally Mobutu, who disliked the new regime in Rwanda because of its alliance with Museveni of Uganda. Also hostile acts were committed against ethnic Tutsi who had been living for years in North Kivu. Thousands of them were killed. Survivors fled to Rwanda where the Tutsi-led RPF had taken power in July 1994.

During the silence of the international community on these developments in 1996, Paul Kagame and his Rwandan Patriotic Army destroyed the camps and killed and brutalized Hutu refugees who were unable or unwilling to return to Rwanda. In October and November 1996 other refugee camps in North and South Kivu provinces of Zaire were also brutally attacked. Search-and-destroy missions against fleeing survivors followed in 1997. It is estimated that as many as 300,000 Hutu refugees in Zaire died of starvation and disease.[21] Zaire was humiliated as its sovereignty was smashed.

The humiliation continued in 1997 when Kagame's RPF, Angolan, and Museveni's Ugandan forces joined a Zairean rebel, Laurent Desiré Kabila, who had actively participated in the 1964 Mulelist rebellion,[22] to overthrow the Zairean government of Mobutu. Kabila promptly renamed the country the Democratic Republic of the Congo.

The ultimate goal of Kagame's alliance with Kabila was not just the overthrow of Mobutu but to make the Congo safe for Rwanda. Kagame saw Kabila as a tool to achieve and sustain this objective. He hoped that he would remain friendly with the ethnic Tutsi in Zaire. However, not long after the overthrow of Mobutu, the RPF-Kabila alliance collapsed for a number of reasons. First, Kagame had come to perceive Kabila as a threat to the security of Rwanda's borders as well as to the Rwanda Tutsi in Zaire. The second reason was the convergence of interests between Kagame and ethnic Tutsi in North and South Kivu provinces of Zaire. These ethnic Tutsi had contributed in no small way to Kabila's victory. They had emerged from the war against Mobutu as a major politico-military force and were determined to exercise rights as bona fide Congolese citizens not just ethnic Tutsi. Kagame shared this interest as a means of guaranteeing Kabila's continuing good intentions after his May 1997 victory.

These converging interests clashed with those of Kabila and most of his Congolese supporters. To Kabila's supporters, ethnic Tutsi represented a foreign presence and were an undue influence on the government. Kabila's political and military reliance upon them seriously eroded his popularity and legitimacy among his supporters. To appease a rising tide of anti-Tutsi sentiment in Kinshasa and to avoid further loss of his popularity and legitimacy, Kabila dismissed his Rwandan Army Chief of Staff, James Kabare, and ordered all foreign troops to leave the Congo. Further, he dismissed three key ethnic Tutsi figures, including his personal secretary, in his government.

By 2 August 1997, Kabila faced a full-scale rebellion in Goma and Bukavu, eastern Congo, engineered and sustained by Kagame and his Ugandan ally, Museveni, as a consequence of these moves. The two were not deterred by their domestic problems. Rwanda was still traumatized by the 1994 genocide. Its economy was in ruins. The mostly Tutsi minority government was not trusted by the Hutu majority. Uganda itself was plagued by two guerrilla movements—the West Bank Liberation Front and the Lord's Resistance Army—in its impoverished and ethnically heterogenous northern region. Both movements were armed and supplied by the Sudanese government in retaliation for the help Museveni provided to the rebel Sudanese People's Liberation Army.

Kabila's opponents joined the rebellion, forming by 16 August 1997 the Congolese Rally for Democracy. In the summer of 1998, the rebellion escalated to what was described as "Africa's first world war," when six countries— Angola, Burundi, Chad, Namibia, Sudan, and Zimbabwe—officially or unofficially joined Kabila to fight the rebels.[23] But it was not long before intense rivalries developed among the insurgent leaders and factions of the rebellion—the Congolese Rally for Democracy, the National Union of Nationalist Republicans, and the Republican Federation Forces—and between them and their external sponsors—Kagame and Museveni. Although neither side to the conflict—Kabila and the rebels and their allies—had a decisive edge in the fighting, the human suffering was appalling. The rebellion took a heavy toll on human lives and resulted in unspeakable atrocities. Both Rwanda and Uganda gained enormously from their intervention through looting by their soldiers and illicit smuggling and export of precious minerals such as gold, diamonds, and coltan, a critical metallic ore used in cell phones. But their involvement aggravated their own internal problems. Angola withdrew to deal with UNITA's increased offensive. Zimbabwe followed suit in order to assuage antiwar protests and to deal with the economic and political costs of the intervention. Rwanda and Uganda persisted for a relatively longer time in spite of several peace conferences to end the rebellion. After much international pressure, Uganda withdrew its troops from the DRC in June 2003.

U.S. Policy on the 1994 Genocide in Rwanda

The story of U.S. policy during the genocide in Rwanda is not a story of willful complicity with evil. U.S. officials did not sit around and conspire to allow genocide to happen. But whatever their convictions about "never again," many of them did sit around, and they most certainly did allow genocide to happen.[24]

The United States had unrivaled military, diplomatic, and political power and so the greatest potential to deter the genocide in Rwanda and the extreme brutalities that accompanied it. Why did the government of William Jefferson Clinton allow the tragedy to occur? During his visit to Rwanda in March 1998, President Clinton said to an audience at Kigali airport: "We come here today partly in recognition of the fact that we in the United States and the world community did not do as much as we could have and should have done to try to limit what occurred…We did not immediately call the crimes by their rightful name: genocide."[25]

What could his administration have done to avert or limit what occurred? To what extent was the failure to prevent the tragedy a function of lack of knowledge or warning about the impending human disaster? Was the failure a deliberate attempt to avoid risking a vital national security interest or paying a political and/or emotional price for intervening in some fashion? How was the Clinton administration able to wield such a negative influence and to justify its policy? Why was there no public outcry against the policy? The Belgians, the French, the United Nations, and the Organization of African Unity investigated their roles in the Rwanda genocide. Why was there no congressional investigation of what the U.S. government did or could have done to avert or limit the scope of the genocide? The rest of this chapter addresses these questions.

Why Did the Clinton Administration Allow the Genocide to Occur?

Although it had enough early warning about the impending human tragedy in Rwanda, the Clinton administration failed on numerous opportunities to intervene. During his visit to Rwanda in March 1998, President Clinton acknowledged in a statement at Kigali airport the failure of the United States and the international community as a whole to prevent or to try to limit the scope of the tragedy. He allowed that it might seem strange, especially to those who had lost family members, that all over the world there were people like himself sitting in offices, day after day, who did not fully appreciate the depth and the speed with which Rwandans were being engulfed by unimaginable terror. In the article "Rwanda in Retrospect" in *Foreign Affairs* (January/February 2000), Alan J. Kuperman argued that President Clinton "could not have known that a nationwide genocide was underway in Rwanda" until about two weeks into the killings. However, declassified documents and interviews with officials of the administration indicate otherwise or at least indicate that the administration knew a lot before then about the killers' intentions.[26] Also, based on warnings of massive slaughter of the Tutsi being prepared in Rwanda, a CIA analyst had predicted in January 1994 that as many as half a million people might die in case of renewed conflict in the country.

Arguably, therefore, President Clinton was disingenuous in this carefully hedged acknowledgment. His failure to appreciate "the depth and speed" of the slaughter was "an artful excuse for not wanting to appreciate the facts which, indeed, were presented to White House and everybody else at the time. They knew. They chose not to know and they chose not to act."[27] In spite of reports from diplomats in Rwanda, during the first three days of the killings, that well-armed Hutu extremists were intent on eliminating the Tutsi, top officials of his administration opted to stay out of Rwanda until peace was restored. The central African nation had never been of more than marginal concern to Washington's most influential policymakers. On 7 April, they decided to evacuate American personnel and nationals from the country.[28] Subsequently, other Western nations landed their troops in Rwanda or Burundi and evacuated their nationals. On 8 April President Clinton assured the families of U.S. nationals in the region that his administration was doing everything it could to be on top of the situation and was taking all appropriate steps to assure their safety. Secretary of State Warren Christopher explained on NBC's *Meet the Press* on the morning that the evacuation of 250 American personnel and nationals was completed that although 300 Marines had been dispatched to neighboring Burundi, there were no plans to send them into Rwanda to restore order. They had been sent into the region, he stressed, as a safety net in case they were needed in the evacuation process. President Clinton himself congratulated the people who had manned the emergency operation's room at the Department of State on a "job well done."

According to Samantha Power, "Once the [American nationals] had been evacuated, Rwanda largely dropped off the radar of most senior Clinton administration officials."[29] Throughout the 100 days of the genocide, neither President Clinton nor his adviser on national security affairs, Anthony Lake, assembled the administration's senior foreign policy advisers to discuss the

Rwanda crisis. At the Department of State, mid-level personnel arranged a daily interagency meeting, often by teleconference to coordinate diplomatic and humanitarian responses to the crisis.[30] Cabinet-level officials focused on crises elsewhere, in Bosnia, Haiti, the Middle East, and North Korea.

Internal intelligence, authenticating American press reports of door-to-door hunting of unarmed civilians, did not produce a change or modification of the administration's policy to stay out of Rwanda. The administration's top policymakers refused to use government technology to jam extremist Hutu radio broadcasts that were a crucial instrument in the initiation, coordination, and perpetuation of the genocide. The broadcasts spread fear and consternation amongst the Rwanda populace while they urged masses of Hutu ethnics to participate in the killing. It many cases, they provided the names and where-abouts of those to be killed and shamed those who were unwilling to participate. As such, the extremist radio broadcasts were essential to the execution of the program of extermination.

The refusal by Clinton administration officials to jam the broadcasts (because of the opposition of the Pentagon) indirectly abetted the program. Pentagon officials argued that jamming would be contrary to constitutional protection of freedom of the press and of speech and, moreover, was ineffective, expensive, and encroached upon international law. Frank Wisner, the third-ranking official at the Pentagon, recommended airlifts to neighboring countries, like Tanzania, to assist in the relief effort.[31] In one area, the policymakers acted. They knew exactly who the leaders of the genocide were and actually spoke with those leaders to urge them to end the violence.[32]

During the first three weeks of the genocide, when, on average, 8,000 Rwandans were being massacred each day, the administration's most influential policymakers shunned the use of the term "genocide" for fear of being obliged to act both on moral grounds and under the terms of the 1948 Genocide Convention.[33] They also believed that to identify the killings as genocide and then do nothing to stop them would damage U.S. credibility and might cost the president's party votes in the 1994 congressional elections. Therefore, they perceived, and indeed chose to portray, the horrendous deaths as "acceptable," if tragic, wartime "casualties"—the deaths of combatants or those caught between them in a civil war. It was not until 21 May, six weeks after the killings began, that Secretary of State Warren Christopher and other top officials in his department agreed that Department of State officials "should be authorized to state the Department's conclusion that 'acts of genocide' have occurred in

Rwanda." This, for the sake of consistency, was the formulation the Department used with respect to Bosnia.

Accordingly, American diplomats were authorized to use the formulation and, in international meetings, to agree to resolutions and other instruments that "provide that "genocide"or "acts of genocide" have occurred in Rwanda. The secretary of state and his senior assistants had concluded that in avoiding the "genocide label," U.S. "credibility [would] be undermined with human rights groups and the general public, who may question how much evidence we can legitimately require before coming to a policy conclusion."[34] In any case, the officials agreed that a statement that acts of genocide had occurred in Rwanda would not have any particular legal consequences because the United States has no criminal jurisdiction over acts of genocide within Rwanda unless they were committed by U.S. citizens or fell under another criminal provision of U.S. law. Even after all these agreements, U.S. diplomats and State Department spokespersons Christine Shelley and Mike McCurry waited for three more weeks before using the term "genocide" publicly.

Earlier, on 15 April, the secretary of state had unequivocally instructed the U.S. Mission to the UN to insist that the international community should give highest priority to full and orderly withdrawal of all UN personnel in Rwanda as soon as possible. Although the United States had no troops in Rwanda, the instruction stressed:

> The United States will oppose any effort at this time to preserve a UNAMIR presence in Rwanda…Our opposition to retaining a UNAMIR presence in Rwanda is firm. It is based on our conviction that the Security Council has an obligation to ensure that peacekeeping operations are viable, that they are capable of fulfilling their mandates, and that UN peacekeeping personnel are not placed or retained, knowingly, in an untenable situation.[35]

Accordingly, the Chief U.S. Representative in the UN Security Council, Madeleine Albright, led a successful effort to remove most of the UN peacekeepers in Rwanda. She aggressively worked to block subsequent authorization of UN reinforcements. This U.S.-led Security Council decision turned out to be the most fateful act of the entire Rwandan tragedy. It sealed the fate of more victims of the genocide by signaling to the Hutu extremists that they had a free hand to kill. Six years later in July 2000, Ambassador Albright, who in keeping with her instructions from the Department of State implemented the obstructionist policy, said in ABC's *This Week* that she had opposed U.S. inaction against genocide in Rwanda. In her entire time at the UN, she revealed, she had violently objected to her instructions regarding the tragedy in the African country because she felt they were wrong.[36]

The rationale for staying out of Rwanda was rooted in the administration's concern that America was being overwhelmed by numerous external involvements that never came to meaningful conclusions and were sapping its resources and provoking the ire of Congress. Illustrative of this concern were the experience and aftermath of the 1993 sequel to Operation Restore Hope in Somalia. It was a traumatizing experience. After the barrage of public and congressional criticism leveled against the Clinton administration over the death and injury of U.S. soldiers in the operation, top administration officials became strongly inclined towards a risk-averse policy. Indeed, some conservative American political observers had regarded Somalia "as an almost welcome inoculation against the temptation to intervene in places such as Rwanda…an epitaph for multilateralism and an object lesson on the United Nations' inadequacies and the need to limit U.S. role in peacekeeping."[37] An editorial in the *New York Times* stressed that Somalia provided ample warning against plunging open-endedly into a "humanitarian mission" and demonstrated the problems of ad hoc force under multinational command on an ill-defined mission.[38]

The Clinton administration internalized these appraisals of the Somalia intervention. Thus, the deaths of ten Belgian members of the UN Assistance Mission in Rwanda only reinforced the internalized appraisals and the inclination not to intervene. In keeping with Clinton's PDD-25,[39] issued 3 May 1994, about a month after the presidents of Rwanda and Burundi died in a plane crash, the administration chose not to risk American lives again in a country in which no vital U.S. security interest was threatened. Samantha Power argues that "with the possibility of deploying U.S. troops to Rwanda taken off the table earlier on—and with crises elsewhere in the world unfolding—the slaughter [in Rwanda] never received the top level attention it deserved."[40] Rather, it had a very low status among seventeen other crisis spots around the world to which the UN was posting 70,000 peacekeepers. Africa specialists, who had the least clout of all regional specialists on policy matters in the U.S. government, were sidelined on the Rwanda decision. Their hands were tied by higher-level officials of their bureaucracy and by Congress.

This policy was reinforced by two other forces. First, for a variety of reasons, Congress had become increasingly suspicious, distrustful, and critical of the UN and its costly and "inefficient" peacekeeping operations. It had refused to authorize the payment of about $1 billion in UN dues and peacekeeping costs and was unhappy about the U.S. obligation to pay one-third of the cost of UN peacekeeping missions. Another probable failed UN mission might complicate, or even damage, relations between Congress and the world organization. On the other hand, Congress would not look kindly upon any unilateral intervention in Rwanda since there was neither a perceived vital security interest of the United States at stake in the Central African nation nor the likelihood of a clearly established exit strategy. For their part, ranking Pentagon officials had become distrustful of the guidance the military had been getting from politicians. And, given the October 1993 experience of a deadly blowup in Somalia, they had already concluded that peacekeeping in Africa meant trouble and that Congress would not support it when the chips were down. Thus, during the first week of the slaughter in Rwanda, they ruled out any military intervention.[41]

Second, the Rwanda genocide generated no sense of urgency in the American public and so was safely avoided by the Clinton administration at no political cost. Domestic political forces that might have pressed the administration or representatives in Congress for action were absent. Many Americans had never heard about Rwanda and its ethnic quarrels. "The editorial boards of the major American newspapers discouraged U.S. intervention... .They, like the [Clinton administration], lamented the killings but believed, in the words of a 17 April 1994 *Washington Post* editorial, that the United States had no recognizable national security interest in taking a role, certainly not a leading role in Rwanda."[42] Some Congresspeople were glad to be free of the expense of another flawed UN mission. A few members of the Africa subcommittees of Congress and the Congressional Black Caucus quietly appealed for the United States to play a role in ending the violence. However, they did not venture to urge involvement on the ground or to kick up a public fuss. Randall Robinson, executive director of TransAfrica, the major lobbying organization for Africa and the Caribbean, was preoccupied with a hunger strike in protest against repatriation of Haitian refugees. Human Rights Watch provided outstanding intelligence on the crisis and established critical one-on-one contacts with the Clinton administration officials but lacked a grassroots base from which to mobilize a broader segment of the American society for action on the genocide.

In summary, here are the reasons for the Clinton administration's posture on the crisis: "a lack of leadership within the administration's foreign policy bureaucracy; the administration's refusal to deal with the crisis as the human rights issue that it demonstrably was; U.S. distrust of peacekeeping in Africa as a consequence of the loss of American soldiers in Somalia in 1993; bureaucratic inertia at the United Nations; U.S. withdrawal generally from engagement in countries for which there is no strong domestic constituency."[43]

The Policy Implementation Process

As we have seen, the UN was a major avenue for implementing the Clinton administration's risk-averse policy on Rwanda. The process began when a decision was made to withdraw UN peacekeepers from Rwanda less than ten days after the slaughter began. As one senior U.S. official explained:

> When the report of the deaths of the ten Belgians came in, it was clear that it was Somalia redux, and the sense was that there would be an expectation everywhere that the U.S. would [become] involved. We thought [that] leaving the peacekeepers in Rwanda and having them confront the violence would take U.S. where we'd been before. It was a foregone conclusion that the United States wouldn't intervene and that the concept of UN peacekeeping could not be sacrificed again.[44]

The decision was fully implemented after the Belgian government, having decided to withdraw its peacekeeping contingent from UNAMIR after the return of the bodies of its slain soldiers to Brussels on 14 April, requested cover from the U.S. Department of State. The Belgian government did not want to be seen as the only one withdrawing from Rwanda, its former colony, and so sought American support for a full UN withdrawal. U.S. Secretary of State Warren Christopher, having appraised the value of bilateral U.S./Belgian relations, provided Belgium the cover it needed by compelling a UN Security Council action to that effect.[45] Earlier, when the killings began on 7 April, Romeo Dallaire, the Canadian commander of UNAMIR, appealed to UN headquarters in New York for reinforcements to improve the quality and effectiveness of the UN presence in Rwanda. The U.S. administration vehemently opposed the idea of sending any reinforcements, regardless of what country they were to come from. Leading the opposition, the Pentagon was apprehensive of a repetition of the October 1993 Somalia experience. It was concerned that what might start as a small engagement by foreign troops could end as a large and costly one by Americans.

Appalled at the scale of the slaughter in Rwanda, nonpermanent members of the Security Council pleaded with the major powers to deploy a stronger and better-armed peace enforcement force to Rwanda. This plea was reinforced by human rights, media, and diplomatic reports of the mounting carnage. In response, the UN met, debated, and eventually decided on 16 May to deploy a more robust and better-equipped force of 5,500 troops (UNAMIR II) under

Chapter VII, which authorizes peace enforcement in a hostile environment. The United States was one of the few countries that could provide the rapid airlift required to deploy the reinforcements to the region. While Vice President Albert Gore explained the administration's specific concerns about basing a humanitarian operation in Kigali in the midst of a civil war with heavy fighting in and around the city and its airport, he pledged its help with the necessary transport in a meeting with Secretary-General Boutros Boutros-Ghali.

As submitted by Dallaire, the plan for the peace enforcement force was to secure Kigali with the reinforcements—up to 5,500 troops—and then to expand outward to provide safe havens for Rwandans who had gathered in large numbers in churches and schools and on hillsides around the country, rescue others, and deliver assistance. A Pentagon representative at the National Security Council, Richard Clarke, who had heavily influenced the instruction to Ambassador Madeleine Albright that culminated in the Security Council withdrawal of UNAMIR personnel, opposed the plan. He proposed an alternative one: the creation of protected zones for refugees at Rwanda's borders. His plan, he argued, would keep U.S. pilots airlifting the peacekeepers safely out of Rwanda. His stress was on avoiding risk to U.S. pilots. Rwandan civilians, on the other hand, would have to move to the proposed but yet undetermined safety zones while negotiating perilous roadblocks on the way.

Clarke was actually attempting to implement America's new peacekeeping doctrine as stipulated in the Clinton administration's PDD-25, of which he was the major architect. Designed to limit military involvement in international peacekeeping, the directive established specific conditions under which U.S. armed forces would participate in multilateral peacekeeping missions under UN auspices.[46] Additionally, the directive crystallized a growing body of resistance to potentially dangerous humanitarian interventions, which had become widespread in the Pentagon and on Capitol Hill. Its stipulated conditions circumscribe U.S. participation in UN peacekeeping missions and limit its support for other states that would normally volunteer to participate in such missions by holding down the number of UN peacekeeping missions.

Dallaire's proposed plan regarding the mission of the reinforcements— UNAMIR II—did not meet aspects of PDD-25's stipulated conditions. In the Rwanda situation the most relevant questions regarded the extent of U.S. vital interests at stake, the acceptable cost, congressional and public support, and an exit strategy. In view of this, U.S. Deputy Secretary of State Strobe Talbott instructed Ambassador Madeleine Albright to inform the Security Council that the United States was not prepared at that point to lift heavy equipment and troops into Kigali. However, it would support a more manageable operation that would create protected zones for Rwandans at the border, secure humanitarian aid deliveries, and promote restoration of a cease-fire and return to the Arusha peace process. The UN was urged "to explore and refine the [U.S.-suggested] alternative and present the Security Council with a menu of at least two options in a formal report from the secretary-general along with cost estimates before the Security Council" could vote on changing UNAMIR's mandate.[47]

When a number of African countries offered troops under a modified version of Dallaire's plan, the Clinton administration acceded to the plan and offered to provide the troops armored support from the U.S. fleet in Germany. But disputes between the Pentagon and UN planners about who would pay for the vehicles and the shipping costs for spare parts stalled the transportation of the armored personnel carriers until 19 June. In the midst of this, the Clinton administration, relying on political advice from the Pentagon, provided no effective leadership to drive the logistical support through. By the time the armored personnel carriers arrived at Entebbe, Uganda, the genocide had been halted by the victory of Paul Kagame-led Tutsi RPF over the Hutu extremists early in July. Otherwise, the carnage would have continued while the United States and other great powers stood by. As the RPF seized control of Rwanda in July, millions of Hutu refugees fled to Zaire and Tanzania. At that point Anthony Lake spearheaded a multilateral aid effort in order to avert a looming humanitarian crisis.

A pervading bureaucratic obstructionism in the Clinton administration[48] which culminated in this eventuality caused one of the officials who kept a journal during the crisis to write:

> A military that wants to go nowhere to do anything—or let go of their toys so someone else can do it. A White House cowed by the brass (and we are to give lessons on how the armed forces take orders from civilians?). An NSC that does peacekeeping by the book—the accounting book, that is. And an assistance program that prefers whites (Europe) to blacks. When it comes to human rights we have no problem drawing the line in the sand of the dark continent (just don't ask U.S. to do anything—agonizing is our specialty), but not China or anyplace else business looks good.
>
> We have a foreign policy based on our amoral economic interests run by amateurs who want to stand for something—hence the agony—but ultimately don't want to exercise any leadership that has a cost.
>
> They say there may be as many as a million massacred in Rwanda. The militias continue to slay the innocent and the educated....Has it really cost the United States nothing?[49]

Conclusion

There were a number of policy options that the Clinton administration could have adopted relative to the tragedy in Rwanda. First, once it knew that the killing of thousands of Rwandans a day had begun, the senior administration officials could have led the world in responding to the tragedy. They could have spent U.S. political capital to rally troops from other nations and to supply strategic airlift and logistic support to deploy the troops to Rwanda. Second, the administration could have deployed U.S. troops to reinforce UNAMIR forces. Third, if there were any concerns about the effectiveness of a multilateral action under UN auspices, the administration could have intervened unilaterally with Security Council authorization as France eventually did in June. Significantly, the French intervention saved tens of thousands of Tutsi lives and facilitated the safe exit of many of the Hutu plotters and perpetrators of the genocide. Lastly, with congressional support, even though such support might have been difficult to obtain, the administration could have intervened on moral grounds without UN Security Council blessing as it was to do five years later in Kosovo.

None of these options was adopted because of the fear of probable risks, given the Somalia experience, and a meticulous adherence to the rigid guidelines of the administration's PDD-25. Even so, there were steps, as enumerated by Samantha Power, that the administration could have taken: Senior officials could have publicly denounced the killings as "genocide" much earlier than they did. They could have used every means and venue at their disposal—the United Nations, telephone, the Voice of America daily radio broadcasts—to warn and threaten those implicit in the genocide. Ambassador Madeleine Albright could have called for the expulsion of the Rwandan delegation to the Security Council. Pentagon assets could have been deployed to jam the extremist Hutu radio broadcasts that fomented the slaughter.

The silence of the American public on the atrocities in Rwanda partly explains why none of these steps were taken. The American public had become so inured by stereotypes about Africa and its perennial mass killings that the genocide in Rwanda failed to arouse their outrage and cause them to put pressure on the government to act.

How did the Clinton administration justify its policy? The administration adopted several measures to stifle enthusiasm for action in Rwanda and to give the public a sense that policy choices on the Rwanda tragedy were both politically astute and morally acceptable. First, President Clinton and his advisers carefully identified the objectives of their policy: to avoid a costly involvement in a conflict that posed no clear threat to American national security interest, narrowly defined; to appease a restless Congress by demonstrating that the administration was cautious in its approach to peacekeeping; and to contain the political costs and avoid the moral stigma associated with allowing genocide to occur.

Second, administration officials overemphasized the extremity of the possible responses. They repeatedly posed the option as either staying out of Rwanda or becoming involved everywhere or as either doing nothing or deploying the Marines. United States could not turn away from ethnic trouble spots, President Clinton told an audience at the Naval Academy graduating ceremony on 25 May 1994. "But our interests," he emphasized, "are not sufficiently at stake in so many of them to justify a commitment of our folks."[50]

A third measure employed by the administration's policymakers was to appeal to "notions of the greater good." They framed U.S. policy not simply as one designed to promote the national interest or avoid U.S. casualties but as one designed to protect human life. Arguing that the UN and humanitarian intervention could not afford another Somalia, they stressed that the UN had more to lose by sending reinforcements to Rwanda and failing than by allowing the killings to occur. More failures in UN peacekeeping, they postulated, might damage the future of United States' relationship with the UN in general and humanitarian intervention in particular.

Normally, when developments of the magnitude of genocide occur, Congress investigates the role of the administration at the time on the event. In the case of Rwanda there was no such investigation.[51] Why? A number of reasons provide the answer. Rwanda is an African country, and historically Africa lies at the very bottom of American foreign policy priorities. U.S. and Congressional interest in the continent is very low. Rampant corruption and political and economic mismanagement in Africa reduced the interest even further during the Rwanda crisis. This situation and the crisis itself created a climate of Afro-pessimism in Congress which was mirrored throughout America. Hence, there was little public pressure on Congress to act, and Congress was not inclined to act, having become leery of UN peacekeeping and being particularly appalled and critical of the Clinton administration following the death of eighteen Rangers in Somalia in 1993. The proliferation and cost of UN peacekeeping after the end of the Cold War provoked a mood of peacekeeping fatigue in Congress, which was apparently satisfied with the Clinton administration's risk- and cost-avoidance policy on Rwanda.

Hutu extremists, who rejected the Arusha Accords and organized and executed the genocide in Rwanda after the death of President Habyarimana on

April 1994, bear full responsibility for the tragedy. To the extent that the United States and the international community failed to prevent the slaughter or limit its scope, they too share responsibility. The UN Department of Peacekeeping Operations at the headquarters in New York under Kofi Annan treated an early warning (cabled to it on 11 January 1994) as a routine bureaucratic matter. The cable detailed an extremist Hutu plan to carry out the genocide and to kill Belgian members of UNAMIR so as to guarantee Belgian withdrawal from Rwanda. Furthermore, as the slaughter began, the UN showed no sense of urgency. It failed to depict the slaughter as genocide. Its European member states were focusing on Bosnia, while its peacekeepers in Rwanda stood by while the genocide went on. They were forbidden to intervene by UN headquarters in New York to avoid a breach of their peace-monitoring mandate. They were only to act in self-defense. The OAU lacked the financial and logistic capability to deploy troops to the country. On 7 May 1998, four years after the calamity, Secretary-General Kofi Annan, who in 1994 had been in charge of UNAMIR, apologized to the parliament of Rwanda in Kigali:

> ...We must and we do acknowledge that the world failed Rwanda at that time of evil. The international community and the United Nations could not muster the political will to confront it. The world must deeply repent. This failure, Rwanda's tragedy was the world's tragedy. All of us who cared about Rwanda, all of us who witnessed its suffering, fervently wish that we could have prevented the genocide. Looking back now, we see the signs which then were not recognized. Now we know that what we did was not nearly enough—not enough to save Rwanda from itself, not enough to honor the ideals for which the United Nations exists. We will not deny that, in their greatest hour of need, the world failed Rwanda....[52]

The failure of the international community to stem the ethnic violence or decelerate the slide towards genocide was not due to any lack of knowledge of the circumstances which led to it. Nor was it due totally to passivity. Growing instability in Rwanda had been evident for several years prior to April 1994. The general situation in the country was well known at the Organization of African Unity, the United Nations, and at foreign ministries worldwide. Extensive human rights reports by international nongovernmental organizations provided ample warning of the impending catastrophe. Regional states, the OAU, and the UN had engaged in preventive diplomacy, which resulted in the Arusha Accords of October 1993. The UN had also deployed peacekeeping contingents (UNAMIR I) to the country, while Secretary-General Boutros-Ghali had a personal representative to keep an eye on developments there.

Those efforts did not prevent the genocide for a variety of reasons. After the end of the Cold War the number of ethnic conflicts increased substantially. The situation in Rwanda was one of those conflicts, but Rwanda was very low in the priority of the great powers compared to the Middle East, North Korea, and seventeen other crisis spots to which the UN deployed about 80,000 troops at a cost of \$3.3 billion in 1994. Financing the peacekeeping missions became especially difficult because of the reticence of the United States and the delinquency of other member states in paying their peacekeeping assessments. The UN did not only operate with such serious financial constraints, it also lacked consensus on specific measures in Rwanda among the permanent members of the Security Council. Also, it lacked the political will to act to strengthen UNAMIR, to give it a stronger mandate to try to stop the killings. Instead, the Security Council, immediately upon the start of the killings, withdrew the strongest (the Belgian) contingent and reduced the mission to less than 10 percent of its former size.

James Woods, deputy assistant secretary for African affairs at the Department of Defense from 1986 to 1994, described what happened as "a failure of leadership throughout the international community—Europe, New York, Washington." The principal problem at the time, he stressed, was

a failure of leadership and it was deliberate and calculated because whether in Europe or in New York or in Washington, the senior-policy making levels did not want to face up to this problem. They did not want to admit what was going on or that they knew what was going on because they didn't want to bear the onus of mounting a humanitarian intervention—probably dangerous—against a genocide. Consequently, instead of planning to move in and address the problem and try to put a stop to it, at a point of a gun, the diplomatic community and the political leadership went into what we in the military called, "escape and evasion." And for two months they nattered on about, "Well, we're not quite sure. There are apparent acts of genocide. There are conflicting reports on casualties." I think much of this was simply a smoke screen for the policy determination in advance. "We're not going to intervene in this mess, let the Africans sort themselves out."[53]

The U.S. share of responsibility for the failure to prevent the genocide derived from two sources. First was its inaction and risk-averse policy. Its policymakers decided early in the conflict to stay out of Rwanda until there was a cease-fire and a return to the Arusha peace process. The policymakers put saving money ahead of saving lives. On 5 May, about a month after the slaughter began, the Clinton administration's adviser on national security, Anthony Lake, said in a press briefing on PDD-25:

When I wake up every morning and look at the headlines and the stories and the images on television of these conflicts, I want to work to end every conflict. I want to work to save every child out there. And I know the president does, and I know the American people do. But neither we nor the international community have *the resources nor the mandate* [emphasis added] to do so. So we have to make distinctions. We have to ask the hard questions about where and when we can intervene. And the reality is that we cannot often solve other people's problems; we can never build their nations for them.[54]

A second indication of U.S. responsibility for failure to prevent or limit the scope of the genocide was the fact that it prevented the international community from taking effective action on the crisis. That obstructionist policy contradicted the official rhetoric that as the world's remaining sole superpower, the United States had obligations to the international community, including maintenance of world peace and support for global human rights. Because of the concern about costs, among other reasons, U.S. officials championed and brought about almost total withdrawal of UN peacekeepers from Rwanda. They slowed the deployment of UNAMIR II to Rwanda. They overemphasized the needs of refugees at the expense of ending the carnage inside Rwanda for fear it might cost American lives in a situation where no vital American security interest, narrowly defined, was at stake. As the sole superpower, with unparalleled leverage over UN Security Council decisions and measures, the United States failed to call for the expulsion of the representative of the Rwandan government complicit in the genocide from the Security Council. It did not sever diplomatic relations with the interim government in Rwanda that was engineering the genocide until 15 July, after the total victory of the RPF. When the Rwanda crisis spilled over into Zaire, U.S. officials still remained so concerned about the proliferation and funding of UN peacekeeping activities that they persuaded the Security Council to delay action when that organ considered the situation on 8 November 1994. They favored a small relief mission and later in 1996 initiated a program of training and equipping African militaries to deal with future crises and emergencies in Africa.

Notes

1.   Tony Hodges, *Angola: From Afro-Stalinism to Petro-Diamond Capitalism* (Bloomington: Indiana University Press, 2001), pp. 154–155.

2.   See "Rwanda: A Historical Chronology," *Frontline*, http://www.pbs.org/wgbh/pages/ frontline/shows/rwanda/etc/cron.html; "The Triumph of Evil: Interview: Philip Gourevitch," *Frontline*, http://www.pbs.org/wgbh/pages/evil/interview/gourevitch.html; Gerard Prunier, *The Rwanda Crisis* (New York: Columbia University Press, 1995); Philip Gourevitch, *We*

Wish to Inform You That Tomorrow We Will Be Killed with Our Families (New York: Farrar, Straus and Giroux, 1995); Alan J. Kuperman, "Rwanda in Retrospect," *Foreign Affairs*, Vol. 79, No. 1 (January/February 2000), pp. 94–118; CIA, *The World Factbook 1999—Rwanda*, http://www.odci.gov/cia/publications/factbook/rw.html; U.S. Department of State, *Background Notes: Republic of Rwanda* (Washington, DC: Bureau of Public Affairs, 1998); Joint Evaluation of Emergency Assistance to Rwanda, "The International Response to Conflict and Genocide: Lessons From the Rwanda Experience," *Journal of Humanitarian Assistance* (March 1996), http://131.111.106.107/policy/pb020.htm; Catherine Newbury, "Background to Genocide in Rwanda," *Issue: Journal of Opinion*, Vol. XXIII, No. 2 (1995), pp. 12–17; René LeMarchand, "Rwanda: The Rationality of Genocide," *Issue: Journal of Opinion*, Vol. XXIII, No. 2 (1995), pp. 8–11; N. Abdulai (ed.), *Genocide in Rwanda: Background and Current Situation* (London: Africa Research and Information Centre, 1994); L. Dorsey, *Historical Dictionary of Rwanda* (London: Scarecrow, 1994); Holly J. Burkhalter, "The Question of Genocide: The Clinton Administration and Rwanda," *World Policy Journal* (Winter 1994/1995), pp. 44–54.

3. René LeMarchand, "The Fire in the Great Lakes," *Current History*, Vol. 98, No. 628 (May 1999), p. 196.

4. René LeMarchand, "A History of Genocide in Rwanda," *Journal of African History*, 43 (2002), p. 308.

5. LeMarchand, "Fire in the Great Lakes," p. 195.

6. Defense Intelligence Agency, Defense Intelligence Report: "Rwanda: The Rwandan Patriotic Front's Offensive," Document 11, in William Ferroggiaro (ed.), *The U.S. and the Genocide in Rwanda 1994: Evidence of Inaction—A National Security Archive Briefing Book*, Washington, DC: 2001; Paul J. Magnarella, "When Victims Become Killers," *Journal of Modern African Studies*, Vol. 40, No. 3 (2002), p. 516.

7. Genocide is the destruction of groups of human beings because of their race, religion, nationality, or ethnic background. The International Genocide Convention of 1948 defines it as acts committed with the intention to destroy, wholly or in part, a national, ethnic, racial, or religious group. Categories of crime recognized in the Convention include killing, causing physical or mental harm, inflicting poor conditions of life, enforced birth control, or transferring children from one group to another. Persons committing or inciting acts of genocide are liable to punishment whether they are public officials or private individuals.

8. Other suspects for shooting down the aircraft included the Rwanda Patriotic Front (RPF), the Belgian government, and senior officials of the Rwanda Army.

9. Reuters, "Reparations Urged for 1994 Rwanda Genocide," http://nytimes.com/reuters/international/international-rwanda.html.

10. LeMarchand, "A History of Genocide in Rwanda," Vol. 43 (2002), p. 311.

11. Arthur J. Klinghoffer, *The International Dimensions of Genocide in Rwanda* (London: Macmillan, 1998), pp. 3–4.

12. Barbara Crossette, "Stinging Report Claims U.S., UN and Others Tolerated Genocide in Rwanda," http://www.nytimes.com/yr/mo/day/late/07rwanda-report.html; Associated Press, "Panel Issues Rwanda Genocide Report," http://www.nytimes.com/ aponline/i/AP-UN-Rwanda-Genocide.htm; "Rwanda Has Right to War Reparations: OAU Panel," http://www.africana.com/news/homepage/2000/07/07ANA/0357-0357-U.S.-Rwanda-OAU....htm.

13. United Nations, "Seventh Annual Report of the International Criminal Tribunal for Rwanda to the General Assembly/Security Council," A/57/163-S/2002/723 (2 July 2002).

14. Danna Harman, "A Woman on Trial for Rwanda's Massacre," *Christian Science Monitor* (7 March 2003), http://www.csmonitor.com/2003/0307/p09s01-woaf.html.

15. See also World Briefing, "Africa: Rwanda: Ex-Minister Jailed for Genocide," *The New York Times* (16 May 2003), Late Edition, Final, Section A, Column 4, p. 6.

16. Sharon LaFranier, "Court Finds Rwanda Media Executives Guilty of Genocide," *The New York Times*, International Section, Africa (3 December 2003).

17. Associated Press, "Belgium Trying Rwandans for Genocide," http://www.nytimes.com/ aponline/i/AP-Belgium-Rwanda.html.

18. LeMarchand, "The Fire in the Great Lakes," pp. 196–197.

19. William Cyrus Reed, "The Rwandan Patriotic Front: Politics and Development in Rwanda," *Issue: A Journal of Opinion*, Vol. XXII, No. 2 (1995), p. 50.

20. See Peter Rosenblum, "Endgame in Zaire," *Current History*, Vol. 96, No. 610 (May 1997), pp. 200–201, 203.

21. LeMarchand, "The Fire in the Great Lakes," p. 169 n.1.

22. For details see Gerard Prunier, "The Great Lakes Crisis," *Current History*, Vol. 96, No. 610 (May 1997), p. 201.

23. Rosenblum, "Endgame in Zaire," p. 201.

24. Samantha Power, "Bystanders to Genocide: Why the United States Let the Rwanda Tragedy Happen," *The Atlantic Monthly On line* (September 2001), p. 3.

25. "The Triumph of Evil: 100 Days of Slaughter/A Chronology of U.S./UN Actions," *Frontline*, http://www.pbs.org/wg...frontline/shows/evil/etc/slaughter.html; "U.S.-Africa: Rwandans Not About to Forget Clinton's Words," http://www.oneworld.org/ips2/mar98/ 18_33_068.html; James Benneth, "Clinton Declares U.S. and the World Failed Rwandans," *The New York Times* (26 March 1998), http://www.mtholyoke.edu/acad/intrel/rwaclint.htm.

26. See William Ferroggiaro (ed.), *The United States and the Genocide in Rwanda 1994*; Kuperman, "Rwanda in Retrospect," pp. 94–118. See a critique of Kuperman's view and his subsequent response in Alison L. Des Forges, "Shame: Rationalizing Western Apathy on Rwanda," *Foreign Affairs*, Vol. 79, No. 3 (May/June 2000), pp. 141–144; "The Triumph of Evil: Interviews: Tony Marley," *Frontline*, http://www.pbs.org/wgbh/pages/frontline/shows/evil/interviews/marley.html.

27. "The Triumph of Evil: Interviews: James Woods," *Frontline*, http://www.pbs.org/wbgh/pages/frontline/shows/evil/interviews/wods.html.

28. On 9 and 10 April 1994, 250 Americans, including Ambassador David Rawson, were evacuated from Kigali and other points. But thirty-five local employees of the embassy, including Ambassador Rawson's steward and his wife, were killed. Power, "Bystanders to Genocide," p. 15.

29. Power, "Bystanders to Genocide," p. 21.

30. "The Triumph of Evil: Interviews: Tony Marley," *Frontline*, http://www.pbs.org/wgbh/pages/frontline/shows/evil/interviews/marley.html.

31. See Document 10 in Ferroggiaro (ed.), *The United States and Genocide in Rwanda 1994*.

32. See Document 5, Statement by the Press Secretary (22 April 1994) and Document 7 in Ferroggiaro (ed.), *The United States and Genocide in Rwanda 1994*; Glenda Cooper, "Memos Reveal Rwanda Delay: U.S. Had Early Notice of Genocide; Pentagon Rejected Action," *The Washington Post* (23 August 2001), p. A 20; Neil A. Lewis, "Papers Show U.S. Knew of Genocide in Rwanda," *The New York Times* (22 August 2001), http://www.nytimes.com/2001/08/22/international/africa/22Rwanda.html.

33. See Action Memorandum from Assistant Secretary of State for African Affairs, George E. Moose et al. to Secretary of State William Christopher, "Has Genocide Occurred in Rwanda?" (21 May 1994), in Document 14, Ferroggiaro (ed.), *The U.S. and the Genocide in Rwanda 1994*, see also Document 6; Douglas Jehl, "Officials Told to Avoid Calling Rwanda Killings Genocide," *The New York Times* International Section (10 June 1994).

34. See Document 14 in Ferroggiaro (ed.), *The United States and Genocide in Rwanda 1994*.

35. See U.S. Department of State Cable Number 099440 to U.S. Mission to the UN in New York, "Talking Points for UNAMIR Withdrawal," 15 April 1994. Confidential. In Ferroggiaro (ed.), *The United States and the Genocide in Rwanda 1994*, p. 25.

36. Associated Press, "Albright Defends U.S. Rwanda Role," *The New York Times* (9 July 2000), http://www.nytimes.com/aponline/i/AP-U.S.-Rwanda-Genocide.html.

37. Chester A. Crocker, "The Lessons of Somalia: Not Everything Went Wrong," *Foreign Affairs*, Vol. 74, No. 3 (May/June 1995), pp. 2–8.

38. *The New York Times* (23 April 1994), p. 24; (3 May 1994), p. A. 22.

39. See "The Clinton Administration's Policy on Reforming Multilateral Peace Operations" (May 1994), Documents 8 and 9 in Ferroggiaro (ed.), *The United States and the Genocide in Rwanda 1994.*

40. Power, "Bystanders to Genocide," pp. 3–4; "The Triumph of Evil: Interviews: James Woods," *Frontline*, in: http://www.pbs.org/wbgh/pages/frontline/shows/evil/ interviews/ woods.html.

41. See: Document 3 in Ferroggiaro (ed.), *The U.S. and the Genocide in Rwanda 1994: Evidence of Inaction*; "The Triumph of Evil: Interviews: James Woods, *Frontline*, in http://www. pbs.org/wgbh/pages/frontline/shows/evil/interviews/woods.html.

42. Power, "Bystanders to Genocide," p. 23.

43. Burkhalter, "The Question of Genocide," p. 44.

44. Power, "Bystanders to Genocide," p. 24.

45. "The Triumph of Evil: Interviews: Tony Marley," *Frontline*, http://www.pbs.org/wgbh/ pages/frontline/shows/evil/interviews/marley.html.

46. Among the specified conditions were whether U.S. vital interests were at stake; there was a threat to world peace; there was a clear mission goal; there were resources to undertake the mission; the costs were acceptable; there was Congressional and public support; and there was an exit strategy.

47. U.S. Department of State, Cable Number 1272262, to U.S. Mission to the United Nations, New York, "Rwanda: Security Council Discussions," (13 May 1994). Confidential. In Document 13, Ferroggiaro (ed.), *The U.S. and the Genocide in Rwanda 1994.*

48. See Ferroggiaro (ed.), *The U.S. and the Genocide in Rwanda 1994.*

49. Quoted in Power, "Bystanders to Genocide," p. 36.

50. Quoted in Power, "Bystanders to Genocide," p. 35.

51. The Subcommittee on International Operations and Human Rights of U.S. House of Representatives Committee on International Relations held a hearing on Rwanda and the continuing cycle of violence on 5 May 1998.

52. Press Release, S/G/SM/6552, "Secretary-General Pledges Support of UN for Rwanda's Search for Peace and Progress," http://www.reliefweb.int/website/RWDOMINO.NSF/ 480fa8736b/88bbc3c12564f60.

53. "The Triumph of Evil: Interviews: James Woods," *Frontline*, http://www.pbs.org/wgbh/pages/frontline/shows/evil/interviews/woods.html.

54. "100 Days of Slaughter: A Chronicle of U.S./UN Action," *Frontline*, http://www.pbs.org/wgbh/pages/frontline/shows/evil/etc/slaughter.htm.

CHAPTER 9
The African Crisis Response
Initiative (ACRI)

The first Bill Clinton administration (1993–1997) confronted a fundamental foreign policy question: How could the United States help to attain regional stability throughout the world with a shrinking foreign policy budget and military force? This foreign policy question had five immediate roots. First, at the time there was a general perception, especially within the Department of Defense and among conservative forces in the Republican Party, that there was not enough spending, staffing, and equipment to cope adequately with United States' ongoing military commitments. At the same time, the number of UN peacekeeping operations requiring U.S. contribution of military personnel and finances had increased from fifteen in 1988 to seventeen in 1994. The cost of the operations had also increased from $230 million to $3.6 billion,[1] consequently increasing the U.S. share of the peacekeeping budget. The number of operations jumped to thirty-one by 1999,[2] increasing further the peacekeeping budget. For the Clinton administration this reality posed an additional problem of dealing with Congress which, focusing primarily on domestic issues, was demonstrating a great deal of reluctance to multilateral peacekeeping action under UN auspices and to the payment of U.S. dues resulting from such action. A proposed but not enacted National Security Restoration Act was one such demonstration.

The second and more immediate root of the question was developments in three African countries—Somalia, Rwanda, and Burundi—during 1991–1996, which, among other things, threatened regional stability and required action by the international community. The third root was the opposition of Congress to U.S. participation in UN peacekeeping missions and humanitarian interventions. Related to this were restrictions on the commitment of U.S. troops abroad without the approval by Congress. American political leaders had become increasingly unwilling to sacrifice the lives of their young people in missions in which, in their view, vital national security interests of the United Sates were not at stake. The fourth root of the foreign policy question was the concerns of the Department of Defense about the commitment of troops to Africa, a region where the Department traditionally believed the United States has "very little traditional strategic interest."[3] The fifth was the end of the ideological conflict between the United States and the Soviet Union, which left the United States as the sole superpower and, according to Secretary of State Madeleine Albright, the "indispensable" nation in world affairs, with a unique ability to shape the terms by which international relations take place. In addition to this outcome, the end of the ideological conflict removed the incentive that had hitherto propelled U.S. intervention in Africa as well as a major constituency—the socialist bloc—that had supported most issues of African concern in the United Nations. These developments increased the difficulty of justifying further U.S. intervention in Africa after the fall of communism and the disintegration of the Soviet Union, and thus placed the continent at the very bottom of American foreign policy priorities.

In the prevailing circumstances, the Clinton administration was confronted with the problem of how the United States should respond to increasing political and humanitarian disasters which threatened regional security and stability around the world. It is significant to note that neither the foreign policy question nor congressional opposition to U.S. participation in multilateral peacekeeping mission and humanitarian intervention under UN auspices arose from conflicts in the Balkan Peninsula—Bosnia, Kosovo—but from those in the three African countries identified above. Why? The reasons are twofold. The United States initially intervened diplomatically to end the conflict in the Balkans and subsequently, bypassing the UN, after hesitation, led NATO countries in the peacekeeping and peace enforcement mission in the region. Besides deploying troops, the Clinton administration contributed American material and financial resources to rebuild the war-torn region. Clinton's successor, George W. Bush, who had criticized the administration during the November 2000 presidential election campaign for, as he charged, spreading U.S. armed forces too thin rather than preparing to withdraw them from the Balkans now contemplated deploying more forces to police a Macedonian cease-fire. All this occurred because U.S. policymakers, including the military, regard Europe as linked to the national security interest of the United States.

The U.S. interests in Africa are not regarded as fundamental or vital by these policy makers. In fact, in *United States Security Strategy in Sub-Saharan Africa,* published in 1995, the Department of Defense reinforced its traditional position on Africa. It insisted that the United States "cannot and should not attempt to resolve Africa's many conflicts." It was also emphasized that America's other global military responsibilities, including its dual containment policy,[4] precluded a major expansion of its role in humanitarian or peacekeeping missions. Therefore, the Clinton administration only continued the initiative of his predecessor, George H.W. Bush to carry out under UN auspices a multilateral humanitarian intervention in Somalia, Operation Restore Hope.[5] The operation ultimately ended in disaster—the death of eighteen American army rangers and the wounding of many others on 3 October 1993. The administration was severely criticized for the disaster in a region in which no perceived U.S. strategic interests were thought to be at stake.[6] Secretary of Defense Les Aspin resigned as a consequence of that outcome. Shortly afterward, President Clinton issued PDD-25[7] defining the conditions under which the United States would participate in multilateral peacekeeping and humanitarian missions under UN auspices. In part, this was done to appease UN critics in Washington for whom the disaster in Somalia had provided an opportunity to bash the organization.

In the case of Rwanda, the Clinton administration was apparently wary of a repeat of the disastrous intervention in Somalia and so was reluctant to act. Therefore, it instructed the U.S. Mission to the UN to mandate that the international community should "give highest priority to full orderly withdrawal of all UN military personnel in Rwanda as soon as possible."[8] In this manner it successfully undermined UN efforts to prevent what culminated in the massacre of an estimated 800,000 Tutsi and their Hutu sympathizers in 1994. It is also appropriate to observe that during his campaign in November 2000 George W. Bush opposed using American military power to stop such tragedies. In his view, such an intervention was a strategic luxury the United States simply could not afford.[9]

The outcome of the Somalia mission and, especially, the Clinton administration's concerns about an emerging crisis in Burundi[10] in 1996 that threatened to duplicate the Rwanda experience forced the foreign policy question. Following the Somalia disaster, crisis prevention became a key concept of the administration's policy towards Africa. In the 1994 White House Conference on Building a Better Future in Africa, the administration stated that one of its goals was to help to bring an end to the many conflicts and crises in Africa and to help the nations of the continent to identify and solve problems before they erupt. However, because of the experience in Somalia, this policy was not implemented in Rwanda. The administration persuaded the UN to withdraw all of its forces in Rwanda in April 1994. The policy was generally criticized.

In light of all this the administration's answer to the ominous political impasse in Burundi in 1996 was an initiative to "create an interoperable African capacity of up to 12,000 troops to respond in a timely and effective manner to peacckeeping and humanitarian assistance contingencies." Special U.S. forces trainers and a number of retired U.S. military contractors would build up the peacekeeping skills of battalion-sized all-African military units by organizing, training, and equipping them to carry out peacekeeping and humanitarian relief operations in Africa or wherever else the United States preferred to avoid. It was hoped that the initiative would be cost-effective and, at the same time, provide the United States and other non-African members of the international community an alternative to either doing nothing or committing forces to a direct military intervention or humanitarian mission in Africa.

Given the significance of the frequency of conflicts in Africa and their tendency to generate refugee problems, humanitarian disasters, and other spill-over effects, the Clinton administration expected that the troops would intervene to prevent more of the recurrent deadly conflicts and humanitarian crises and thus contribute to a more stable and peaceful future for Africa as a whole. It was also believed that when militaries, through the initiative, "know each other, work together, and train together, they would build up the contacts that will instill confidence, foster cooperation, and encourage long-term relationships that [would be] in the interests of both the partner country and the United States."[11]

The plan was initially entitled the African Crisis Response Force. Later, after consultations with African states, the nomenclature was modified in 1996 to African Crisis Response Initiative (ACRI), with the word "initiative" reflecting those consultations. After hearings by its relevant committees, Congress endorsed the concept as one seeking maximum security at minimum cost. Its rationale for approving the concept was that rather than remain intimately engaged in managing Africa's conflicts at considerably higher cost, the United States should assist nations of the continent to strike their own politico-military balance. Therefore, it proceeded to fund the Clinton administration's proposed ACRI as a significant U.S. initiative to the tune of $20 million for the first year. This amount was several times less than U.S. military assistance to the Middle East, especially to Israel and Egypt. Some observers saw the policy either as a U.S. plan to help African nations help themselves to resolve their own problems while it disengaged from events in Africa or as a plan to use Africans to promote American interests on the continent.

ACRI was immediately put under the management of the U.S. Department of State instead of the Department of Defense, even though it involved the training of militaries. However, the Department was intimately involved in the initiative. Its primary trainers were the Special Forces of the U.S. Army. Several other elements of the Department of Defense were close partners in the initiative, maintaining a symbiotic relationship with the Department of State in the process and implementation of the initiative.

In addition to the summary description of the origins of the Clinton administration's ACRI provided above, this chapter attempts to ascertain (1) the nature of national security interests served by the Clinton administration proposal, (2) why Africa was the target of the initiative, given the Clinton administration's concern for regional security throughout the world. It also examines the response of African states, Western European allies of the United States, and the UN to the initiative. It looks at the philosophy of the initiative as well as its implementation. Finally, it evaluates the policy at the end of the Clinton administration in January 2001, especially as to the extent it had contributed to maintain or advance regional stability in Africa.

Responses to African Crisis Response Initiative

Before any discussion of the responses of African states to ACRI it is necessary to establish why Africa became the particular target of Clinton administration policy as well as the nature of U.S. interests it served. Africa became the focus of the initiative because of the frequency with which African nations engaged in intra-, especially, and interstate wars which they were unable to manage and resolve. From the 1960s to 1996 when ACRI was proposed, Africa was the scene of many of the world's most devastating conflicts. Wars in Angola, Ethiopia, Mozambique, Somalia, Sudan, and Uganda, for example, claimed between 500,000 and one million lives each, either as direct battlefield casualties or indirectly as results of war-induced famine and disease. These figures do not include the 800,000 victims of the genocide in Rwanda nor the more than 200,000 lives that were lost in two other conflicts in Burundi and Liberia, nor those who died from ethnic and religious conflicts in Nigeria. More lives were lost in the eight civil wars between 1960 and 1980 and in ten more that were waged during decade that ended in 1990. Eleven of the thirty-five genocides the world witnessed between 1960 and 1998 occurred in Africa. The continent was also the scene of sixty-one military coups d'etat between 1963 and 1985.[12] The military coups and the wars not only killed millions of Africans, they also created more than eight million refugees and internally displaced persons. This record, in general, earned Africa, already the world's poorest region, the notoriety of being the world's most war-ravaged region and the most heavily burdened with conflict-generated problems such as fatalities, collapsed states, and developmental and environmental disasters.

The number of violent and destructive conflicts in Africa required more and more internal and external funds for their management and resolution, emergency relief, and reconstruction. In requiring these, they caused external donor fatigue and diverted funds away from sustainable development programs that could have contributed towards building a more solid foundation for long-term peace and stability in a society as well as between societies.

The significance of these conflicts and their strategic, political, and economic ramifications for the United States are apparent. The conflicts threaten, and frequently damage, regional security. Breakdowns in regional or subregional stability threaten virtually all U.S. regional interests. They promote such transnational threats as terrorism and transits of illegal narcotics and arms. Strategically, the African region, among others, provides bases for America's Rapid Deployment Force (RDF). It has tremendous mineral wealth essential to continued American industrial growth. About 20 percent of America's oil is imported from Africa. The coastal waters of the continent support huge fisheries. Its potential as a market and as a source of commodities is great. To protect these and other interests the U.S. government carried out several interventions in the continent from 1990 to 1997. Examples of those include noncombatant evacuations, largely of American citizens, from Liberia (1990, 1996), Somalia (1991), Zaire/Congo (1991), Sierra Leone (1992, 1997), Rwanda (1994), and Central African Republic (1996); humanitarian relief operations in Somalia (1992), Rwanda (1994), and Central African Republic (1996); election support in Angola (1992); and support to deployment of the monitoring group of the Economic Community of West African States (ECOMOG) in Liberia (1997). In addition, the United States was a major contributor to the relief of refugees generated by the violent conflicts, and to the grant of asylum to refugees from Ethiopia, Sudan, and Togo, for example.

These costly activities were carried out at a time when Congress was cutting the foreign aid budget and when Russia, the former communists countries of Eastern Europe, and the members of the Commonwealth of Independent States had become competitors with African states for the available U.S. foreign aid. These activities and the interventions in response to crises in Africa demonstrated an inability or lack of interest on the part of U.S. administrators and their agencies involved in Africa to shape the regional security environment in the continent, especially after the end of the Cold War when the United States became the sole superpower. The death of eighteen U.S. soldiers in Somalia in October 1993 and the widespread international criticism of the United States for preventing the UN from averting the 1994 genocide in Rwanda served as a wake-up call for the United States to address the task of managing the regional security environment in Africa. Donor fatigue and the impending crisis in Burundi provided the impetus for doing so and thus the proposal in 1996 for an African Crisis Response Force.

Secretary of State Warren Christopher's announcement of the Clinton administration's proposal to establish an African Crisis Response Force in October 1996 generated responses from the major actors in Africa. These principal actors were the African states themselves, America's Western European allies which still have substantial interests and wield significant influence in the continent, and the United Nations Chapter VI of whose charter provides the guidelines for the setup and operation of such a proposal. A summary of the response by each of the respective actors to ACRI follows.

Responses by African States

After the end of the Cold War African nations stressed the need to set up regional security structures that would manage proliferating conflicts and the problem of collapsed states in their region. They acknowledged their own responsibility for managing such conflicts as well as the effects of donor fatigue outside Africa. Their experience with UN peacekeeping missions from the first Congo crisis (1960–1964) to the mass killings in Rwanda (1994) had eroded their confidence as to what the organization could do to foster peace in war-prone and war-torn countries. The UN secretary-general's Millennium Report admitted as much when it stated that the organization "does not know what works or even possible in peacekeeping operations."[13]

Consequently African states advocated African solutions for African problems. The Economic Community of West African States' Monitoring Group (ECOMOG) intervened in Liberia (1990), Sierra Leone (1998), and Guinea-Bissau (1999) under the regional and organizational umbrella of the Economic Community of West African States (ECOWAS). On a lesser scale, Southern African Development Community (SADC) undertook similar peacekeeping efforts in its region. Acting in its name, Botswana, the Republic of South Africa, and Zimbabwe mobilized forces for a military intervention in Lesotho, following a miliary coup and a threatening political crisis in the southern African country.[14] During its summit in Yaounde, Cameroon, in July 1996, the Organization of African Unity (OAU) resolved to establish a Continental Peacekeeping and Intervention Force, a formal departure from its traditional policy of nonintervention in the internal affairs of member states. Given the fact that African countries lack the financial and logistical means to respond effectively to humanitarian crises and peacekeeping missions, this resolution and the regional effort in West Africa may have contributed to inspire the Clinton administration's ACRI proposal.

However, despite their new enthusiasm for military intervention in internal conflicts of OAU member states, African states did not immediately embrace the Clinton administration's proposal. They were cautious and a little fearful of American intentions. They were puzzled by the lack of prior consultation and total disregard for the growing role of subregional organizations like ECOWAS and SADC in seeking resolution of conflicts within Africa. Therefore, the proposal was greeted by mixed and lukewarm reactions.[15] Some saw it either as a "knee jerk" reaction to the volatile situation in Burundi or as an excuse for U.S. disengagement from Africa. Such countries as Mali, Ethiopia, Senegal, and Uganda which had internal conflicts and believed that alignment with the United States through participation in the initiative would meet their security needs supported the proposal. Kenya expressed qualified support. Others, such as Nigeria, the Republic of South Africa, Tanzania, and Zimbabwe, stressed African solutions to African problems and were noncommittal. Reflecting this stance, President Nelson Mandela stated that Africans would prefer to handle African problems themselves and not act in response to outside suggestions.

An additional concern of the group of African states that remained noncommittal was the question of command structure and the extent of the role of the proposed military force in a regional crisis. Those states that were receptive to the idea expressed the need to tie the initiative closely to other peacekeeping training activities that were already ongoing in the continent with British and French assistance. This, they believed, would obviate any perception of competition. Later, Tanzania flatly declined participation "because it was not satisfied that the objectives of the ACRI were consistent with its national interests."[16] For his part, OAU Secretary-General at the time, Salim Ahmad Salim advised that further consultations and clarification were needed before any acceptance or rejection of the proposal.

Following these responses, the U.S. government initiated such consultations and clarification with the OAU and its member states. As a consequence, the proposed name was modified to African Crisis Response Initiative. Also, as requested by African states during the consultation, and in keeping with the philosophy of cooperation as an essential component of the program, the Clinton administration agreed to work in tandem with America's European allies to ensure that various peacekeeping initiatives would complement rather than compete with each other. While these details were being worked out, OAU

Secretary-General at the time Salim Salim harked back on the concept of "African solutions for African problems." In his address at the Second Meeting of the Chiefs of Defense Staff of Member States of the OAU Central Organ at Harare, Zimbabwe (25 October 1997), Salim said:

> OAU Member States can no longer afford to stand aloof and expect the International Community to care more for our problems than we do, or indeed to find solutions to those problems which, in many instances, have been of our own making. The simple truth that we must confront today is that the world does not owe us a living and we must remain in the forefront of efforts to act, and act speedily, to prevent conflicts from getting out of hand.[17]

By 1997 eight African nations—Senegal, Uganda, Malawi, Mali, Ghana, Benin, Côte d'Ivoire, and Ethiopia—embraced ACRI. Their militaries were to receive "training with emphasis on commonality of communications, basic soldiering skills, and specific military activities required in peacekeeping."[18] The training was to continue until the end of fiscal year 2001 when continued U.S. support would be evaluated on the basis of the effectiveness of the initiative and the capability of the trained militaries to command and control their own multinational operations in Africa. In general, those countries that embraced the program did so for their own interests and stability. Nigeria, which did not embrace the program, participated in Operation Focus Relief (OFR), for which the United States provided the military training of seven Nigerian, Senegalese, and Ghanaian battalions to serve in war-torn Sierra Leone.

Responses by Western European Allies

Among United States' Western European allies, Britain, France, and Belgium have long-standing historical, cultural, and economic ties with African countries as a consequence of their imperial presence in the continent. The three powers continued to play key roles in their former colonies after the termination of colonial control through a variety of means, including trade and commercial relations, economic aid, security assistance, and arms sales. France, in particular, maintained a military presence in its former colonies and intervened militarily in such countries as the DRC and the Central African Republic (CAR) to sustain (as in the DRC) or remove (as in the CAR) the ruler.

Before the proposal for ACRI was made Britain and France had already demonstrated a diminishing will to use their own troops for conflict resolution in Africa. To obviate their military presence or intervention in African conflicts it seemed to them reasonable and more cost-effective to assist African countries to build their capacity for conflict management in their continent.[19] Hence, they began to help augment Africa's peacekeeping capacity building much earlier than the Rwanda and Burundi crises. The two leading European allies were, therefore, appalled by the lack of prior consultation before the announcement of the Clinton administration's initiative. However, because the proposed ACRI naturally dovetailed with their new thinking, it received the support of these key European allies that have substantial interest in Africa. After consultations in 1997, the United States agreed with Britain and France to strengthen and coordinate their policies and to attract other members of the European Community interested in a capacity-building program for conflict resolution in Africa to support the Clinton administration initiative.

The UN Response

The United Nations, like the U.S. government, has a major interest in regional and global stability. The organization attempted to provide mechanisms for conflict resolution for a long time and in several occasions authorized humanitarian or peacekeeping operations in several African countries. But it prefers that regional and subregional organizations should resolve problems without any direct involvement by the UN. Undersecretary-General Kofi Annan, who had been in charge of the failed mission in Rwanda and later succeeded Boutros Boutros-Ghali as secretary-general, shared the evolving concept within the OAU of military intervention in internal conflicts in Sub-Saharan Africa. He believed that only a credible show of force by the international community, modeled after the 40,000-strong NATO Implementation Force (IFOR) in the former Yugoslavia, could prevent a repeat of the Rwanda experience in Burundi. Because of limited funds available to the UN for peacekeeping missions and other related uses, such as consensus within the UN Security Council to undertake such missions, Annan enthusiastically supported efforts by regional organizations to resolve problems within their own region.

The U.S. initiative to promote such efforts in the African region was, therefore, favorably viewed by Kofi Annan. This provided the initiative the support it clearly needed from the United Nations. High-level consultations and coordination between U.S. government agencies and the UN ensured firm UN support for the initiative and the training program. To further cement that support, the program of instruction for all ACRI training was supplied to the UN for its input prior to the implementation of the training exercise.

Guiding Principles and Philosophy

The principles and philosophy of ACRI were rooted in U.S. interest in regional and global stability as the preeminent world power after the end of the Cold War. Indeed, the United States is committed to a global order in which no region is dominated by a hostile power and where regions perceived as of vital importance to the world order are stable and at peace. Besides its interest in promoting an environment conducive to political stability and economic growth, it wishes to protect its citizens from transnational threats. Conflicts and the high incidence of collapsed states that they cause perpetuate economic misery and stagnation, which threaten regional stability and world peace. At the same time they provide terrorist groups and other international criminals with safe havens for operation. Illegal narcotics and weapons trafficking, money laundering, and terrorist acts originating from such havens severely impact not only regional security and stability but possibly the security and well-being of the United States and its people. The role of Osama bin Laden's agents in the death of eighteen U.S. army rangers in Somalia in October 1993[20] and the subsequent 7 August 1998 bombs that destroyed U.S. embassies in Kenya and Tanzania and killed more than 200 Africans and Americans demonstrate this. The terrible events of 11 September 2001 at the World Trade Center in New York and the Pentagon in Washington, DC, and the consequent war in Afghanistan also emphasize the significance of failed states as havens and training grounds for terrorists that can menace global peace and stability.

In spite of the traditional perception of Africa as of limited strategic and minimal economic importance to the United States, American leaders still recognize Africa's vast potential—its current (2004) population of about 800 million, its vast wealth of natural resources, its geostrategic significance, and its potential markets—and hence the need for stability in the region. As already indicated, during the period 1990–1997, the United States intervened militarily in African nations about sixteen times to carry out evacuation, humanitarian, election support, and military transport missions.[21]

The Clinton administration's policy towards the human tragedy in Rwanda in 1994 denied Africa's importance. ACRI was an attempt to assuage a national conscience betrayed by a policy that also violated the traditional idealist belief that America's foreign policy should be guided by American values. The Rwanda policy undercut the claim by U.S. administrators that democracies truly protect and promote human rights. In a world essentially operated and dominated by the United States and other industrial democracies, the apparent indifference reflected by the Clinton administration's Rwanda policy weakened the credibility and moral authority of the United States as a global leader. Therefore, its proposed ACRI represented a decision to redeem that credibility and authority. It was an attempt to help promote peace and stability in Africa and to prevent destabilizing situations such as those that occurred in Somalia (where American soldiers became casualties of a civil war), in Rwanda (where genocide provoked widespread outcry against the United Nations and the United States, in particular, for not acting quickly to stop the massacre), and in Burundi (where a precarious political stalemate which had claimed more than 150,000 lives was about to replicate the tragic events in neighboring Rwanda).

The Clinton initiative was, above all, designed to reduce U.S. troop deployment around the world as military budgets and manpower continued to shrink while maintaining a leading role in Africa as part of America's worldwide security policy. The initiative was a reflection of the rigid political and budgetary parameters within which the administration operated.

The essential element of the philosophy of ACRI was cooperation in accordance with aspects of the New World order enunciated by Clinton's predecessor George H.W. Bush after the end of the Cold War. Clinton did not repudiate that strategy. The strategy's multilateral approach, including burden sharing, to world problems under UN auspices but with U.S. leadership was reflected by the Clinton administration's proposal to train and equip African militaries for peacekeeping in Africa. Such U.S. initiative was regarded as an essential catalyst that, with the cooperation of others—the United Nations and the European Union for example—would lead to real change to be brought about by Africans themselves. The spirit of cooperation resulted in consultations and consensus among the United States and the other principal participants in the program.

An additional element of the program was interoperability. The training was based on a common doctrine and equipment for all participating states. It emphasized interoperable communications equipment so as to enable multinational units to work together more effectively. It sought to obviate or limit the risks of training and equipment being used for military operations outside an intended or possible peacekeeping zone by providing only training in and the delivery of nonlethal equipment. It was not to be a separate peacekeeping force that would be available for every crisis that erupted in Africa. Such a potential force was to be conceived, developed, and controlled by African nations themselves.

African countries interested in participating in the training program were required

1. to have a democratic civilian government and military forces under civilian control;
2. to respect human rights; and
3. to have a significant military capacity, including evidence of forces that have demonstrated some professional military capabilities, such as previous participation in a peacekeeping mission.

Other militaries, such as those of Britain and France, and such UN agencies and international organizations as the UN High Commission for Refugees, UN World Food Program, UN International Children's Fund (UNICEF), the International Institute for Humanitarian Law, and the International Federation of the Red Cross were to be allowed to participate in the training program. The participation of these agencies and organizations in the training program was deemed essential because they would be on the ground wherever there was a humanitarian crisis. Additional rationale for their participation was that their input would make the exercise more realistic; the military would become aware of the needs of the humanitarian organizations; and the humanitarian organizations would recognize the needs of the military and what the military could do for them.

Observers from various regions of Africa were to be allowed to observe ACRI training program so that they would develop an interest in the program and become potential participants. Members of the European Union were also to be allowed to observe the training exercises and to donate equipment to trained battalions deployed in a conflict zone.

The training program was conducted in three phases: an initial phase, a follow-up, and reinforcement. Once the capability was created, further assistance would be provided to the participating militaries in order to sustain their capability, including power projection.

Deployment of ACRI-trained troops was to be a decision made by ACRI partner nations "in response to a request from international organizations such as the United Nations, or the Organization of African Unity, or a sub-regional organization such as the Economic Community of West African States."[22]

Implementation of the Initiative

As indicated above, ACRI was under the management of the U.S. Department of State. Ambassador Aubrey Hooks was appointed special coordinator. The Department worked out the political aspects of the program, set the priorities for the assessment and training schedules, and evaluates potential partners and other critical criteria. The Special Forces of the U.S. army in the Department served as the lead trainers and emphasized commonality of communications, basic soldiering skills, and specific military activities required in peacekeeping and humanitarian missions. They were also required to instill in the trainees the standard peacekeeping doctrines and humanitarian relief practices used by the United States, the UN, NATO, the United Kingdom, and the Nordic countries. The training was designed specifically to promote interoperability so that African military forces could blend more easily with each other and with contingents from the United States and Western European nations in future peacekeeping missions.

In 1997 U.S. Army Special Forces conducted the initial battalion training in seven African nations—Senegal, Uganda, Malawi, Mali, Ghana, Benin, and Côte d'Ivoire. The initial training included six months instruction in military operational skills, command and staff operations, computer-simulated exercises, negotiation and mediation, and other humanitarian concerns relevant to peacekeeping. Initial and subsequent training activities included instruction in observance of human rights and issues in humanitarian law. Follow-up training, designed to reinforce initial training and to allow a progressive building-block process focused on commanders and staff at all levels. It began six months after the initial training and resumed every six months for two-and-a-half years. It was based on the "train the trainer" concept, which combined classroom instruction with field training and computer simulation.

Initial and follow-up training in Ethiopia was deferred until a resolution of its war with Eritrea, while follow-up training for Uganda was to resume after a successful implementation of a cease-fire agreement in the DRC. ACRI activities in Côte d'Ivoire were suspended in December 2000 because of the military overthrow of the civilian government.

A third phase in the training program involved activities and exercises that reinforced the initial and follow-up training. One example was the Joint Combined Exercise Training, a training exercise of the U.S. military in African countries and in other nations around the world. Conducted with local troops, the exercises complemented the force protection skills being imparted to the African trainees. By the year 2000 ACRI had trained 6,500 troops and spent a total of $75 million to further its goal of broad-based peacekeeping cooperation throughout Africa.

Peacekeeping Deployment

ACRI-trained military forces from Kenya, Ghana, Mali, and Senegal participated in peacekeeping missions to attempt to stop the military conflict in Sierra Leone. Similarly, forces from Benin and Senegal were sent to Guinea-Bissau. Senegal sent its ACRI-trained troops and military observers to the DRC. Senegalese peacekeepers also engaged under UN auspices in the Central African Republic. ACRI equipment was used by Malawi to provide humanitarian relief to Mozambique in the wake of the devastating flood that ravaged the country in 2000.

Evaluation

The death of eighteen U.S. army rangers in Mogadishu in October 1993 had a profound and traumatic effect on the way President Clinton and his foreign policy team looked at peacekeeping, especially in Africa and under UN auspices. After the disaster and UN bashing in Washington, they developed a greater aversion to peacekeeping in Africa. The proposal for an African Crisis Response Force represented their alternative to doing nothing. Some saw the initiative as an insurance policy against U.S. involvement in peacekeeping operations in Africa.

The Clinton administration overcame an initial mixed and lukewarm reaction to the proposal. After a series of consultations with African states and America's Western European allies, it achieved a broad-based cooperation to promote capacity building for peacekeeping and humanitarian missions in Africa under Article VI of the UN Charter. Thus, as it eventually developed, ACRI provided a rare opportunity in the atomized and unharmonious world of international policymaking for all the participants in the program—the trainers, the trainees, and other participants—to work together and concentrate resources in pursuit of a common goal. By the end of the administration's term in office about 6,500 soldiers had been trained. This number was less than the anticipated 12,000 but was expected to increase as the program's "train-the-trainer"concept succeeded in integrating new soldiers into ACRI units and elevated them to the required skill and proficiency. Five of the eight African partner nations in the program had participated in peacekeeping missions in Africa by the time Clinton left office in January 2001. Also, by that time, more than $75 million authorized by Congress had been spent on the project. What the succeeding George W. Bush administration intended to do with the training program remained, upon its inauguration, an open question. Not long, however, the administration decided to review the program in order to decide whether to continue it.

It was apparent by the end of the Clinton administration that ACRI had provided African states with an opportunity to pursue regional stability, a much-needed objective that had eluded them over the years, by crafting a new security system. Thus, it was expected that in the long run the security system would become, on the one hand, an effective way to prevent conflicts or resolve them peacefully and, on the other, it would incorporate a regional military and political capability to manage those conflicts that could not be prevented. Trained African militaries were likely to perform more effectively in peacekeeping operations with their acquired skills. A realization of the key objective of interoperability would enhance the performance of African forces in regional peacekeeping missions. Civil-military relations were likely to improve, depending on the length of the training period and the time spent by trained troops in their national militaries and the spillover effect that the trained militaries would have on their comrades. All of these benefits were expected in the future.

The Clinton administration's initiative did even more for the United States. It enhanced U.S. leadership in Africa and provided it an opportunity for consultation and cooperation with its Western European allies and African states in a noncrisis environment. It gave U.S. administrators a means of managing rigid domestic political and budgetary constraints as well as promoting the safety and well-being of American citizens in Africa and the economic interests of Americans in the continent. On many occasions, U.S. administrators had to act when such citizens and business interests were threatened by the high incidence of conflicts and instability in various regions of Africa.

ACRI allowed the U.S. army Special Forces units, which provided the instruction and training for the African militaries, "to practice their skills and advance their understanding of the African operational environment. It was a very effective training for the foreign internal defense mission, which involved training friendly armed forces among other tasks, assigned to Special Forces groups who participated."[23]

The greatest influence on the choice of the first countries to participate in ACRI was the security interests of the United States rather than the established criteria for participation. In the east and in the Horn of Africa, the two countries chosen to participate, Uganda and Ethiopia, were countries that U.S. authorities regarded as anchors of stability in their region. They constituted, in the Clinton administration's view, the "new frontline states" against the fundamentalist

Islamic regime in Sudan, which was perceived as a terrorist base and so a threat to regional stability and international security. In 1996 $20 million was approved for military aid to the two countries and Eritrea for the defense of their territories against Sudan's Nationalist Islamic Front incursions.[24] The security interest of the two African countries converged with the national interest of the United States. Uganda was battling insurgent groups—the Lord's Resistance Army in the north, and the Allied Democratic Front in the south, while Ethiopia was internally threatened by Oromo-based opposition groups and Islamic groups as well. Furthermore, although they were undergoing some form of democratic transition, the two countries had governments that came to power through armed struggle rather than free and fair elections. In Uganda, the civilian government of Yoweri Museveni, who had contested the presidency without resigning from the armed forces and still remained on active duty, did not control the military. In his country the "military are actively involved in political decision-making, and are represented in parliament as a special group. Military personnel compete for public office without having to resign from active military service. They can also be appointed to the public service without having to resign from active duty."[25]

Five shortcomings of the Clinton administration's ACRI can be identified. First, there was no stipulation that required the trained militaries to participate in a regional crisis or peacekeeping mission. Participation in a peace mission within or outside Africa was the decision of each participating country, which could adduce any number of reasons to avoid participation in any or all peacekeeping operations. The participating countries were, therefore, more likely to use the trained militaries internally in repressing opponents and dissidents.

The relationship between ACRI and such existing subregional structures as ECOWAS and SADC, which also were engaged in conflict resolution in their respective regions, was not clear. There was no explicit structure linking them or at least their most dominant members—Nigeria and South Africa—with ACRI. It was not clear whether their peacekeeping role would cease (apparently it did not) or whether they would work as parallel structures with ACRI. Would it have been more fruitful to provide financial and political support for these already existing subregional structures to establish regional security regimes than to embark on ACRI?

A third shortcoming of the initiative was that it did not provide for any augmentation of the peacekeeping role of the police who play an important role in such operations. The peacekeeping mission in Bosnia took cognizance of this fact by creating an international police force—CIVPOL. Earlier, United Nations Operations in the Congo (ONUC) had provided for such linkage during the first Congo crisis (1960–1964).

Another shortcoming of the Clinton administration was its "failure to establish a credible linkage between capacity-building and capacity utilisation."[26] It did not include provisions whereby African states themselves would take further steps to develop their peace operations capabilities without relying on the UN or powers outside Africa to fund, organize, control, and support future peacekeeping missions in Africa. This would not augur well for regional stability in Africa.

Finally, ACRI was a hasty reaction to events in Africa over which the United States had little control. The proposal was announced with no advance warning to or consultation with U.S. diplomatic missions, African governments, and American allies with significant interests in Africa. It demonstrated a major flaw in U.S. African policy: the tendency to react to events and developments in Africa rather than actively seeking to shape them. Accordingly, the policy devoted little thought to the compounded effects of enhancing the military capacity of African countries in which basic human needs like a living wage, freedom from oppression, a stable government, and the rule of law remained unmet. Furthermore, the policy did not explicitly define how Africans might structure or use ACRI-trained militaries. In 1998, Ugandan troops trained under the program were redeployed, shortly after the training, as a major counter-insurgency campaign against the Allied Democratic Forces in Western Uganda. Equally important, the policy did not truly indicate visionary efforts to fundamentally alter or shape the security environment in Africa. It did not lead automatically to an organic African capability for peacekeeping as demonstrated by the civil wars that continued and resumed in the DRC and Liberia, respectively. Essentially, of course, these are tasks that leaders of African states themselves should undertake.

Sequel to ACRI: African Contingency Operations Training and Assistance (ACOTA)[27]

In early 2001 there was some concern among African political observers and students of U.S.-Africa policy that the George W. Bush administration was likely to ignore Africa's priorities, especially attempts to resolve conflicts, manage peace negotiations, and achieve lasting peace and stability in the continent. During the 2000 presidential elections campaign, Bush had expressed his opposition to using American troops to stop such tragedies as those that occurred in Rwanda in 1994. "I don't like genocide," he said in January 2000. "But I would not commit our troops." He also had expressed the view that Africa was not important and had pledged to avoid what he described as President Clinton's policy of "nation building" in Somalia and elsewhere.

But as president, Bush was compelled to abandon his campaign rhetoric. Months after his inauguration, his administration undertook an extensive interagency review of the ACRI program. Given increased concern with international terrorism after 11 September 2001 and the global implications of the fluid security situation in Africa, the review focused mainly on the need to increase the capacity of African states to fight terrorism and to prevent, mitigate, or resolve regional instability. During the review process, the interagency group, including the Departments of State and Defense and the National Security Council, consulted with many African governments, international organizations, and ACRI-partner countries. The review process confirmed the need for continued U.S. support for African capacity building and the development of a new program—African Contingency Operations Training and Assistance (ACOTA)—to provide such support. Thus, ACOTA became the sequel to the Clinton administration's ACRI program.

Upon the recommendations of the interagency review group, the Bush administration decided that U.S. support for the follow-up program would continue to be largely on a bilateral basis with the inclusion of active participation of appropriate regional organizations. Two major goals were highlighted:

1. To improve Sub-Saharan African militaries' sustainable capacity to conduct peace support and humanitarian relief operations in Africa.
2. To improve the interoperability of these militaries in order to facilitate joint peace and humanitarian operations.

As was the case with ACRI, ACOTA is managed by the Department of State. It is coordinated by an interagency Program Development and Oversight Committee, which includes representatives from the Departments of State and Defense and the National Security Council. It is funded with a combination of peacekeeping operations and foreign military financing funds.

The guiding principles and philosophy of the program remain the same as those of ACRI. It emphasizes training trainers and working with African training structures and institutions so that African countries themselves might have the capacity to prepare their troops for peace support and humanitarian relief operations. The training is primarily designed for partner-nation trainers who will be able to mold ACOTA instruction to local needs. The training is provided by a combination of U.S. citizen contractors, the U.S. government, and third-country military trainers.

Subject to U.S. government resource levels, participation in ACOTA is open to all Sub-Saharan African nations eligible for U.S. security assistance. As in the ACRI program, initial priority for participation in ACOTA is given to those countries that have demonstrated commitment to providing forces for peace support or humanitarian operations outside their own borders. Sub-Saharan regional or subregional defense and security organizations that have Secretariat support are eligible for training under the ACOTA program as well as participation in its hosted exercises and seminars.

In keeping with these provisions, ACOTA offered a thirteen-week training program to Ghanaian Air Force trainers, who, in turn, trained a Ghanaian replacement battalion deployed for the United Nations Mission in the Democratic Republic of the Congo (MONUC) duties. Similarly, it trained Ethiopian peacekeepers in preparation for their peace-support activities in Burundi under African Union mandate. It provided resources and logistical support to ECOWAS forces in the Côte d'Ivoire. Training was provided for Senegal, Kenya, and Botswana for multinational exercises in late 2003. Beyond these, it was not possible to ascertain other activities and accomplishments of ACOTA. Massive U.S. commitment of resources to the reconstruction of Iraq and budget constraints may very likely affect its future.

In the meanwhile, there is overwhelming evidence that the Bush administration is shifting its focus away from ACOTA to the global war on terrorism.[28] It is eager to keep Africa's poor nations and shaky governments from becoming breeding grounds and safe havens for terrorists. Hence, Africa was identified as a crucial sector of that global war. It is suspected that suicide bombers who attacked five targets in Casablanca, Morocco, in May 2003 had links with Al Qaeda. Prior to those attacks, Al Qaeda had already been linked to an attack on a synagogue in Tunisia in April 2002 that killed twenty-one people as well as to the car bombings of the U.S. embassies in Kenya and Tanzania in 1998, in which 224 people died. In June 2003 U.S. intelligence and military officials revealed that vast swaths of the Sahara desert, from Mauritania in the west to Sudan in the east, used as smuggling routes for centuries, were becoming areas of choice for terrorist groups, including Al Qaeda, and that United States and the NATO maritime armada in the Mediterranean had forced international drug smugglers, weapons traffickers, Islamic extremists, and other terrorists south to overland routes through Africa.

Since 2002, more than 1,800 American troops have been stationed in Djibouti to conduct counterterrorism operations in the Horn of Africa. After the major combat in Iraq in 2003, the United States diverted reconnaissance aircraft and satellites to watch Mauritania, Algeria, Morocco, and Tunisia in northwest Africa. Also, significantly, the United States military embarked upon plans to expand its presence in north and Sub-Saharan Africa through basing agreements and training exercises intended to combat a growing terrorist threat in the entire region. In the process the Pentagon began to seek to enhance military ties with Morocco and Tunisia. It also embarked on plans to gain long-term access to bases in such countries as Mauritania and Algeria which American forces could use to strike at terrorists. In addition, the Pentagon aims to build on aircraft refueling agreements negotiated earlier with Ghana, Senegal, Gabon, Namibia, Uganda, and Zimbabwe to allow American aircraft flying through Africa to refuel at their local bases. Notably also, amid fears that terror networks would use ships for attacks, the United States and Liberia signed an accord on 11 February 2004. The accord allows U.S. Navy sailors to board thousands of commercial ships, under Liberia's shipping registry, in international waters to search for unconventional weapons.[29]

The United States European Command, which oversees military operations in most of Africa, initiated a plan to rotate U.S. troops stationed in Europe more frequently into bare-bones camps or airfields in Africa and to train soldiers in the Maghribian countries to patrol and gather intelligence. There are also plans for the Marines to spend more time sailing off the coast of West Africa and to initiate a $6.25 million program by the Defense and State Departments to provide training as well as radios and Toyota pickup trucks to company-size army units in Mauritania, Mali, and Niger. In his remarks to the Corporate Council on Africa's U.S.-Africa Business Summit in Washington, DC, on 26 June 2003, President Bush announced that the United States would devote $100 million over the subsequent fifteen months to help African countries increase their own counter terror efforts. He promised that the United States would work with Kenya, Ethiopia, Djibouti, Uganda, and Tanzania to improve their air and seaport capabilities as well as their coastal and border patrols. His administration, he said, would also provide these East African nations with computer databases to track terrorists and the means to cut off terrorist financing while promoting intelligence sharing with the United States.

So far, responses from African countries to these plans to assist them and to expand U.S. military presence in the continent have been positive.[30] African countries and the United States have a mutual interest in preventing terrorism and terrorist acts in Africa. However, there is concern that the United States commitment to the global war on terrorism might replicate U.S. policy in Africa during the Cold War. That policy relegated African realities and priorities to the dictates of the Cold War and simply used African states as pawns in that ideological struggle with the Soviet Union. This time around, Africans expect greater understanding and cooperation in addressing Africa's problems.

Notes

1. United Nations, "Supplement to an Agenda for Peace: Position Paper of the Secretary-General on the Occasion of the Fiftieth Anniversary of the United Nations," A/50/60,S/1995/1 (January 1995).

2. U.S. Institute of Peace, *Peacekeeping in Africa: Special Report Newsbyte* (Washington, DC, 26 March 2001) http://www.usip.org/oc/newsrom/sr66nb.html.

3. U.S. Department of Defense, "U.S. Security Strategy for Sub-Saharan Africa" (Washington, DC: DOD, Office of International Security Affairs, 1995), p. 3.

4. Dual containment refers to U.S. military strategy of effectively and successfully fighting two wars simultaneously against Iran and Iraq, the two countries perceived to be hostile to American interests in the Persian Gulf.

5. George H.W. Bush, "Humanitarian Mission to Somalia: Address to the Nation," Washington, DC (4 December 1992), *U.S. Department of State Dispatch,* Vol. 3, No. 49 (7 December 1992).

6. Walter Clarke and Jeffrey Herbst, "Somalia and the Future of Humanitarian Intervention," *Foreign Affairs,* Vol. 75, No. 2 (March/April 1996), pp. 70–85.

7. For details see F. Ugboaja Ohaegbulam, *A Concise Introduction to American Foreign Policy* (New York: Peter Lang, 1999), p. 309; also note 25, p. 326.

8. Glenda Cooper, "Memos Reveal Rwanda Delay: U.S. Had Early Notice of Genocide; Pentagon Rejected Action," *The Washington Post* (23 August 2001), p. A 20; Neil A. Lewis, "Papers Show U.S. Knew of Genocide in Rwanda," *The New York Times* (22 August 2001), http:/www.nytimes.com/2001/08/22/international/africa/22Rwanda.html. Documents published on 20 August 2001 show that the United States lobbied the UN for a total withdrawal of the organization's troops in Rwanda; Secretary of State Warren Christopher refused to authorize official use of the term "genocide" until 21 May, and even then, U.S. officials waited for three more weeks before public use of the term; and U.S. officials knew leaders of the genocide and did urge them to stop the killings.

9. See Michael E. O'Hanlon, "How to Keep Peace in Africa Without Sending Troops," *The New York Times* (8 January 2001), http://www.brook.edu/views/oped/ohanlon/ 20010108. htm.

10. A political turmoil had continued to bedevil the central African state of Burundi, Rwanda's neighbor, since an attempted coup in October 1993. In that event, Melchior Ndadayi, the first of the Hutu majority to be elected Burundi's president, was killed. His successor, Cyprian Ntaryamira, another Hutu, died on 6 April 1994 when the plane in which he and the Rwandan president, Juvenal Habyarimana, also Hutu, were traveling was shot down over Kigali, capital of Rwanda. This incident precipitated the Rwanda genocide of 1994. Burundi itself remained in a state of political impasse. This provoked strong fears of a repetition of the 1994 ethnic massacres in Rwanda and a potential threat to the stability of the entire region and thus highlighted the urgency of a regional action. This need for an urgent action, in the light of U.S. policy in Rwanda, provided the immediate background for the Clinton administration's African Crisis Response Initiative.

11. U.S. Department of State, "ACRI: Working with African Nations to Build Regional Stability" (An interview with Ambassador Aubrey Hooks), http://usinfo.state/gov/region al/af/acri/intervie.htm.

12. Michael E. Brown (ed.), *The International Dimensions of Internal Conflict* (Cambridge, MA: MIT, 1996), p. 238.

13. Dianna Ayton-Shenka and John Tessitore (eds.), *A Global Agenda: Issues Before the 56th General Assembly of the United Nations* (New York: Rowman & Littlefield, 2002), p.1.

14. Khabele Matsola, "The Recent Political Crisis in Lesotho," *Africa Insight,* Vol. 24, No. 4 (1994), pp. 225–229.

15. "OAU Cool on U.S. Idea of African Force," Pan-African News Agency, Electronic News Wire (14 October 1996); Lionel Williams, "E.U. Supports South African Stand on African Peace Force," Pan-African News Agency, Electronic News Wire (15 October 1996).

16. Paul Omach, "The African Crisis Response Initiative: Domestic Politics and Convergence of National Interests," *African Affairs*, 99 (2000), p. 87.

17. Quoted in Mark Malan, "Peacekeeping in Africa: Trends and Responses," Institute for Strategic Studies, Occasional Paper No. 31 (June 1998), http://www.iss.co.za/Pubs/PAP ERS/31/Paper31.html.

18. Dan Henk and Steven Metz, *The United States and the Transformation of African Security: The African Crisis Response Initiative and Beyond* (Carlisle, PA: Strategic Studies Institute, U.S. Army War College, 5 December 1997), p. 25.

19. The two had started two programs to this effect. The British: *The UK African Peace Training and Support Program,* and the French: *Reinforcement of African Military Peacekeeping Capacity (RECAMP).*

20. See Karl Vick, "Fighting in Somalia Draws U.S. Attention," *The Washington Post* (29 November 2001), p. A28, wysiwgy://8/http://www.washingtonpost.c...-dyn/world/africa/A31119-2001Nov28.html.

21. Henk and Metz, *The United States and the Transformation of African Security*, pp. 41–42.

22. U.S. Department of State, *Summary of the African Crisis Response Initiative*, http://usinfo.state.gov/regional/af/acri/acrisumm.html.

23. Henk and Metz, *The United States and the Transformation of African Security*, p. 28.

24. "Africa/United States: Madeleine's Mission," *Africa Confidential,* Vol. 38, No. 24 (5 December 1997), pp. 1–2.

25. Omach, "The African Crisis Response Initiative," pp. 89–90.

26. Henk and Metz, *The United States and the Transformation of African Security*, p. 29.

27. I am indebted to Mr. Scott Fisher of ACOTA, U.S. Department of State, for the bulk of the information included here.

28. See Richard W. Stevenson, "New Threats and Opportunities Redefine U.S. Interests in Africa," *The New York Times*, International Section—Africa (7 July 2003), http://www.nytimes.com/2003/07/07/international/africa/07AFRI.html?th.

29. The Associated Press, "Deal Lets U.S. Search Ships," *The New York Times* (14 February 2004) in http://www.nytimes.com/2004/02/14/international/africa/14SHIP.html.

30. "Pentagon Seeking New Access Pacts for Africa Bases," *The New York Times*, International Section (5 July 2003).

CHAPTER 10
Conclusion

At the end of World War II, the United States became the most dominant power in the world. It enjoyed a remarkable international credibility and the expectation that it would use its unique position, given especially its leading role in the establishment of the United Nations, to strengthen the foundations of lasting world peace and a more equitable international political and economic order. In particular, because of its political and democratic ideals, emergent African nationalists expected its support for the liberation of their countries from European colonial domination. They also hoped that it would assist them in their political and economic development. These expectations and hopes were dashed.

Soon after the end of the world war, U.S. leaders became preoccupied with what they passionately believed was a communist and Soviet threat to their vital national security interests. Instead of assisting in promoting the principle of national self-determination and the related issues of political and economic development in Africa, the United States chose to preserve the colonial and international economic status quo as a means of protecting and enhancing its global security interests. That was not an easy choice, made without sufficient or calculated deliberation at the expense of American political values. The conduct of foreign policy requires the ordering of priorities in accordance with a hierarchy of perceived national security interests as well as some pragmatic trade-offs. Accordingly, American political leaders decided to align with the European imperial powers. They rejected the role of a champion of the principle of national self-determination or an impartial arbiter in the colonial and postcolonial conflicts that arose in Africa. U.S. policy towards Africa—its realities and traumas—was predicated on this calculated choice and on the contemporary international situation, essentially the Cold War.

In the foregoing chapters we discussed various dimensions of U.S. role in conflicts in postcolonial Africa. The United States contributed to the onset, escalation, and prolongation of some of those conflicts. It attempted through a variety of measures, successfully or unsuccessfully, to help find peaceful resolution of others. What follows is an outline summary of the various ways, including the extent, the United States became involved in conflicts in postcolonial Africa.

1. In a number of instances—most conspicuously in the DRC (in 1960 especially) and in Angola (in the 1960s and 1970s)—the United States engaged in covert (and in cases overt) operations which aggravated the conflicts. In such cases it shunned diplomatic negotiations, undermined them, or gave them short shrift. The destructive consequences of such a policy on African states such as the DRC and its neighbors were usually enormous and persistent. Patrice Lumumba, the Congo's first prime minister, was assassinated thanks to the plots and maneuvers by President Dwight Eisenhower in Washington and political authorities of the Belgian government in Brussels.[1] The elimination of Lumumba and subsequent elevation of Mobutu Sese Seko to power marked a major phase in the Congo's unending crisis. As a legacy of covert activities in the Congo, Angola, and elsewhere in postcolonial Africa, every legitimate American businessman, educator, journalist, and official is perceived as a probable CIA operative, capable of dangerous betrayals. True or false, such American citizens are suspected of being in Africa to recruit agents for the CIA, to bribe officials to promote U.S. interests, and to support covert adventures that undermine or destabilize African nationalists perceived as radical by U.S. administrations.

2. In many a postcolonial African conflict, the United States, its sponsored arms smugglers, and arms industries largely outside government regulations and civilian oversight, transferred arms to preferred parties—client states or insurgent leaders. A corollary to this measure was the military training of units of the insurgents or armed forces of the de jure government. Most of the African countries engaged in such conflicts during the Cold War (1950–1989) received U.S. weapons and military training. Ethiopia, Morocco, the DRC, Liberia, Somalia, Sudan, and the Jonas Savimbi-led UNITA rebels in Angola are the most conspicuous examples. Thus, throughout the period of the ideological struggle, the United States transferred more than $1.5 billion worth of weapons to Africa.[2] Four of the leading recipients of U.S. arms transfers—Liberia, the DRC, Somalia, and Sudan—became the top basket cases of the 1990s and the new millennium in terms of violence, instability, and economic collapse.

U.S. arms transfers to Africa continued after the end of the Cold War. From 1991 to 1998, U.S. weapons and training deliveries to fifty of the continent's fifty-three nations totaled more than $227 million. Direct weapons transfers and international military education and training in the region in 1998 alone totaled $20.1 million.[3] This figure does not include $64 million in weapons sales by licensed U.S. manufacturers during the same year. The bulk of the arms transfers were financed by loans (subsidized by U.S. taxpayers) which increased the debt burden of the recipients. For example, in 2000, the DRC alone owed more than $150 million, while Liberia, Somalia, and Sudan collectively owed $160 million.[4]

The United States, as the world's leading weapons supplier, shares responsibility with other major weapons suppliers for the legacy of a plague of weapons in Africa. Its arms shipments to crisis areas in Africa and elsewhere in the world during and after the Cold War could be viewed as part of public policy, fostered by the military-industrial-congressional complex, to support American arms industry.[5]

3. In the Nigerian civil war (1967–1970), the United States deferred to Great Britain, the former colonial power, as the authority with primary responsibility for seeking a resolution to the conflict. In the Eurocentric vision of Secretary of State Dean Rusk, "Nigeria was a British baby." The United States, therefore, was officially neutral on the conflict, to the political benefit of Nigeria, while there was a great deal of sympathy officially and privately for Biafra.

4. Diplomatic support was provided, in and outside the United Nations, for the white minority regimes—the Republic of South Africa, Imperial Portugal until the collapse of the empire in 1974, the Ian Smith regime in Rhodesia (Zimbabwe)—in southern Africa and other clients of the United States such as Morocco. The support tended to exacerbate and prolong conflicts such as the ongoing one in the Western Sahara which began in November 1975.

5. The U.S. government became directly or indirectly involved in diplomatic negotiations for the resolution of some conflicts. Negotiations that produced the UN Security Council Resolution 435 and its sequels for the independence of Namibia typified U.S. direct involvement in search of a negotiated settlement of an African conflict. The United States was similarly involved in developing the aborted Anglo-American Plan for the independence of Rhodesia-Zimbabwe. Ultimately, the Carter administra-

tion pressured the government of Margaret Thatcher to embark on such negotiations at Lancaster House in 1979. Those negotiations led to the independence of Zimbabwe in April 1980. Similarly, after the flight of Mengistu Haile Mariam from Ethiopia in 1991, the United States played a direct role in the eventual diplomatic solution to the protracted and multifaceted civil war in Ethiopia that culminated in the independence of Eritrea and a modicum of political stability in the rest of Ethiopia. The George W. Bush administration became directly involved in diplomatic negotiations in Sudan after the events of 11 September 2001, not solely to resolve the eighteen-year-old civil war but also to promote stability and to reduce the chances of international terrorists using the territory as a safe haven for terrorist acts and other crimes. Pressured by American evangelical Christians and African Americans outraged by the religious discrimination against southern Sudanese Christians, the administration became truly engaged in the country. It maintained sanctions imposed on Sudan during the Clinton administration. Eventually, the Sudanese government was pushed by American and European financial sanctions and citizen pressures against investors into negotiations with the southerners.

After the release of Nelson Mandela from prison in 1990, the United States indirectly assisted South African parties—the National Party, the African National Congress, the Inkatha Freedom Party, especially—to reach agreement on a new constitution for a multiracial democracy. It provided funds and requisite assistance to facilitate the resulting elections that made Nelson Mandela the first elected black president of the republic. In other cases, such as Mozambique, Rwanda, Burundi, and the DRC after 1997, U.S. administrations supported third parties and provided funds and logistical support to African regional organizations which sought peaceful solution through diplomatic negotiation.

6. In a number of cases, U.S. administrations exerted pressure on parties in conflict in order to foster diplomatic negotiations. In such cases economic or other sanctions or condign measures were imposed, or the U.S. embassy was closed to elicit appropriate response. Although the Byrd Amendment negated the U.S. commitment to the UN to impose limited sanctions on the British rebellious colony of Rhodesia, the U.S. government was a prime mover of the multilateral sanctions. President Johnson had imposed the sanctions by executive order, and President Carter worked to reimpose them by obtaining a repeal of the Byrd Amendment

in 1977. The Comprehensive Anti-Apartheid Sanctions Act (1986) contributed towards political change in the Republic of South Africa.

7. Humanitarian intervention represents another dimension of the U.S. role in conflicts in postcolonial Africa. Operation Restore Hope in Somalia, initiated by the George H.W. Bush administration under UN auspices, was the first and most conspicuous U.S. humanitarian military intervention in Africa. The operation reduced famine, death, and starvation due to clan wars and state failure in the country. Its follow-up by the Clinton administration, which sought to address the core of the problem—state failure— ended in a fiasco. Elsewhere, the United States actively assisted in providing relief for millions of refugees and displaced persons produced by wars in postcolonial Africa. It also provided asylum to refugees from such troubled African countries as Ethiopia, Sudan, and Togo.

8. The adoption and implementation of the African Crisis Response Initiative and its sequel, the African Contingency Operations Training and Assistance, represents another dimension of U.S. involvement in conflict resolution in postcolonial Africa. Among others these programs were designed to improve and sustain the capacity of Sub-Saharan African militaries to conduct peace support and humanitarian relief operations in their region. However, the programs have not enhanced such capacity as the resumed civil war in Liberia, for which the Bush administration after much agonizing and delay had to deploy 2,300 Marines to the coast of Liberia in July 2003, demonstrated.

U.S. Intervention and Local Forces in Africa's Postcolonial Conflicts

There are limits to the extent to which foreign intervention can successfully reshape local forces—such as colonial legacy, ethnic and religious animosities, poverty, political exclusion—that have caused conflicts in postcolonial Africa. The motivations, goals, and objectives of the intervening power tend to be critical factors in the process and its outcome. These critical factors may not be congruent or coincide with the interests of the local forces because the activities of the intervening power are guided mainly by the goals and objectives it seeks to achieve or promote. Thus, local forces and realities tend to be ignored. This was the case with the U.S. intervention and role in such conflicts as those in the Horn, the DRC, and Angola, for example. U.S. intervention in these conflicts, therefore, failed to address their historical and indigenous origins. Its motivations did not coincide with the interests of the local people—the belligerents.

U.S. policy in the conflicts in the Horn of Africa was conducted along predetermined lines that gave priority to U.S. military, strategic, and geopolitical interests, including concern for stability in the region. The policy devoted insufficient attention to the region's political-economic health and the historical inequities that fueled rebellion, especially in Ethiopia. The rationale for the policy's support of the status quo in Haile Selassie's Ethiopia was that his regime, although internally unpopular, was anticommunist. It was the only one in the Horn, it was believed, that "could serve as an effective counterweight to a Somalia aligned with the Soviet Union."[6] Therefore, U.S. administrators allowed Emperor Haile Selassie to exploit his association with the United States to shore up his arbitrary power. They failed to pressure him to institute meaningful social, economic, and political reforms but simply blinked at the dangers and domestic problems inherent in his policies. These eventually brought about the collapse of his imperial throne.

Regarding the Ethiopia-Somalia border dispute, U.S. administrations were mainly interested in deterrence and not in settlement of the dispute by means of diplomatic negotiations. They pursued a similar policy on Ethiopia's determination to retain Eritrea as an integral part of Ethiopia. Large U.S. arms shipments to the region were a legacy of the U.S.-Soviet rivalry. The arms did not create the region's conflicts and subsequent political and economic instability, but they played a significant role in exacerbating their magnitude and the instability of the region.

The rationale in both Angola and the DRC was similar to that of the Horn: To prevent the spread of communism and Soviet influence in the "heart" of Africa. Again, local forces and realities were ignored. In the Congo the policy was: "Mobutu or chaos." In Angola, it was support for the opportunist Jonas Savimbi, who was regarded by President Reagan as a "freedom fighter."

The lack of congruence between the local forces in Africa's postcolonial conflicts and the motivations of U.S. intervention was only one of the constraints on the U.S. role. The high incidence of conflicts in Africa constituted a major obstacle to U.S. involvement in their resolution. The proliferation of conflicts in the continent in the 1980s and 1990s generated intra-African competition for limited American resources. The risks and the humanitarian crises such as flows of refugees and displaced persons, famine, disease, and collapsed states that frequently accompanied the conflicts made them more complex and very costly. U.S. administrations tended to play a leading role in addressing the humanitarian crises, but direct U.S. military involvement in Africa has been rare. Consistently, the administrations have been very reluctant to risk American lives by sending armed forces into combat zones in Africa. The vagaries of domestic politics, including the post-Vietnam climate in the United States, constrained the scope of the rare U.S. military intervention in Somalia in 1992/93 and prevented altogether intervention in Rwanda in 1994. Clinton's political opponents had made much political capital out of the October 1993 casualties in Somalia, which, like other African crisis areas, lacked an effective U.S. domestic constituency.

During and after the Cold War, conflicts in other regions of the world such as Nicaragua, Chile, Czechoslovakia in 1968, Bosnia, Kosovo, the intractable Israeli-Palestinian conflict, Lebanon, Haiti, and the Cuban-U.S. refugee situation competed with African conflicts for American human and material resources. Needless to say, those in Africa received the least of America's attention and resources. The end of the Cold War reduced the attention and resources further. It significantly eliminated the importance of some of the crisis areas such as Liberia, Ethiopia, and Somalia to United States' interest in sustaining client governments in Africa.

A further constraint on U.S. involvement in African conflict management is the fact that the vast majority of American citizens, including their elected representatives, have very little or no knowledge about the actual roots and circumstances of African conflicts. Therefore, they are naturally unwilling to risk the lives of members of U.S. armed forces in regions of Africa, like Somalia in 1993, that were perceived as peripheral to the national security interests of the United States.

Legacies of the U.S. Role

Through their Cold War policies, U.S. administrations helped to create conditions that contributed to intractable and prolonged conflicts that raged in Africa. Those in the Horn, the DRC, Angola, and the Western Sahara are typical examples. Policy miscalculations arising from U.S. rapprochement with Emperor Haile Selassie of Ethiopia after World War II reinforced local conditions to prolong conflicts in the Horn. U.S. diplomatic support for the emperor in and outside the United Nations facilitated the incorporation of Eritrea, a former Italian colony, as an autonomous federated unit within Ethiopia. When Emperor Haile Selassie flagrantly violated the terms of the incorporation, the United States, a major sponsor of the incorporation, raised no objections and consistently supplied him with weapons to crush a group of determined Eritrean rebels who made enormous sacrifices over a period of thirty years to establish, as they did in 1993, an independent state of Eritrea. Thus, U.S. concern for stability in the Horn, which, in part, motivated the support for Haile Selassie against the Eritrean nationalist rebels, did not only strengthen the power and unwillingness of the emperor to negotiate, it increased the determination and persistence of the rebels in the conflict. In the long run, as we have stated, the rebels won but at a considerable cost to themselves and to Ethiopia. Similarly, successive U.S. administrations ostensibly failed to encourage the Ethiopian emperor to undertake transparent social, economic, and political reforms to allay domestic discontent. His failure to undertake such reforms caused prolonged civil discontent and eventually cost him his throne.

Another miscalculation that contributed to prolonged warfare in the Horn of Africa was the embrace of the Mohammed Siad Barre regime in Somalia by Presidents Carter and Reagan during and after the Ogaden war (1977–1978). Barre, who had lost that war, used American weapons transferred to his regime to suppress his people, especially the other clans. In 1989, the United States and members of the European Union abandoned him because of his poor human rights record and failure to liberalize the political system in his country. When he was ousted from power in 1991, clan warfare, fueled by U.S.-supplied arms, erupted. The effects of the warfare, including the collapse of Somalia as a sovereign state, continue to be felt in the Horn and beyond.

The scale and character of U.S. military involvement in the Horn greatly helped to promote the development of a low-intensity arms race among the Ethiopians, Somalis, and Eritrean rebels.[7] In the process, scarce resources were diverted from the region's basic social and economic needs to arms purchases. Furthermore, tensions that arose from the intensified arms race in the region caused Ethiopia and Somalia not only to "outfox" each other but also to seek and obtain the military means to sponsor guerrilla campaigns against each other.

The situation in the Horn was replicated in central Africa. There massive U.S. intervention in the mineral-rich and strategically located DRC prolonged a conflict that began immediately after independence on 30 June 1960. The intervention catapulted Joseph Desiré Mobutu, later Mobutu Sese Seko, into office, where he ruled with U.S. diplomatic, economic, and military support for a period of more than thirty years. For the entire period, Mobutu was transparently corrupt and authoritarian. U.S. leaders ignored these defects and rescued him on several occasions from the wrath of Congolese rebels who sought to overthrow his regime. As a result, the Congo experienced unending crisis, a stagnant economy, a collapsed economic and social infrastructure, and a crisis of leadership. In 2003 it remained a cauldron of civil war and a collapsed state.

The civil war that continued in the central African country after the overthrow of Mobutu in 1997 is a prime example of the devastating legacy of U.S. arms sales policy on Africa. From the 1960s to the end of the Cold War in 1989, Washington prolonged the rule of Mobutu by providing the dictator more than $300 million in weapons and $100 million in military training. Mobutu used his U.S.-supplied arsenal to repress his own people and plunder his nation's economy for three decades without shame and without honor until his brutal regime was overthrown by Laurent Kabila's forces.

Immediately after Kabila overthrew Mobutu, the Clinton administration offered the new Congo ruler military support by developing a plan for new training operations with his armed forces. When factional fighting began in the country not long after the demise of the Mobutu regime, neighboring countries which had received decades of U.S. weapons transfers and military training intervened on both sides in the war. Thus, U.S. military transfers in the form of direct government-to-government weapons deliveries, commercial sales, and International Military Education and Training (IMET) to six states directly involved in the war facilitated such intervention. The intervention culminated in what the Clinton administration's Assistant Secretary of State for African affairs, Susan Rice, described as Africa's "first world war."

In Angola, the Ford administration deliberately facilitated a war of political succession that ravaged the country for nearly three decades. The administration accomplished this through covert operation, military collaboration with the government of South Africa and Mobutu, and military support for two of the three Angolan factions that sought to succeed Portuguese colonial rulers. The administration's policy undermined the Alvor Accord by which the departing Portuguese government and the three Angolan nationalist movements had agreed to a transitional government with shared ministries and a subsequent independence election.

Congress' amendment initiated by Congressman Dick Clark of Iowa to negate that policy was not entirely successful in the long run. While President Ford's successor, Jimmy Carter, observed the provisions of the amendment and carried out negotiations with the de facto government of Angola, he failed to offer it formal diplomatic recognition, a critical step that could have shortened the war. In the name of anticommunism and reviving the credibility of the United States, President Carter's successor, Ronald Reagan, persuaded Congress to repeal the Clark Amendment. Subsequently, President Reagan resumed U.S.

support, directly and indirectly through Morocco and Israel, for the rebel UNITA movement. For eight more years the Angolan war raged. It continued beyond the four years served by Reagan's successor, George H.W. Bush who himself continued U.S. military and moral support for the rebel group.

U.S. support for UNITA during the period 1975–1992 hindered Angola's development for more than two decades. It increased its dependence on Cuba and the Soviet Union for most of that time. Even after the Clinton administration formally recognized the Marxist-oriented MPLA government in 1993, congressional support for UNITA still lingered and caused further economic and political damage in the nation. It raised the cost of the conflict and weakened the capacity of the government to penetrate and regulate its society. The support enabled Savimbi to persist beyond reasonable limits but ultimately contributed to his death. In general, America's Cold War global strategy that required that Washington should support such African opportunists as Savimbi and Mobutu undermined U.S. credibility in most of Africa. The support was also antithetical to basic American democratic values, but it was part of the trade-off the administrations carried out in pursuit of what they regarded as vital security interests of the United States.

The modalities of U.S. role in the Western Sahara conflict and the genocide in Rwanda differed from those in Angola and the Congo. Minimal covert operations were involved in the Western Sahara. In Rwanda, for reasons already articulated, the Clinton administration failed to intervene to prevent or minimize the scope of the tragedy. There was no motivation to protect or promote any ideological interest as in the days of the Cold War. The policy of nonintervention was guided by "cost and risk avoidance" in a country where no obvious U.S. national security interest was threatened. Only purely moral and humanitarian interests were at stake, and in this case were not considered worth sacrificing American lives and overextending material resources. A military humanitarian mission in nearby Somalia had ended in disaster for U.S. soldiers. The widely publicized killings of those soldiers by Somali militiamen hardened attitudes among American policymakers and the public about the costs and efficacy of U.S. military intervention in Africa. Therefore, the Clinton administration did not only refuse to undertake another risk but also prevented the UN Security Council from authorizing any military intervention. A U.S. mission, narrowly confined to delivering humanitarian relief to Rwanda and to refugees in camps in neighboring countries, was carried out by U.S. troops after the worst of the brutality had eased. Four years after the genocide, President Clinton expressed his regrets before an audience in Rwanda for the failure of his administration and the international community to prevent or limit the scope of the tragedy.

In the Western Sahara, U.S. administrators made no pretense of playing the role of an honest broker. From the beginning of the conflict in 1975 to 2003 they consistently and solidly supported Morocco.[8] Thereby the United States became the major obstacle to attempts by the UN to resolve the national self-determination issue in the territory after so much expenditure of resources and suffering by the people of Western Sahara. In general, although the policy may have promoted American arms industries whose exports sustained the war, it repudiated basic American values and principles, blatantly displayed U.S. double standards,[9] and served no vital interests of the nation.

We conclude this book with the following observations:

1. This study copiously illustrates the interplay and power sharing between the chief executive and Congress in the conduct and management of American foreign policy and role in world affairs. Both branches of the government (the executive branch more so than the legislative) were involved in U.S. role in the postcolonial conflicts in Africa examined here. This is in accordance with American constitutional provisions, but the study shows that under this established constitutional system, the United States failed to exercise effective leverage to end any of the four conflicts examined in detail.

2. Counterproductive Cold War policies defined U.S.-Africa relations for far too long. As a consequence, the contemporary problems of violent conflict, political instability, and the lowest regional rate of economic growth worldwide that have plagued Africa and its peoples are in part a legacy of those policies and of U.S. involvement in the continent since the end of World War II. This view neither ignores local forces nor exonerates the leaders of African nations from their responsibility for their own palpable failures. It suggests that the rest of the world—the former Cold Warriors and those other powers that historically had a hand in creating the political and economic conditions under which African states function—shares the responsibility for the African condition.

3. As politically and economically powerful as it is, the United States lacks both the domestic and the international capacity to resolve internal conflicts in other societies or even to monitor and control transnational developments that threaten U.S. citizens at home or abroad. This reality is reflected in the creation of the Clinton administration's ACRI and the enormous effort by the George W. Bush administration, in spite of its unilateralist tendencies, to

mobilize the nations of the world in a crusade against international terrorism. Thus, in spite of the United States' overwhelming military and economic superiority, the contemporary world, together with its problems, is beyond its ability as the sole superpower to manage and control. Resolving intrastate and interstate conflicts, defeating terrorism and countering the proliferation of weapons of mass destruction, promoting democracy and economic prosperity, sustaining the global environment, and containing HIV/AIDS pandemic all require the active cooperation of other countries. This fact underscores the need for local actors, non-governmental organizations, subregional and regional organizations in Africa to respond first to conflicts in their region. Further, it emphasizes the need for outsiders to assist them as necessary, but especially when the crisis goes beyond their capacity to manage and resolve. However, ultimately, it is the Africans themselves who must shoulder the responsibility for the stability, security, and prosperity of their nations.

Notes

1. "Who Killed Lumumba?" http://www.africawithin.com/lumumba/whokilled lumuumba. htm; "Lumumba's Legacy and the Crisis in the Congo," wysiwyg://main.2/http://www. afri cana com/index20010117.htm; U.S. Senate, *Alleged Assassination Plots Involving Foreign Leaders: An Interim Report of the Select Committee to Study Government Operations with Respect to Intelligence Activities* (Washington, DC: U.S. Government Printing Office, 1975); Madeleine G. Kalb, *The Congo Cables: The Cold War in Africa—From Eisenhower to Kennedy* (New York: Macmillan, 1982).

2. U.S. Department of Defense, "Foreign Military Sales, Foreign Military Construction Sales and Military Assistance Fact As of 30 September 1998," (1999); William D. Hartung and Bridget Moix, "Deadly Legacy: U.S. Arms to Africa and the Congo War," World Policy Institute (11 January 2000), http://www.worldpolicy.org.

3. Hartung and Moix, "Deadly Legacy," http://www.worldpolicy.org.

4. U.S. Department of Defense, "Report on the Status of the Department of Defense Direct Loans As of 30 September 1998," (1999); Hartung and Moix, "Deadly Legacy," http://www.worldpolicy.org.

5. See for example Tony Hodges, *Western Sahara: The Roots of a Desert War* (Westport, CT: Lawrence Hill, 1983), p. 362; Karin von Hippel, "The Noninterventionary Norm Prevails: An Analysis of the Western Sahara," *The Journal of Modern African Studies*, Vol. 33, No. 1 (1995), p. 75. See also p. 75 n. 29; p. 75 n. 30.

6. Robert H. Selassie, "The American Dilemma in the Horn," in Gerald Bender et al. (eds.), *African Crisis Areas and U.S. Foreign Policy* (Los Angeles: University of California, 1985), p. 172.

7. For details see Edmond J. Keller, "United States Foreign Policy on the Horn of Africa: Policy-making with Blinders on," in Gerald Bender et al. (eds.), *African Crisis Areas and U.S. Foreign Policy,* p. 181.

8. Stephen Zunes, "U.S. Should Reassess Policy in Western Sahara," *The Christian Science Monitor* (10 January 1989), in *AF Press Clips*, Vol. xxiv, No. 2 (Washington, DC: 13 January 1989), p. 9.

9. For example in Afghanistan, U.S. administrations regarded the Mujaheden who fought against Soviet invaders as "freedom fighters," but labeled as "terrorists" Polisario nationalists resisting Moroccan imperialism in the Western Sahara. Also, the administrations accorded any African nation whose sovereignty was threatened by external aggression the right to request British, French, and even American troops but refused Angola the same right when its sovereignty was threatened by South Africa.

Index